Criminal Networks and Law Enforcement

This collection presents an analysis of illicit networks and discusses implications for law enforcement and crime prevention. The contributors draw on a range of methodologies and apply them to diverse international criminological settings, from illegal fishing in the Indo-Pacific to 'money mule' networks in the Netherlands. Using a variety of examples, the book elucidates how and why criminals form networks of cooperation and how they can be disrupted. It is expected to be of interest to those who study criminology or criminal law, as well as law enforcement practitioners.

Dr Saskia Hufnagel is a Senior Lecturer in Criminal Law at Queen Mary University of London. She previously worked as a Research Fellow at the Australian Research Council Centre of Excellence in Policing and Security (CEPS), Griffith University, Australia, and was a Leverhulme Fellow at the University of Leeds. She taught at the ANU College of Law, Canberra, and held a permanent teaching position at the University of Canberra. Her main research areas encompass law enforcement cooperation in Asia, North America, the EU and Australasia, comparative constitutional and human rights law with a focus on terrorism legislation and the policing of art crime. She has widely published on national and international police cooperation, security, comparative constitutional law and art crime. Dr Hufnagel is a qualified German legal professional and accredited specialist in criminal law.

Dr Anton Moiseienko is a Research Fellow at the Centre for Financial Crime & Security Studies of the Royal United Services Institute, London. He holds a PhD in law from Queen Mary University of London. He has published on international law and criminal law, including in the *International & Comparative Law Quarterly* and *Criminal Law Review*.

Transnational Criminal Justice

Series Editor
Saskia Hufnagel, Queen Mary University of London, UK

The concept of 'transnational criminal justice' has frequently been interpreted in academic literature as 'international criminal justice' or 'global criminal justice'. Many publications that use the term 'transnational' therefore discuss international criminal justice and international legal frameworks. Another form of studies that has developed under the umbrella of transnationality in the field of criminal law is comparative. There has hence been a move from the terminology of 'international', 'global' and 'comparative' criminal justice towards 'transnational' criminal justice.

This series considers these developments but focuses primarily on publications that adhere to a more literal interpretation of the term 'transnational'. The aim of the series is to provide a forum for discussion of bilateral and multilateral relationships between nations in the field of criminal justice. International law influences these relationships but is not the focus here. Equally, to explain transnational relationships, comparative analyses are required. While incorporating comparative studies in this series, their aim is the explanation of challenges to criminal justice cooperation in bilateral or multilateral relationships.

Titles in this series:

Police Cooperation and Sovereignty in the EU
Norway's Lessons for Europe
Synnøve Ugelvik

Criminal Networks and Law Enforcement
Global Perspectives On Illegal Enterprise
Saskia Hufnagel and Anton Moiseienko

For more information about this series, please visit:
https://www.routledge.com/Transnational-Criminal-Justice/book-series/TRANSCJ

Criminal Networks and Law Enforcement

Global Perspectives on Illegal Enterprise

Edited by
Saskia Hufnagel and Anton Moiseienko

Routledge
Taylor & Francis Group
LONDON AND NEW YORK

First published 2020
by Routledge
2 Park Square, Milton Park, Abingdon, Oxon OX14 4RN

and by Routledge
605 Third Avenue, New York, NY 10017

First issued in paperback 2020

Routledge is an imprint of the Taylor & Francis Group, an informa business

British Library Cataloguing-in-Publication Data
A catalogue record for this book is available from the British Library

Library of Congress Cataloging-in-Publication Data
A catalog record has been requested for this book

ISBN 13: 978-0-367-72697-3 (pbk)
ISBN 13: 978-0-8153-8600-1 (hbk)

Typeset in Galliard
by Deanta Global Publishing Services, Chennai, India

Contents

List of contributors

Synøve N. Andersen works as a researcher at the Unit for Social and Demographic research at Statistics Norway and as Associate Professor of Empirical Legal Studies at the University of Oslo. Her research focuses on quasi-experimental analyses of the effects of Norwegian correctional policies on reoffending and labour market outcomes, as well as on the dynamics of co-offending, co-offending networks and criminal careers.

David Bright is a Criminologist and Forensic Psychologist. He has worked in a range of clinical and forensic settings including community mental health services, police agencies, courts and prisons. Associate Professor Bright's research interests include organised crime and criminal networks, intelligence collection and law enforcement interventions against organised crime, offender rehabilitation and treatment, offender recidivism and illicit drug policy.

Chiara Broccatelli is a Research Assistant at MRC/CSO Social and Public Health Sciences Unit at the University of Glasgow. She received her PhD Sociology at the University of Manchester, then received her MSc in Sociology and Social Research from the University of Trento. Chiara also worked as a Research Assistant at Transcrime – Joint Research Centre on Transnational Crime and <ahref Foundation in Italy.

Eric R. Cheney is a Professor of Sociology at Central Washington University. His research interests include social networks and the sociology of deviance and white-collar crime.

Martin Everett holds a Chair in Social Network Analysis in the School of Social Sciences at the University of Manchester. After he was awarded his DPhil at Oxford, he worked at East London, Westminster and Greenwich universities. He joined the University of Manchester in 2009, where he helped co-found the Mitchell Centre for Social Network Analysis. Martin is a co-author of the software package UCINET and has made significant contributions to methods for social network analysis.

Robert R. Faulkner is Professor Emeritus, University of Massachusetts. His current research is on zealotry in secret societies.

Samuel Hardy is a Post-Doctoral Research Fellow in Cultural Heritage and Conflicts at the Norwegian Institute in Rome, University of Oslo; an Honorary Research Associate at the Institute of Archaeology, University College London; an Adjunct Professor at the American University of Rome; and an Expert at the Association for Research into Crimes against Art (ARCA). He blogs at https://conflictantiquities.wordpress.com/

Saskia Hufnagel is a senior lecturer in Criminal Law and co-director of the Criminal Justice Centre at Queen Mary University of London.

Edward R. Kleemans is Director of Research/Vice-Dean of the Faculty of Law and Full Professor (Serious and Organised Crime and Criminal Justice) at the VU School of Criminology, Faculty of Law, Vrije Universiteit Amsterdam, the Netherlands. He graduated with a degree in Public Administration and Public Policy (with the highest possible distinction) and earned a PhD (with the highest possible distinction) from Twente University, the Netherlands.

Johan Koskinen is a Lecturer in Social Statistics at the University of Manchester. He was awarded his PhD in Statistics from Stockholm University and worked at the Universities of Stockholm, Melbourne and Oxford. He joined the University of Manchester in 2011. Johan has contributed to the development of a number of statistical models and inference procedures for social networks, in particular exponential random graph models (ERGM) and stochastic actor-oriented models (SAOM). He co-edited an introductory book on ERGM with Dean Lusher and Gary Robins at the Universities of Melbourne and Swinburne that was recently published with CUP.

Panos Kostakos is the author of various articles on organised crime. He is currently a postdoc researcher in the Center for Ubiquitous Computing working on Big Data, Machine Learning and Decision Support Systems, at the University of Oulu, Finland.

Siobhan Lawler is a PhD Candidate at the National Drug and Alcohol Research Centre (NDARC), UNSW Sydney. Siobhan's research examines the role of alcohol and other drug use as a risk factor for aggression and future violent behaviour. Siobhan has been involved with a number of interdisciplinary research projects and currently works part-time to increase the uptake of evidence-based drug education in Australian schools.

Rutger Leukfeldt is Senior Researcher and the Cybercrime Cluster Coordinator at the Netherlands Institute for the Study of Crime and Law Enforcement (NSCR). Furthermore, Rutger is director of the Cybersecurity & SMEs Research Center of the Hague University of Applied Sciences. Over the last decade, Rutger worked on a number of cybercrime studies for the Dutch government and private companies. Examples include studies into the modus operandi and characteristics of cybercriminals, a nation-wide cybercrime victim survey and a study into the organisation of Dutch law enforcement agencies responsible for the fight against cybercrime.

Jade Lindley holds a PhD in Criminology and is based at the University of Western Australia Law School and UWA Oceans Institute. Her research focuses on the intersection of transnational crimes, international law and regulation. She is particularly interested in marine-based crimes such as maritime piracy and illegal fishing.

Anna Markovska is a Principal Lecturer in Criminology, Anglia Ruskin University. She has written and researched widely on issues of corruption, organised crime and prohibition in Ukraine. She has completed British Academy-sponsored projects on migrant workers and policing. She is currently conducting two empirical research projects on practicalities of policing modern-day slavery and on the study of illegal markets in Ukraine.

Anton Moiseienko is a Research Fellow at the Centre for Financial Crime & Security Studies of the Royal United Services Institute, London. He holds a PhD in law from Queen Mary University of London. He has published on international law and criminal law, including in the *International & Comparative Law Quarterly* and *Criminal Law Review.*

Erika Techera is a Professor of Environmental Law at the University of Western Australia Law School and UWA Oceans Institute. Her research focuses on international and comparative environmental law, particularly in relation to marine governance and small island states.

Anna Sergi holds a PhD in Sociology (2014), with specialisation in Criminology, from the University of Essex, where she currently is a Senior Lecturer. Her specialism is in organised crime and comparative criminal justice. She has published extensively in renowned journals and she has authored three books. Prior to her PhD, Anna completed her degree in law at the University of Bologna, and a Master of Law (LL.M.) in Criminal Law at Kings College London. Anna has worked in the private sector briefly too, first in Forensics for Pricewaterhouse Coopers in Milan and afterwards in the Italian Desk of Withers LLP in London.

Petrus C. van Duyne, Psychologist and Jurist, carried out research at the Dutch Ministry of Justice and as a Professor until 2011 at Tilburg University, the Netherlands. He researched decision making by public prosecutors and judges, after which he undertook research on fraud, economic and organised crime in the Netherlands and surrounding countries and participated in organised crime projects in the Western Balkans. He has researched money laundering and corruption in Serbia. He followed the unfolding anti-laundering policy critically and published extensively on this subject. Since 1999, he has organised Cross-Border Crime Colloquium.

1 Introduction

Saskia Hufnagel and Anton Moiseienko

Organised crime by definition involves collaboration among criminals. This collaboration and the networks it involves are increasingly complex, which is why efforts to understand it represent a crucial area in criminological research. Not only does scholarly research in this area enrich our knowledge of how criminals operate, but it also offers insights of practical relevance to law enforcement work. Most obviously, focusing investigatory and prosecutorial resources on key criminal actors – such as gang leaders or prolific criminal enablers – causes greater disruption to crime than merely pursuing rank-and-file offenders. On a more systemic level, addressing the conditions that enable criminal groups to (co-)operate effectively, be it access to specific markets or the ability to recruit low-level accomplices on the internet, can provide further intervention opportunities for policy-makers and law enforcement.

In light of this, the present edited collection provides an overview of global perspectives on global networks. Its objective is to contribute to the existing knowledge on why and how criminals form stable or fluid networks of cooperation, what patterns of interaction within those networks are observable in various contexts and how they can be disrupted. Intended audiences of the book include researchers, policy-makers, law enforcement officers and anyone else with an interest in criminal justice generally and organised crime specifically.

This volume draws on the updated and revised versions of papers presented at the 8th Illicit Networks Workshop held at Queen Mary University of London in December 2016. The annual Illicit Networks Workshop brings together scholars from around the world with an interest in the study of illicit networks. The book reflects the international and interdisciplinary ethos of the workshop.

Thus, contributions address illicit networks in Australia, the Indo-Pacific region, South Asia and a number of European countries, such as Italy, the Netherlands, Norway and Ukraine. Methodological approaches taken by authors are similarly diverse. While several chapters use social network analysis to elucidate the operation of illicit networks,[1] among the variety of methods applied by

1 Chapter 3: 'Sticking together: Evidence of co-offending partnerships in two-mode covert networks' by Chiara Broccatelli, Martin Everett and Johan Koskinen; Chapter 4: '"It's just

other authors are statistical analysis of the prevalence of co-offending,[2] qualitative analysis of over a hundred police interrogations,[3] the use of routine activity theory to explain the attractiveness of illegal fishing to criminal groups[4] and case-study analysis of corrupt networks.[5] Finally, one author employs social network analysis to analyse the proliferation not of crime but of the *literature* on organised crime to identify trends in knowledge production.[6]

This eclectic array of contributions fulfils two interrelated aims. First and foremost, it showcases the constructive role that analysis of illicit networks can fulfil in various contexts, ranging from co-offending in Norway to trafficking in metal-detected cultural goods in South Asia. Second, it highlights the variety of methods that can be fruitfully applied. In doing so, the book makes a modest contribution to filling in some of the existing knowledge gaps while also pointing to directions for future research, which we will explore further in the final and concluding chapter.

The book opens with two chapters that deal with the formation of illicit networks by exploring co-offending patterns. Synøve Andersen's statistical analysis provides a rare glimpse into co-offending in Norway, a country that differs in many ways from the Anglo-American jurisdictions that typically constitute a focal point for similar studies. While the Norwegian co-offending landscape is broadly similar to those of other states discussed in the existing literature, some divergences – such as a lower level of female co-offending – reaffirm the value of conducting such analysis in various geographies.

The comparative aspect is also prominent in the chapter by Chiara Broccatelli, Martin Everett and Johan Koskinen on co-offending in several covert networks, both contemporary and historical. The consideration by the authors of the early 20th-century British suffragettes is particularly instructive. While the objective of attaining female suffrage would be universally considered laudable today, some of the suffragettes' actions caused them to run afoul of the law and therefore operate covertly. The similarities and distinctions between such borderline groups and genuinely criminal organisations or terrorists can be of relevance for understanding, to take one example, today's animal-rights activists.

---

business:" Leaders' strategies for risk management in criminal networks' by Siobhan Lawler and David Bright; Chapter 10: 'The social organisation of treason: Anti-Hitler networks in the Third Reich' by Robert R. Faulkner and Eric R. Cheney; and Chapter 8: 'Meet the in-betweeners: Exploring the quality and strength of ties in the "Mafia Capitale" network in Rome' by Anna Sergi.

2 Chapter 2: 'Co-offending in Norway: A comparative perspective' by Synøve N. Andersen.

3 Chapter 5: 'Cybercrime, money mules and situational crime prevention: Recruitment, motives and involvement mechanisms' by E.R. (Rutger) Leukfeldt and E.R. (Edward) Kleemans.

4 Chapter 7: 'Using routine activity theory to explain illegal fishing in the Indo-Pacific' by Jade Lindley and Erika Techera.

5 Chapter 9: 'Power and trust networks in the organisation of crime in Ukraine' by Anna Markovska and Petrus C. van Duyne.

6 Chapter 11: 'Organised crime research 1985–2014: Mapping research dynamics through social network analysis' by Panos Kostakos.

The second part of the book considers the management of illicit networks. Based on the information about a drug trafficking syndicate active in Australia in the 1970s, Siobhan Lawler and David Bright analyse how leaders in criminal groups manage the tension between maintaining contacts with a large number of criminal associates and avoiding increased visibility that may lead to detection. Although one possibility to successfully coordinate a criminal network is to liaise with a select circle of key accomplices, the authors find that reliance on strategies such as the use of corruption or threat of violence, the latter generally being underrated because of its 'irrationality', is much more widespread than previously assumed.

While Lawler and Bright focus on gang leaders, Rutger Leukfeldt and Edward Kleemans examine the recruitment of so-called money mules, individuals who wittingly or unwittingly transfer funds for the benefit of a criminal. Despite their low level in the criminal hierarchy, money mules are vital to cybercrime, in particular as they enable the 'cashing out' of funds stolen online. The authors' proposals for framing awareness-raising campaigns among potential money mules will no doubt be of interest to law enforcement in EU member states that have already taken steps in that direction, for instance, with Europol's successive Money Mule Actions.

The third part of the book investigates two previously underexplored types of transnational illicit trafficking, the movement of cultural artefacts illegally retrieved by metal detecting across international borders and illegal international fishing. In addition to that, both chapters underscore the utility of methods other than social network analysis for studying illicit networks. Using open-source information from online forums for metal detectorists, Samuel Hardy sheds light on how modern-day treasure hunters find and sell cultural heritage objects in South Asia. As he makes clear, although one cannot presume all such detectorists to breach local laws, many of them probably do; such open-source analysis is therefore a useful barometer for researchers and policy-makers.

The chapter by Jade Lindley and Erika Techera looks at another area of transnational crime that does not always attract the attention it deserves, namely illegal fishing in the Indo-Pacific region. By looking at the phenomenon through the lens of Routine Activity Theory, the authors identify measures that have the potential to mitigate the impact of this type of crime, focusing not only on governmental intervention but also on the role that consumers can play by affecting relevant markets.

The fourth part of the book continues the theme of exploring the boundaries in the study of illicit networks. Although illicit networks often operate in the criminal underground, occasionally they affect governance structures or even actively seek to impact political life. Hence, the following three chapters are centred around the subject of illicit networks and politics. Anna Sergi paints in depth the symbiotic relationship that Rome's 'Mafia Capitale' had managed to establish with certain strata of the city's political elite before the trial of its leaders in 2015–2016.

A similar theme of collusion between criminal entrepreneurs and public officials is examined in the analysis of the illegal gambling business in Ukraine by

Anna Markovska and Petrus van Duyne. Drawing on a detailed case study, the authors show how the legislative prohibition of gambling in Ukraine has shaped an environment where entrepreneurs, organised criminals and state authorities negotiate the limits of permissible behaviour on a case-by-case basis. In such circumstances, interpersonal trust replaces reliance on the rules; yet it remains a scarce commodity in relations among crooks.

In contrast to the two preceding chapters, the one by Robert Faulkner and Eric Cheney is not concerned with profit-driven criminality. Instead, it looks at anti-Nazi networks during the Third Reich and analyses the impact of the plotters' personal background on the objectives they pursued, such as the assassination of Hitler or clandestine negotiations with Allied Powers. As with the 20th-century suffragette networks, the characterisation of such networks as 'criminal' is not a moral judgement but merely a reflection of the fact that they were operating in defiance of their country's law at the time. Since they aimed to change Germany's political system, this analysis represents a rare study of a historical group that pursued purely political objectives in a clandestine manner without engaging in indiscriminate terror attacks.

Finally, the book concludes with a section on advancing the field. It consists of two chapters, with one taking stock of the existing scholarship and the other outlining directions for future research. By measuring the density and centrality of certain topics in organised crime research over the past three decades, Panos Kostakos uses quantitative analysis to map out thee evolution of the literature in the field. In doing so, he shows that subjects explicitly related to the real-life need of policy-makers and law enforcement agencies score higher on density and centrality than other domains of study. While this attests to the existence of a continuing dialogue between the academic and practitioners' communities, Kostakos sounds a note of caution in that research should not be entirely subordinated to the needs of the day. The balance between academic pursuit of knowledge and real-world relevance is also a central theme in the editors' conclusions, which reflect on the ways in which further exploration of criminal networks can facilitate criminal justice policy-making and law enforcement.

As the pages that follow aim to demonstrate, research that focuses on criminal networks as a focal point for analysis can make a significant contribution to the study of organised crime. Importantly, such work is not the exclusive preserve of those who conduct social network analysis. This book will succeed in its objectives if its content gives a flavour of the methodological variety, geographical diversity, interdisciplinarity and originality of contemporary research on criminal networks.

Part I

Formation of criminal networks

2 Co-offending in Norway

A comparative perspective

Synøve N. Andersen

2.1 Introduction

The notion of co-offending has been known to criminologists for about a century (Breckinridge and Abbot, 1912; Shaw and McKay, 1931), and, as a phenomenon, co-offending is of interest both in itself and because it can provide insights into other criminological phenomena, such as gangs, organised crime and peer effects (Carrington, 2014; van Mastrigt and Farrington, 2009; Weerman, 2014). While theoretically salient, the empirical literature on co-offending has remained relatively limited up until recent years. Much promoted by the entry of social network analysis into the social sciences (see, e.g., Butts, 2008, for an overview), as well as the increasing availability of large-scale official datasets that include information on co-offending, new and exciting opportunities to advance the ways in which criminal phenomena are analysed and understood now dominate this field of study (Bouchard and Amirault, 2013).

While the co-offending literature has developed significantly in recent years, it is important to recognise that most of the co-offending literature – as the criminological literature more generally – comprises empirical contributions from the United States, the UK and Canada (see, e.g., Andresen and Felson, 2012; Bouchard and Nguyen, 2010; Carrington, 2002, 2009; Stoltzenberg and D'Alessio, 2008; van Mastrigt and Farrington, 2009).[1] An important question is, therefore, whether the patterns found in these countries extrapolate to other national, institutional and penal contexts. The purpose of this chapter is to explore the nature and characteristics of co-offending and co-offending groups in Norway, using the rich – and relatively unexplored – information about co-offending that is found in Norwegian official registers. Norway as a country is commonly considered both a geographical, social and penal outlier, characterised by a relatively small and heterogenous population, a generous welfare state, high rates of trust and life satisfaction, and low rates of both crime and recidivism (see, e.g., Pratt, 2008). This makes Norway a unique and interesting setting for

1 Some co-offending studies are also based on data from Sweden (Sarnecki, 2001) and the Netherlands (Bernasco, 2006).

exploring the generalisability of co-offending patterns that are derived from studies conducted (primarily) in Anglo-American countries. Norwegian registry data are moreover a rich and largely untapped source of information on criminological phenomena (Hovde Lyngstad and Skardhamar, 2011), which, amongst other things, enable the identification of co-offenders and co-offending groups in a very similar manner to what has been done in other countries. Notably, a substantial part of the cross-national comparison of co-offending in Canada, England and the United States conducted by Carrington and van Mastrigt (2013) can be replicated using Norwegian registers.

2.2 Co-offending: A brief descriptive overview

Before exploring the prevalence and characteristics of co-offending in Norway, a quick overview of the current knowledge status of key co-offending measures is in order. Co-offending is defined as the commission of an offence by more than one person, and one of the most well-established findings in the study of co-offending is that it is relatively common (Carrington, 2014). However, the generality of this conclusion is called into question by the wide variety of prevalence estimates found in the literature so far – ranging from, e.g., 10 percent in van Mastrigt and Farrington (2009) to 82 percent in Shaw and McKay (1931).[2] Co-offending is known to vary systematically by crime type, and is more common in, e.g., burglaries, robberies and vehicle thefts than in, e.g., drug possessions or violent and sexual offences (Carrington, 2002, 2014; Piquero, Farrington and Blumstein, 2007; Reiss and Farrington, 1991). Co-offences are typically more serious than solo offences (Erickson, 1971) – a phenomenon referred to as group polarisation (Lamm and Meyers, 1978) or social amplification (Kasperson et al., 1988).

Compared to solo offenders, co-offenders typically have higher offending rates (McCord and Conway, 2002; Ouellet, Boivin, Leclerc and Morselli, 2013; Reiss and Farrington, 1991; Sarnecki, 2001). In terms of demographics, co-offending is more common among young offenders than among older offenders, and although the literature is somewhat inconclusive, women seem to co-offend slightly more often than men and ethnic minorities somewhat more often than the ethnic majority (Carrington, 2002, 2009; Reiss, 1988; van Mastrigt and Farrington, 2009). In terms of criminal experience, co-offending is also more common at the onset of the criminal career than at the end of it (Carrington, 2009; Reiss, 1988; Reiss and Farrington, 1991).

As co-offending is defined as the commission of an offence by more than one person, co-offending networks (or groups) comprise actors who are defined based upon event participation (i.e., committing a crime together) (Kreager et al., 2016). Co-offences typically take place in small groups of two or three offenders

2 Important sources of variation include the definition of co-offending, the level of measurement, the data used, the historical and geographical setting, and the samples criteria; see, e.g., Table 1 in Carrington (2014, pp., 550–551).

(Carrington, 2002; Reiss and Farrington, 1991; van Mastrigt and Farrington, 2009), and co-offending relationships tend to be relatively short-lived; most co-offending pairs only commit one (recorded) crime together (Carrington, 2014; Reiss and Farrington, 1991; Sarnecki, 2001). Offenders also tend to choose as co-offenders people who are similar to themselves in terms of age, ethnicity and criminal experience (Sarnecki, 2001; van Mastrigt and Farrington, 2009; Weerman, 2003), giving co-offending groups a strong homophilous tendency.

2.3 Empirical analysis

The analyses in this chapter are based on data from Norwegian administrative registers as kept and provided by Statistics Norway. Information from different data sources is combined using an 11-digit personal identification number (PIN), which is issued by the Norwegian Tax Administration to all individuals with a temporary or permanent residence permit. This allows for a population-wide dataset comprising information on offending and other socio-demographic states and events.

2.3.1 Co-offending data

Information on (co-)offending is based on the statistics on criminal charges against individuals (Statistics Norway, 2017), which rely on police data on completely investigated offences where there is one (or more) identified suspect(s) at the end of the police investigation. A limitation of using police data is, of course, that the question of guilt has not yet been decided by the court, and that the data material hence will include some offenders who eventually will be acquitted. The main reason for choosing police data is that these data are structured with offences and offenders nested within offence participations, meaning that every time an offender engages in one offence this is entered as one record in the data material.[3] Each record therefore includes information on both the offence (e.g., date of offence, crime type, severity, offence ID, police district, etc.) and the offender (e.g., sex, age and PIN), and by combining the offence ID and the offender PIN it is possible to determine who co-offended with whom in committing what offence. Due to the structure of the data, this cannot be done using court or prison data. It is moreover important to stress that the data extraction takes place at the *end* of the police investigation, i.e., when the question of guilt has been decided by the prosecution authorities, and that many (primarily less serious) offences never reach the court system. Relying on police data hence

3 Suppose, for instance, that individuals *A–C* are all charged with committing offence *1* (e.g., an auto theft) and individual *A* with offences *2–4* as well. The data then includes one data record per offender for offence *1* (*A1, B1, C1*) and one data record per additional offence *2-4* for individual *1* (*A2, A3, A4*) – i.e., a total of six data records, with four records for individual *A*, one record for individual *B* and one record for individual *C*.

provides a more complete overview of offences that come to the attention of the criminal justice system than would court or prison data (see Hovde Lyngstad and Skardhamar, 2011, p. 623, for an overview of the course of an offence through the Norwegian legal system).

The data on investigated offences are available from 1992 until 2015 and include both felonies and misdemeanours. In the following analyses, information on co-offending will be explored using two units of analysis: offences and offence participations.[4] An offence (also known as an incident) is a criminal event in which one or more people are identified as offenders. An offence participation (also referred to just as a participation) is the involvement of an offender in an offence. Offence participations are particularly valuable as they allow for the simultaneous examination of both offence and offender correlates of co-offending. The analyses in this chapter are based on, and compared to, measures on the offence and/or participation level as appropriate.

Statistics Norway differentiates between nine[5] main types of offences, and the relative distribution of these offences in the data material is summarised in Table 2.1. The largest offence categories are traffic offences and drug and alcohol offences, which make up just over 24 percent of all offences and around 23 percent of all offence participations each.

The third largest offence category is property theft (17 and 19 percent of all offences and offence participations, respectively), followed by public order and integrity violations (13 and 12 percent of all offences and offence participations, respectively). The smallest proportion of offences are sexual offences, criminal damage and so-called other offences, making up approximately 1, 3 and 1.3 percent of all offences and offence participations, respectively.

2.3.2 Data on individual characteristics

The analyses in this chapter also rely on information from the population registry to explore variations in co-offending depending on the offender's sex, age at offence and immigrant background. The age at offence is calculated by combining information on the date of birth from the population registry with the date of offence in the data on criminal charges. Age at offence is used both as a continuous variable and as a dummy separating those who were under the age of 18 when committing their offence, from those who were older (labelled

4 Offenders, i.e., persons who can appear more than once in the data as a participant in different offences, is a third unit of analysis (Carrington and van Mastrigt, 2013; Ouellet, Boivin, Leclerc and Morselli, 2013; van Mastrigt and Farrington, 2009) that will not be analysed here.

5 These are based on the Norwegian Penal Code of 2005, and I use the current legislation for offences committed both before and after the new law was effective. For instance, while the Penal Code of 1905 defined an incident of driving under the influence (DUI) as a traffic offence, the Penal Code of 2005 defines it as a drug and alcohol offence. All DUI incidents will therefore be characterised as drug and alcohol offences, irrespective of when they took place.

Table 2.1 Relative distribution of different offence types measured on offence and offence participation level

	Offence	*Offence participation*
Property theft (e.g., theft, other unlawful use and possession of property)	17.30%	18.76%
Other offences for profit (e.g., fraud, embezzlement, money laundering, corruption, tax evasion, smuggling)	8.91%	10.01%
Criminal damage (e.g., damage to property, public danger from fire and other criminal damage)	2.53%	3.10%
Violence and maltreatment (e.g., assault, threats, robbery and extortion, coercion, deprivation of liberty, human trafficking, terrorism, murder)	7.82%	8.01%
Sexual offences (e.g., rape, sexual abuse, incest)	0.99%	0.95%
Drug and alcohol offences (e.g., possession and use of narcotics, selling narcotics, doping, driving under the influence)	24.50%	23.25%
Public order and integrity violations (e.g., public order violations, harassing public servant, perjury, violation of entry ban, ID or document forgery)	12.53%	12.15%
Traffic offences (e.g., speeding, non-possession of driving license, personal injury)	24.15%	22.49%
Other offences (e.g., offences against nature and the environment, work environment offences)	1.28%	1.28%
Number of observations	**3 659 837**	**3 975 261**

'youths' and 'adults', respectively). This cut-off is set at 18 years because this is the age of majority in Norway, and because this is a commonly applied cut-off in the literature which facilitates direct comparisons between studies. To measure ethnicity[6] or immigrant background, I create a dummy variable set to 1 for those who are born outside of Norway, i.e., for first-generation immigrants and 0 for those born in Norway. Another approach would be to group first and second-generation immigrants together in the 'minority' category. Second-generation immigrants are, however, a relatively small group, which comprised

6 Note that ethnicity is a complex concept that is captured using measures on, e.g., own/parents'/grandparents' country of birth, citizenship, race and self-reported ethnic/cultural background or identity throughout both the co-offending literature and the criminological literature more broadly. A detailed analysis of variations in co-offending by the choice of ethnicity measure is outside the scope of this chapter, and studies that report on ethnic differences are cited without detailed information on the underlying ethnicity measure being provided. Norwegian authorities do not obtain information on race or perceived cultural/ethnic identity, and a measure based on country of birth will therefore be used throughout.

only 0.5 percent of the total population in 1992 and 2.9 percent of the total population in 2015. The majority of second-generation immigrants are also relatively young, and the treatment of this group will most likely have no substantial impact on the results presented here. It is still important to recognise that this is a crude categorisation of immigrant background, which is likely to mask variations in both overall offending and co-offending between immigrants who come to Norway from different countries and for different reasons. As the low prevalence of co-offending among immigrants (see Table 2.7) makes it challenging to conduct robust subsample analyses, and information on immigrant status is easy to come by in official registers, this approach is chosen in order to simplify the analysis and enhance comparability.

2.3.3 Method of analysis

The purpose of this analysis is to give a descriptive overview of the prevalence and nature of co-offending and co-offending groups in Norway. Moreover, the goal is to contextualise these estimates in light of the international literature to assess whether co-offending in Norway resembles or differs from co-offending in other countries. The comparative approach can be characterised as empirical and quantitative, and direct comparisons will be made only to previous studies that meet the following three criteria:

- They rely on similar data sources as applied here, preferably retrieved from registers of offences investigated by the police and/or prosecution authorities;
- Analyses are based on the same measuring level as applied here (i.e., offence and/or offence participation);
- The data material covers the entire (or a random sample of the entire) population of offence participations, and/or subsamples defined according to the same characteristics as in the current study.

Based on these criteria, there is one study that stands out as a particularly relevant basis of comparison, namely Carrington and van Mastrigt's (2013) cross-national comparison of co-offending in Canada, England and the United States. This study draws on datasets from police reports on cleared criminal incidents in all three countries in which offence participations include both offence and offender characteristics. This means that the data follow the same structure as the Norwegian data, and similarly include cases where the question of guilt has been evaluated by the prosecution authority but not the courts. These three datasets are used by Carrington and van Mastrigt (2013) to provide a comparative and comprehensive overview of key co-offending measures in three of the most commonly cited countries in the co-offending literature. All country-specific measures provided in this analysis can be replicated using Norwegian data, and this provides a unique opportunity to create precise and directly comparable estimates. In addition to the direct comparisons between the Norwegian analysis and that of Carrington and van Mastrigt (2013), the relative uniqueness and generalisability of the Norwegian findings are also assessed drawing parallels to the co-offending literature more generally.

2.4 Co-offending in Norway

The following three sections explore the nature and characteristics of co-offending and co-offending groups in Norway. The first section considers the prevalence of co-offending, and the second section explores the characteristics of co-offending groups. Here, all estimates are based on the offence level. Finally, the third section explores offence and offender correlates of co-offending, using information on both the offence and offence participation level. All results are contextualised with the results of previous studies, with a particularly strong parallel to Carrington and van Mastrigt's (2013) comparative study of co-offending in Canada, England and the United States.

2.4.1 Prevalence

The prevalence of co-offending (measured as the proportion of all offences or offence participations that includes more than one offender) is the attribute that has most frequently been subjected to comparison across datasets and countries. While both readily available and of fundamental importance, prevalence rates vary drastically depending on, e.g., the definition of co-offending, the level of measurement, the data used, the historical and geographical setting, and the sample criteria (Carrington, 2014). Limiting the focus to prevalence rates based on large-scale administrative datasets similar to the one analysed here, the numbers vary somewhat in the Norwegian datasets and those used in previous studies.

Table 2.2 shows that there are approximately 3.7 million offences and nearly 4 million offence participations in the data material. Of these two units, the prevalence of co-offending is approximately 5.7 percent at the offence level and 13 percent at the participation level. These numbers are approximately 50 percent lower than those that have been reported elsewhere; for instance, the co-offending prevalence varied from 10.6 to 14.5 percent at the offence level and from 21.9 and 29.1 at the participation level in Carrington and van Mastrigt (2013; see also Hashimi, Bouchard, Morselli, and Ouellet, 2016; Ouellet et al., 2013). The relatively low Norwegian numbers may be a result of a combination of (at least) four different factors: co-offending is less common in Norway; the

Table 2.2 Co-offending prevalence measured on offence and offence participation level

	Offence	*Offence participation*
Solo offending	94.34%	86.96%
Co-offending	5.66%	13.04%
Number of observations	**3 659 837**	**3 975 261**

Norwegian data on criminal charges consistently underestimate co-offending, for instance, due to the reporting and/or registration practices of police; the inclusion of all offences (rather than only 'street crimes') deflates Norwegian prevalence rates, especially as compared to older co-offending studies (e.g., Shaw and McKay, 1942); or, more co-offences than solo offences are dropped during the police investigation due to, e.g., police priorities and resources, or the state of evidence in co-offending cases.

2.4.2 Co-offending groups

While estimates of the prevalence of co-offending differ, previous studies tend to converge more with regards to the common characteristics of co-offending groups. That is, they tend to be small, impermanent and homophilous (i.e., people tend to co-offend with others that are similar to themselves in terms of age, sex, ethnicity, etc.) (Carrington, 2002; Reiss and Farrington, 1991; Sarnecki, 2001; van Mastrigt and Farrington, 2009; Weerman, 2003). The following sections will explore the characteristics of co-offending groups in Norway, focusing first on their size and then on their demographic composition.

2.4.2.1 Size

The size of the co-offending groups in the Norwegian data is shown in Table 2.3 below. The size distribution reflects the well-documented pattern of co-offending being a 'small-group' phenomenon (cf., Carrington, 2002; Reiss and Farrington, 1991; van Mastrigt and Farrington, 2009): about 75 percent of all co-offences involve only two offenders, while only 3.3 percent include 6 offenders or more. These numbers are very similar to the offence level measures in, e.g., Carrington and van Mastrigt (2013) and Hashimi et al. (2016), with only a few percentage points distinguishing the results in these studies.

The average co-offending group size is, as a result, also very similar; at 2.5 offenders in Norway and between 2.3 and 2.4 offenders in Carrington and van

Table 2.3 Co-offending group size in percent of all co-offences. Measured on offence level

Number of offenders	*Offence*
2	74.55%
3	15.37%
4	4.75%
5	2.03%
6+	3.30%
N	**207 029**
Mean size	2.50 (1.21)
Maximum size	41
99th percentile	8

Mastrigt (2013). It is the slightly higher proportion of co-offending groups with 5 or more offenders in Norway that drives this average marginally upwards. In sum, however, these numbers suggest that while the prevalence of co-offending is lower in Norway, the size of co-offending groups is remarkably similar across nations.

One result that is less consistent between studies is that of maximum group size. Carrington and van Mastrigt reported groups of up to 20 offenders in England and up to 75 offenders in Canada, and several groups of this size can be seen in the literature (see Carrington, 2014, for an overview). The Norwegian data include groups of 41 offenders at the most. It is, however, worth emphasising that the size distribution is highly left-skewed, and that there is only one group of this size in the dataset. The second largest group consists of 31 offenders (N=2 groups) and the third largest of 27 offenders (N=3 groups). The 99th percentile is at 8 offenders.

2.4.2.2 Demographic composition

The demographic composition of the co-offending groups is shown in Table 2.4. Each panel breaks down the group into three categories: two homophilous categories (e.g., for all male and all female) and one mixed category for groups where the offenders have different demographic characteristics.

Panel (a) shows the sex composition of the co-offending groups in the sample. All-male groups are the most common (77 percent), followed by mixed groups (19.7 percent) and finally all-female groups (3.3 percent). This overall pattern confirms that co-offending groups have strong homophilous tendencies (Sarnecki, 2001; van Mastrigt and Farrington, 2009; Weerman, 2003).

Table 2.4 Sex, age and immigrant composition of co-offending groups in percent of all co-offences. Measured at the offence level

	Offence
(a) Sex	
All male	77.00%
All female	3.26%
Mixed	19.74%
(b) Age	
All adult	65.94%
All youth	21.06%
Mixed	13.00%
(c) Immigrant	
All immigrants	3.01%
All Norwegian-born	88.29%
Mixed	8.70%
N	**207 029**

However, the proportion of all-female groups is substantially lower here than in Canada, England and the United States (with 12.8, 11.5 and 16.4 percent all-female groups, respectively) (Carrington and van Mastrigt, 2013, p. 130). The proportion of all-male groups is consequentially higher (77 vs. 57.7, 68.4 and 48 percent in Canada, England and the United States, respectively), while the proportion of mixed groups is about the same as in England (19.74 ca. 20.1 percent) and somewhat lower than in Canada (29.5 percent) and the United States (35.5 percent). These differences can, at least in part, be linked to the relative composition of the overall pool of offenders, as the relatively low proportion of female participants in the overall Norwegian offender population might suggest that the availability of potential co-offenders that are female is more limited (see Table 2.5(b)). The tendency for women to co-offend is also lower in Norway (see Table 2.5(a)): 14.3 percent of all co-offence participation in Norway involve a woman, compared to 20.1 percent in England, 26 percent in Canada and 32.8 percent in the United States (Carrington and van Mastrigt, 2013, p. 130).

The age composition is shown in panel (b) of Table 2.4. All-adult groups are the most common and mixed age groups the least common, a pattern that reflects that in Carrington and van Mastrigt (2013). The age distribution in the Norwegian data is relatively similar to that found in US data, where 69.9 percent of co-offending groups were all-adult, 17.8 were all-youth and 12.3 were mixed (Carrington and van Mastrigt, 2013, p. 131). In the data from both England and Canada, the proportion of all-adult groups was lower (52.9 and 54.9 percent, respectively) and the proportion of all-youth groups higher (29.7 percent and 30.7 percent, respectively) than in both Norwegian and American data. This can again be linked to the proportion of adult and young co-offenders in the four datasets, where the relative distribution of the two groups is quite similar in Norway and the United States (72 and 70 percent of co-offenders are adults and 28 and 25 percent are youths (see Table 2.6 (a)), while there is a higher proportion of youth co-offenders in both England and Canada (Carrington and van Mastrigt, 2013, p. 131).

Finally, panel (c) of Table 2.4 shows the immigrant distribution of co-offending groups in Norway. All Norwegian-born groups are by far the most common (88 percent), while 9 percent are mixed, and 3 percent are all-immigrant. The immigrant background of offenders has less often been included in studies of co-offending than information about age and sex, and it is therefore more challenging to find valid comparisons. In one study based on police data on co-offending among youths[7] in Stockholm, Sarnecki (2001) explored the composition of co-offending *dyads* and found that 47 percent were all-Swedish, 32 percent were mixed and 21 percent all-immigrants (see Sarnecki, 2001, p. 127). The relative distribution of the three groups is hence the same as in the Norwegian data, although the numbers differ substantially.

7 Defined as individuals aged 20 or younger (Sarnecki, 2001, p. 37).

2.4.3 *Correlates of co-offending*

The frequency of co-offending has consistently been shown to vary with both offence and offender characteristics. The offence type and the age of the offender have been particularly strong predictors, but weak relationships have also been found for sex, ethnicity and criminal experience (Carrington, 2002, 2009; Carrington and van Mastrigt, 2013; Reiss, 1988; van Mastrigt and Farrington, 2009). The following section first explores the relationships between the sex, age and immigrant background of the offender and co-offending, before moving on to differences in co-offending in different types of crimes. All estimates are measured on the participation level.

2.4.3.1 *Sex, age and immigrant background*

Table 2.5 shows the sex distribution of offence participations using three different measures. Panel (a) shows the relative distribution of men and women in co-offence participations, and panel (b) the relative distributions in *all* offence participations. Comparing these numbers makes it possible to explore whether co-offending is more common in one of the groups than overall offending. Finally, panel (c) shows the proportion of all offence participations that were co-offences, by the sex of the offender. The contents and structure of Tables 2.6 and 2.7 reflects that of Table 2.5, but the moderator variable of Table 2.6 is the offender's age and the moderator variable of Table 2.7 is the offender's immigrant background.

As we see from panel (a) of Table 2.5, 14.3 percent of all co-offence participations were committed by a woman and 85.7 percent by a male. The corresponding

Table 2.5 Sex distribution of participations in co-offences (a); sex distribution of participations in all offences (b); proportion of participations that were in co-offences, by the sex of the offender (c). Measured on offence participation level

(a)	
Male	85.68%
Female	14.32%
N (co-offence participations)	**518 442**
(b)	
Male	86.14%
Female	13.86%
N (all offence participations)	**3 975 261**
(c)	
Male	12.97%
N (all offence participations)	**3 424 200**
Female	13.47%
N (all offence participations)	**551 061**
Odds ratio (female:male)	1.05

number for *all* offence participations (panel (b)) is 13.9 and 86.1 percent, respectively, showing that the proportion of women is higher among co-offenders. Panel (c) reflects this, and shows that for women, 13.5 percent of all offence participations were co-offences. The corresponding number is 13.0 percent for men. This leads to an odds ratio of 1.05, indicating that the odds of committing a co-offence is 5 percent higher for women than for men. This finding is consistent with what we know about sex differences in co-offending from other countries (Carrington, 2002, 2009; Reiss, 1988; van Mastrigt and Farrington, 2009).

Comparing the numbers in Table 2.5 to those in Table 2.3 in Carrington and van Mastrigt (2013, p. 130), the proportion of female co-offenders and female offenders is lower in Norway than in Canada, England and the United States. The proportion of female offenders is lowest (and hence most similar to Norway) in England, where 20 percent of all co-offence participations and 18 percent of all offence participations involve women. The difference is largest between Norway and the United States; in the United States, 32.8 percent of all co-offence participations and 27.8 percent of all offence participations involve women. While the relative proportion of female offenders differs substantially both within Carrington and van Mastrigt (2013) and between their study and this Norwegian analysis, the finding that there is a higher proportion of women that co-offend is consistent across all four studies as well as with the general literature (Carrington, 2002, 2009; Reiss, 1988; van Mastrigt and Farrington, 2009). However, the odds ratio is smaller in Norway than in the other countries: 1.05 vs. 1.18, 1.33 and 1.40 in England, Canada and the United States, respectively (Carrington and van Mastrigt, 2013, p. 130). There are therefore variations in how much more common co-offending is among women than among men in different countries.

Table 2.6 Age distribution of participations in co-offences (a); age distribution of participations in all offences (b); proportion of participations that were in co-offences, by the age group of the offender (c)

(a)	
Adult	71.78%
Youth	28.22%
N (co-offence participations)	**518 442**
(b)	
Adult	89.09%
Youth	10.91%
N (all offence participations)	**3 975 261**
(c)	
Adult	10.51%
N (all offence participations)	**3 541 529**
Youth	33.73%
N (all offence participations)	**433 732**
Odds ratio (youth:adult)	4.34

The age distribution of offence participations is shown in Table 2.6, and the highest proportion of both co-offence participations and all offence participations involve an adult offender. However, the relative distribution of the two age groups differs substantially depending on whether co-offences or all offences are considered: 28 percent of all co-offence participations involve an offender aged 17 or younger while the corresponding number for all offences is 11 percent. Panel (c) moreover shows that 34 percent of all offence participations committed by youths were co-offences, while this only applies to 11 percent of all offence participations by adults. This corresponds to an odds ratio of 4.34, indicating that youths are 334 percent more likely to co-offend than adults. This confirms the well-established finding that co-offending is most common during adolescence and less so among adult offenders (see, e.g., Carrington, 2002, 2009; Reiss, 1988; van Mastrigt and Farrington, 2009).

Compared to the analyses in Carrington and van Mastrigt (2013), the proportion of co-offence participations involving youths is relatively similar in Norway and the United States (28 percent vs. 25 percent), but lower than in both Canada and England (both at 40 percent). At the same time, the proportion of *all* offence participations involving youths is lower in Norway than in all the other countries (10.9 percent of all offence participations in Norway as compared to 16 percent in the United States and 23 percent in both Canada and England) (Carrington and van Mastrigt, 2013, p. 131). This seemingly contradictory pattern reflects the low co-offending prevalence rates in Norway (see Table 2.2), which entail that the patterns observed for co-offending have a relatively small impact on the overall picture as compared to the countries where co-offending is more common. This pattern also means that the relative difference between youth and adults' co-offence participation is larger in Norway than the three other countries; while the odds ratio between youth and adults is 4.3 in Norway, it is 2.4 in the United States, 2.8 in England and 3.6 in Canada.[8]

To explore the relationship between age and co-offending in more detail, Figure 2.1 displays the proportion of all offence participations committed at a given age that were co-offences. This figure shows the left-skewed relationship between age and co-offending that is well-known from previous studies (see, e.g., Carrington, 2002, 2009; Reiss, 1988; van Mastrigt and Farrington, 2009), where co-offending is most common during adolescence before it decreases with age. Compared to the age-co-offending curves in Carrington and van Mastrigt (2013), three features of Figure 3 stand out. First, and, as expected, given the low prevalence of co-offending in the dataset, the overall level of co-offending is lower than in other studies for all ages. Second, rather than seeing a concave slope peaking at 13–15 years, the slope in figure 2.1 decreases consistently already

8 Carrington and van Mastrigt (2013) do not calculate odds ratios for their analysis of age, and odds ratios are therefore calculated based on the numbers in panel (d) of Table 4 using the following formula: $OR_{youth}=Odds_{adult}/Odds_{youth}=(1/P_{adult}-1)/(1/P_{youth}-1)$, where P is the percentage of co-offence participations in Table 4 (Carrington and van Mastrigt, 2013, p. 131).

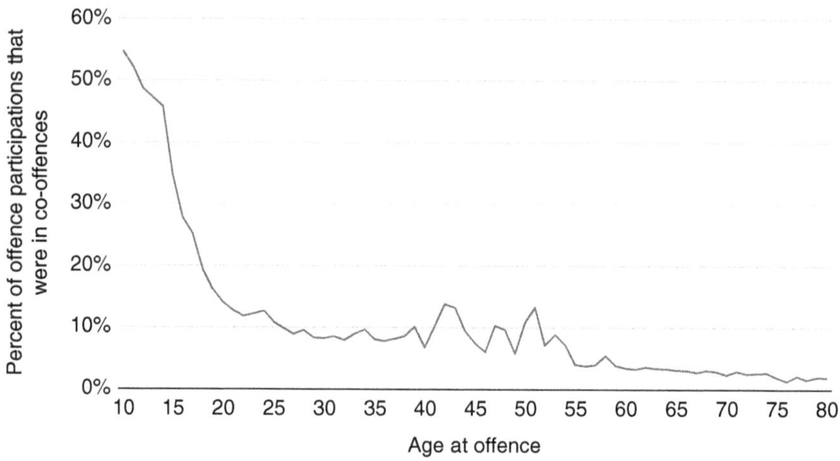

Figure 2.1 Age co-offending curve. Age 10–80 years

from 10 years. It is challenging to determine the cause of this pattern, but one plausible explanation is that Norwegian police to a greater extent than Canadian, English and American police discharge young solo offenders and therefore end up with a high proportion of co-offences in the cases where young offenders are charged. The empirical support for this argument should, however, be explored in future analyses. Finally, there is an *increase* in the proportion of co-offences for some ages between 40 and 55. This is the result of a large investigation that was concluded in 2008, in which a group of individuals in this age range was charged with a high number of co-offences. As this is an age at which both offending and co-offending is relatively rare, these offenders make a substantial impact on the data material. Overall, however, the relationship between age and co-offending in Norway corresponds very well with what we know from other countries.

The immigrant distribution of offence participations is shown in Table 2.7. The highest proportion of both co-offence participations and all offence participations involve a Norwegian-born offender. This is natural given the relative distribution of immigrants and Norwegian-born in the total population; in the period considered here, immigrants have comprised between 3.8 percent (1992) and 13 percent (2015) of the Norwegian population. The pool of potential offenders and accomplices is hence more limited among individuals with an immigrant background than among individuals born in Norway. Comparing the proportion of immigrants in panels (a) and (b), we see, however, that the proportion of immigrants is higher for all offence participations than for co-offence participations, indicating that co-offending is less common among immigrants than the native population. This is reflected in panel (c), where we see that 11 percent of all offence participations involving an immigrant were co-offences, while the same is true for 13 percent of offence participations involving a person

Table 2.7 Immigrant background distribution of participations in co-offences (a); immigrant background distribution of participations in all offences (b); proportion of participations that were in co-offences, by the immigrant background of the offender (c)

(a)	
Immigrant	6.80%
Norwegian-born	93.20%
N (co-offence participations)	**518 442**
(b)	
Immigrant	8.21%
Norwegian-born	91.79%
N (all offence participations)	**3 975 261**
(c)	
Immigrant	10.81%
N (all offence participations)	**326 215**
Norwegian-born	13.24%
N (all offence participations)	**3 649 046**
Odds ratio (immigrant:Norwegian-born)	0.80

Table 2.8 Odds ratios with 95 confidence intervals (CI) from logistic regression of the probability of a co-offence. Offence participations

	Odds ratio	*Lower 95% CI*	*Upper 95% CI*
Intercept	0.120		
Female	0.975	0.967	0.984
Youth	4.345	4.314	4.376
Immigrant	0.783	0.774	0.792

born in Norway. This is somewhat different to patterns shown in some other studies; while somewhat inconclusive on this point, the literature tends to show that ethnic minorities co-offend somewhat more often than the ethnic majority (Carrington, 2002, 2009; Reiss, 1988; van Mastrigt and Farrington, 2009).

An important question is how much of the difference between the two groups is driven by an unequal distribution of other characteristics than the moderator variable. Is, for instance, co-offending less common among immigrants because many of them arrive in Norway after the 'peak age' of co-offending? To explore this and related questions, Table 2.8 includes the results of a logistic regression model where all three offender characteristics are included. As we see, the results remain relatively unchanged even when the other variables are accounted for.

2.4.3.2 Type of offence

Crime type is one of the most widely explored correlates of co-offending, and co-offending is typically found to be more common in, e.g., burglaries, robberies and vehicle thefts than in, e.g., drug possessions or violent and sexual offences (Carrington, 2002, 2014; Piquero et al., 2007; Reiss and Farrington, 1991). Table 2.9 compares co-offending across the nine broad categories of offences as presented in Table 2.1. As we see, there are substantial variations in the prevalence estimates for different offence types, and co-offending is most common in offences categorised as criminal damage (21 percent), property theft (13 percent) and other offences for profit (9 percent). Co-offending is the least common for traffic offences (1 percent), drug and alcohol offences (2 percent) and sexual offences (3 percent). Hence, there is a substantial overlap in the co-offending prevalence for different offence types in the Norwegian data and what we know from previous studies (cf., Carrington, 2002, 2014; Piquero et al., 2007; Reiss and Farrington, 1991). One exception is the prevalence of co-offending in drug offences, where co-offending is substantially less common in Norway than in both Canada and the United States (2.4 vs. 21.6 and 17.3 percent at the offence level), but more similar to the levels of England (4.5 percent) (Carrington and van Mastrigt, 2013, p. 133). In this regard, it is interesting to note that co-offending is the least common in traffic and drug offences, two offence types that intuitively differ in terms of both their nature, typical offender characterises and incentives of group offending. The precursors and nature of co-offending in drug-related offences should therefore be explored in more detail in later analyses.

Table 2.9 Co-offence prevalence in various crime types. Offences characterised based on nine categories (a) and three categories (b)

	Offence	*Offence participation*
(a) Nine categories		
Property theft	13.19%	26.16%
Other offences for profit	9.26%	25.51%
Criminal damage	20.70%	40.37%
Violence and maltreatment	7.75%	17.00%
Sexual offences	3.02%	7.06%
Drug and alcohol offences	2.39%	5.21%
Public order and integrity violations	3.87%	8.64%
Traffic offences	1.00%	2.09%
Other offences	6.31%	13.25%
N	**3 659 837**	**3 975 261**
(b) Three categories		
Persons	7.22%	15.94%
N, offences against persons	**322 151**	**356 094**
Property	12.63%	27.34%
N, offences against property	**1 051 879**	**1 267 006**
Other	2.23%	4.9%
N, other offences	**2 285 807**	**2 352 161**
N, total	**3 659 837**	**3 975 261**

Making direct comparisons between the offence categories applied in various studies is challenging given the complex nature of the data material upon which the categories are based. Another approach than the one taken by Statistics Norway is to apply a broader categorisation, e.g., a distinction between 'offences against property', 'offences against persons' and 'other offences'. Taking this approach, the original offence categorisation in the Norwegian data can be recategorised in the following way: property theft, other offences for profit and criminal damage as 'offences against property', violence and maltreatment, as well as sexual offences, as 'offences against the person', and drug and alcohol offences, public order and integrity violations, traffic offences and other offences as 'other offences'. Applying this categorisation, panel (b) of Table 2.9 shows that co-offending is most common in offences against property (12.6 percent), followed by offences against persons (7.2 percent) and finally other offences (2.2 percent). It is interesting to note that the co-offending prevalence in offences against both property and persons resembles those reported in Carrington and van Mastrigt (2013), while the prevalence for other offences is substantially lower. This suggests that the comparatively low co-offending prevalence rate in Norway is primarily driven by a low rate of co-offending in this heterogeneous 'Other' category, which includes both traffic and drug offences (that collectively account for nearly 50 percent of all offences committed; see Table 2.1).

2.5 Summary

This chapter has explored the prevalence and characteristics of co-offending and co-offending groups in Norway by analysing a comprehensive dataset from the police and prosecution authorities covering all offence participations taking place between 1992 and 2015. In sum, it seems that co-offending in Norway – as represented in these data – is somewhat less common than in the Anglo-American countries that dominate the international literature (cf. Carrington and van Mastrigt, 2013; Ouellet et al., 2013; van Mastrigt and Farrington, 2009). This supports the notion that the prevalence of co-offending, as reported on in the international literature, might be somewhat exaggerated (Carrington, 2014). At the same time, it is important to acknowledge that using data on all offenses (as is done here) likely drives prevalence estimates downwards as compared to more 'traditional' analyses focusing on street crime (e.g., Shaw and McKay, 1942). We also see that the prevalence rates are particularly low for some of the most common offence types in Norway, including traffic and drug offences, which is likely driving the overall estimates downwards.

While co-offending is less common, it seems that the co-offending that takes place shares many of the same characteristics as in other countries. First, the size distribution of co-offending groups is remarkably similar to what we have seen in comparable datasets from Canada, England and the United States (cf. Carrington and van Mastrigt, 2013; Ouellet et al., 2013; van Mastrigt and Farrington, 2009). Only a few percentage points distinguish the results in these studies, and our finding therefore supports the notion of co-offending as a small-group phenomenon. Second, focusing on the sex, age and immigrant background of offenders, the results show that offenders tend to choose as co-offenders people who are similar to themselves. This gives co-offending groups in Norway a strong homophilous tendency (cf., Sarnecki, 2001; van Mastrigt and Farrington, 2009; Weerman, 2003). Third, the Norwegian data replicate the well-known correlation between age and co-offending and show that co-offending is most common during adolescence before it decreases with age (cf., Carrington, 2002, 2009; Reiss, 1988; van Mastrigt and Farrington, 2009). Of the correlates of co-offending that have been explored, age is the most influential. Fourthly, and also related to demographic predictors of co-offending, the results show that women co-offend at a slightly higher rate than men. The literature is somewhat inconclusive on this point, but the finding corresponds to those of, e.g., Carrington and van Mastrigt (2013). Finally, the results show that the rate of co-offending differs substantially between different crime types, and is most common for property offences (including property theft, criminal damage and offences for profit), less common for offences against the person (including sexual and violent offences) and the least common for so-called other offences (including traffic and drug and alcohol offences) (cf., Carrington, 2002, 2014; Carrington and van Mastrigt, 2013; Piquero et al., 2007; Reiss and Farrington, 1991). This is interesting as it suggests that irrespective of national context, co-offending is most common in offence types where co-offending has the most obvious instrumental advantages, for instance, in the form of criminal capital and the opportunity to collaborate and divide roles and responsibilities in the planning and execution of an offence.

In addition to these overall similarities, there are some interesting disparities between previous studies and the findings from Norway. These disparities can primarily be seen on a more detailed level of analysis, and do therefore rely on the comparison with Carrington and van Mastrigt's (2013) cross-national analysis of co-offending in Canada, England and the United States (in which the data and measures are relatively similar). From these two analyses, we can observe four points of contrast. First, there is a lower proportion of both female co-offenders and all-female co-offending groups in Norway than in both Canada, England and the United States. The sex difference in co-offending is also smaller in Norway, and while the common finding of women co-offending at a somewhat higher rate than men is replicated, the *rate* of overrepresentation varies between countries. Second, the age distribution in Norway is relatively similar to that found in the United States, but less left-skewed (i.e., with a lower proportion of youth co-offenders) than in both England and Canada. The proportion of *all* offence participations involving youths is furthermore lower in Norway than in all the other countries, meaning that the relative overrepresentation of youths as co-offenders is largest in Norway.[9] Third, the co-offending prevalence

9 Note that the sex distribution in co-offending in Norway most resembles that in England (and at least more than in the US) while the age distribution most resembles that in the US (and at least more than in England). This illustrates that similarities on one measure cannot necessarily be extrapolated to all other measures for the same two countries.

in some offences outside the typical property/person dichotomy is much lower in Norway than in other countries. This applies to drug and alcohol offences in particular. Finally, and this is the one point of divergence that pertains to the co-offending literature more generally, the results show that co-offending is less common among immigrants than individuals born in Norway. It should be noted that the literature is not conclusive on this point, but the results still provide no support for the finding that immigrant minorities co-offend somewhat more often than the majority (Carrington, 2002, 2009; Reiss, 1988; van Mastrigt and Farrington, 2009). To what extent different measures of ethnicity contribute to these differences cannot be explored in more detail using the current data material.

It is not possible with the data material at hand to assess the extent to which differences (and similarities) in co-offending in Norway are driven by national variations in the distribution of key co-offending correlates. It is also important to acknowledge that the use of registry data is accompanied by 'dark figures', meaning that the true prevalence of co-offending remains unknown. Despite these caveats, the current study has provided an overview of the prevalence and characteristics of registered co-offending and co-offending groups in a country that has not been represented in the co-offending literature thus far. This contributes to a more diverse empirical literature upon which conclusions about co-offending can be based, and furthermore provides a better foundation for tapping into the potential impact of social and institutional context for the patterns observed. The current analysis has thoroughly demonstrated that co-offending in Norway shares many of the same characteristics as in the Anglo-American countries that are better-represented in the international literature, supporting the notion that co-offending has some universal features that are prevalent independent of national context. Replicating this study across even more countries would constitute an important step in advancing our knowledge of the causes and consequences of this fundamental, yet still understudied, aspect of criminal behaviour.

References

Andresen, M. A., and Felson, M. (2012) Co-offending and the Diversification of Crime Types. *International Journal of Offender Therapy and Comparative Criminology*, 56, pp. 811–829.

Bernasco, W. (2006). Co-offending and the Choice of Target Areas in Burglary. *Journal of Investigative Psychology and Offender Profiling*, 3, 139–155.

Bouchard, M., and Amirault, J. (2013) Advances in Research on Illicit Networks. *Global Crime*, 14, pp. 119–122.

Bouchard, M., and Nguyen, H. (2010) Is It Who You Know, or How Many That Counts? Criminal Networks and Cost Avoidance in a Sample of Young Offenders. *Justice Quarterly*, 27, pp. 130–158.

Breckinridge, S. P., and Abbot, E. (1912) *The Delinquent Child and the Home*. New York, NY: Russel Sage Foundation Charities Publication Committee.

Butts, C. T. (2008) Social Network Analysis: A Methodological Introduction. *Asian Journal of Social Psychology*, 11, pp. 13–41.

Carrington, P. J. (2002) Group Crime in Canada. *Canadian Journal of Criminology*, 44, pp. 277–315.

Carrington, P. J. (2009) Co-offending and the Development of the Delinquent Career. *Criminology*, 47, pp. 1295–1329.

Carrington, P. J. (2014) Co-offending. In: G. Bruinsma and D. Weisburd (Eds.), *Encyclopedia of Criminology and Criminal Justice* (pp. 548–558). New York, NY: Springer-Verlag.

Carrington, P. J., and van Mastrigt, S. B. (2013) Co-offending in Canada, England and the United States: A Cross-National Comparison. *Global Crime*, 14, pp. 123–140.

Erickson, M. L. (1971) The group Context of delinquent Behavior. *Social Problems*, 19, pp. 114–129.

Hashimi, S., Bouchard, M., Morselli, C., and Ouellet, M. (2016) A Method to Detect Criminal Organizations from Police Data. *Methodological Innovations*, 9, pp. 1–14.

Hovde Lyngstad, T., and Skardhamar, T. (2011) Nordic Register Data and Their Untapped Potential for Criminological Knowledge. *Crime and Justice*, 40, pp. 613–645.

Kasperson, R. E., Renn, O., Slovic, P., Brown, H. S., Emel, J., Goble, R., Kasperson, J. X., and Ratick, S. (1988) The Social Amplification of Risk: A Conceptual Framework. *Risk Analysis*, 8, pp. 177–187.

Kreager, D. A., Schaefer, D. R., Bouchard, M., Haynie, D. L., Wakefield, S., Young, J., and Zajac, G. (2016) Toward a Criminology of Inmate Networks. *Justice Quarterly*, 33, pp. 1000–1028.

Lamm, H., and Myers, D. G. (1978) Group-Induced Polarization of Attitudes and Behavior. *Advances in Experimental Social Psychology*, 11, pp. 145–195.

McCord, J., and Conway, K. P. (2002) Patterns of Juvenile Delinquency and Co-offending. In: E. Waring, D. Weisburd, L. Sherman and F. Earls (Eds.), *Advances in Criminological Theory* (vol. 10, pp. 19–39). New Brunswick, NJ: Transaction.

Ouellet, F., Boivin, R., Leclerc, C., and Morselli, C. (2013) Friends With(Out) Benefits: Co-offending and Re-arrest. *Global Crime*, 14, pp. 141–154.

Piquero, A. R., Farrington, D. P., and Blumstein, A. (2007) *Key Issues in Criminal Career Research: New Analyses of the Cambridge Study on Delinquent Development.* Cambridge, MA: Cambridge University Press.

Pratt, J. (2008) Scandinavian Exceptionalism in an Era of Penal Excess. Part I: The Nature and Roots of Scandinavian Exceptionalism. *British Journal of Criminology*, 48, pp. 119–137.

Reiss, A. J. (1988) Co-offending and Criminal Careers. In: N. Morris and M. Tonry (Eds.), *Criminal Justice*, (vol. 10, pp. 117–170). Chicago, IL: University of Chicago Press.

Reiss, A. J., and Farrington, D. P. (1991) Advancing Knowledge about Co-offending: Results from a Prospective Longitudinal Survey of London Males. *The Journal of Criminal Law and Criminology*, 82, pp. 360–395.

Sarnecki, J. (2001) *Delinquent Networks.* Cambridge, MA: Cambridge University Press.

Shaw, C. R., & McKay, H. D. (1942). Juvenile Delinquency in Urban Areas. Chicago, IL: University of Chicago press.

Shaw, C. R., and McKay, H. D. (1931) *Juvenile Delinquency in Urban Areas.* Chicago, IL: University of Chicago Press.

Statistics Norway. (2017) Offenses Investigated, 2016. Retrieved from www.ssb.no/en/sosiale-forhold-og-kriminalitet/statistikker/lovbrudde.

Stolzenberg, L., and D'Alessio, S. J. (2008) Co-offending and the Age-Crime Curve. *Journal of Research in Crime and Delinquency*, 45, pp. 65–86.

van Mastrigt, S. B., and Farrington, D. P. (2009) Co-offending, Age, Gender and Crime Type: Implications for Criminal Justice Policy. *British Journal of Criminology*, 49, pp. 552–573.

Weerman, F. M. (2003) Co-offending as Social Exchange. Explaining Characteristics of Co-offending. *British Journal of Criminology*, 43, pp. 398–416.

Weerman, F. M. (2014) Theories of Co-offending. In: G. Bruinsma and D. Weisburd (Eds.), *Encyclopedia of Criminology and Criminal Justice* (pp. 5173–5184). New York, NY: Springer-Verlag.

3 Sticking together

Evidence of co-offending partnerships in two-mode covert networks

Chiara Broccatelli, Martin Everett and Johan Koskinen

3.1 Introduction

Research on social networks and crime has argued that individuals keep their relationships secret to limit their overexposure and protect their network from law enforcement (Sparrow, 1991; Everton, 2012a, 2012b; Lauchs, Keast and Le, 2012). It is assumed that the risk of incarceration, injury and death manifests itself in a both conscious and unconscious need to keep these types of relationships hidden (Erickson, 1981). This implies that individuals reduce their communications to a minimum (Koschade, 2006; Enders and Su, 2007; Eilstrup-Sangiovanni and Jones, 2008; Lindelauf, Borm and Hamers, 2009; Enders and Jindapon, 2010; Morselli, 2010). Consequently, criminals tend to act more autonomously (Krebs, 2002; Kirby, 2007) and, perhaps, limit their participation in activities. Yet, the collective behaviour of those individuals leads to a disconnected network structure, also characterised by a low level of cohesion (Raab and Milward, 2003; Brinton Milward and Raab, 2006; Morselli, 2009; Crossley et al., 2012; Stevenson and Crossley, 2013). In addition, criminal networks appear to be arranged along mutual trust relationships (Bruinsma and Bernasco, 2004) and kinship ties (Malm and Bichler, 2011), and fostered by individuals' belonging to different overlapping social circles (Papachristos and Smith, 2014).

The bulk of criminological research that investigates the dynamics of cohesion in covert networks is generally focusing on co-offending networks, and it has mainly focused on street gangs and juvenile groups. The phenomenon of co-offending has been defined as 'the act of committing a crime together with one or more accomplices' (Carrington and van Mastrigt, 2013, p. 124). Despite the burgeoning interest among scholars in studying which factors increase the individual preference to commit a crime with usual partners, disagreement still exists as to what extent co-offending partnerships should be evaluated and assessed.

Based on the sociological tradition, our basic premise here is that people's interactions can express individuals' motivations. One can argue that interactions within covert networks are subject to several constraints, mainly deriving from the need to act in secrecy. However, one can also suggest that the individuals choose to take part in illicit activities either because they already knew someone else involved, or because they had other types of influences reinforcing their motivations. We also consider that individuals participating together in crime events are likely to coordinate their actions. In this context, their relationships provide them with a fertile ground for nurturing their abilities and improving their performances because they can share their knowledge and expertise. Therefore, we suggest that stable co-offending partnerships not only better preserve secrecy but can also reduce the costs of changing accomplices and establishing new trust relationships.

The rest of the chapter is organised as follows. In the next section, we briefly review the literature on co-offending networks and co-participation in crime. We present our hypotheses in Section 3.3 and describe the strategy we used for detecting and analysing co-offending partnerships in Section 3.4. In later sections of the chapter, we demonstrate the value of this approach by analysing four real-world covert networks.

3.2 Co-offending networks

Traditionally, criminological theories explain changes in co-offending partnerships starting from delinquent roles and criminal careers. Warr (1996) argued that juvenile offenders tended to belong to multiple groups over the course of their delinquent careers and were likely to change accomplices frequently when they shifted roles from one type of offence to another. He concluded that the transitory and unstable nature of juvenile street gangs in the US was, perhaps, a consequence of the need to preserve secrecy since joint offending with the same accomplice may increase an individual's exposure. This idea is in line with Erickson's claim that operating in risky conditions provides a good motivation to maximise individuals' secrecy (Erickson, 1981). The tendency for offenders to take part in several offences while playing different roles was also confirmed by Sarnecki (1990). In his work, he used police information about suspected joint participation in offences in the population of juveniles up to age 20 in the city of Borlänge (Sweden). By looking at the delinquent careers and the tendency to co-offend along with others, Sarnecki confirmed the presence of shifting membership previously elaborated by Warr (1996). Sarnecki highlighted that

> the juveniles enter and leave the gangs very rapidly. They commit offenses together for a time and then cease, or start to commit offenses together with others—occasionally returning later to their former companions.
>
> (Sarnecki, 1990, p. 39)

He concluded that juveniles who move frequently from one gang to another might erase the boundaries between gangs because they essentially have multiple gang affiliations. This is in line with the idea formulated by Yablonsky, who defined a co-offending network as a 'near-group' by virtue of its impermanence, lack of cohesion and unclear role division (Yablonsky, 1959, p. 109).

Research on co-offending networks has found associations between the tendency to co-offend and individuals' personal characteristics. Some studies reported sex differences and suggest that females seem to be more likely to commit a crime with male partners, rather than males who, instead, tend to prefer same-sex accomplices (see Carrington, 2011, pp. 244–248; van Mastrigt, 2014, pp. 560–561). Moreover, other studies suggest that ethnicity can play a certain role in the selection of the offenders (Sarnecki, 2001; Pettersson, 2003). Partners in crime tended to be selected from the same ethnic group, although this was confirmed mainly for the US, with evidence less clear for other countries due to a lack of studies (van Mastrigt, 2014, pp. 562–563, for a review of those studies).

The probability of committing crimes with accomplices has also been related to both the age and the delinquent career of individuals involved. Carrington (2009) suggested that juvenile offenders were more active than adults and that the tendency to commit crimes together decreased with age, especially for individuals with only a few recorded offences. Concerning individual criminal experiences, findings reported that individuals with fewer than eight recorded offences were more likely to commit a crime with accomplices at the beginning of their career, presumably due to their initial need to learn. Individuals with high records of offences, instead, seemed not to show any particular pattern, equally favouring solo and co-offences (Carrington, 2009). In addition, it has been suggested that offences involving three or more accomplices were likely to occur during the adolescence rather than the adult age, although typically they involve only two offenders (McGloin and Nguyen, 2014).

Moving on towards measuring cohesion dynamics over time, McGloin and colleagues (2008) developed a standardised measure of co-offender stability as a proportion of the number of pairs for each offender and his number of offences, and the total number of offenders (McGloin et al., 2008, p. 164). They found that the co-offending activity of juvenile offenders in Philadelphia is characterised by multiple delinquent trajectories. This restricted the possibility to identify clear-cut patterns notwithstanding the identification of some pathways, e.g. subjects with more arrests who offended with larger groups in the past were more likely to co-offend more often. In general, authors argued that delinquents generally tended not to re-select past partners when committing crimes, but, due to the presence of several variations, evaluating the stability of co-offending activity is a complex matter that requires deep analysis.

Tayebi and Glasser (2012), who used a big longitudinal crime dataset with 4.4 million records, highlighted the complexity of the co-offending phenomenon when time is taken into account. They argued that if, on the one hand, co-offending networks did not last for long and showed different levels of activity during all the five temporal snapshots considered, on the other hand, cliques tended to overlap, stressing, in turn, that individuals belonging to different crime groups were likely to collaborate. Similar evidence had also emerged in Sarnecki (2001), who analysed delinquent youth groups suspected of criminal offences in Stockholm between 1991 and 1995. He reported the tendency for small groups to be subsets of larger networks. Finally, Iwanski and Frank (2014) revealed that offenders were effectively organised in clusters, which emerged over time as the groups evolved, parallel to the recruitment of new people, resulting in an increase of the internal network cohesiveness (Iwanski and Frank, 2014, p. 70).

With the exception of the last study, the research by and large seems to suggest that in co-offending networks the tendency to form clusters declines over time. It appears that co-offending partnerships do not last longer and that the act of committing a crime with the same accomplices is, eventually, an isolated phenomenon rather than a consistent one. Together with the need to keep individual's visibility low, this could also reflect the offender's need to assume different delinquent roles and functions and carry out different types of crime. In sum, consistent co-participation in co-offending networks seems to be a myth.

Research on criminal networks remains explorative and descriptive to a large extent (Morselli, 2014, p. 3; Campana, 2016, p. 1). Although the use of social network analysis is becoming more extensive, studies which applied SNA to analyse the co-offending phenomenon are only few, and in those, some limitations could be highlighted. First, limitations can reflect the data collection process. Limiting the number of offences recorded for each criminal (Warr 1996) and only focusing on ego-networks (Morselli and Tremblay, 2004; McGloin and Piquero, 2010) can lead to an underestimation of the general co-offending patterns within those networks. A second limitation concerns the practice of transforming the genuine two-mode network of co-offending into one-mode networks, in order to increase the range of possible SNA measures to use for the analysis. Projecting a two-mode network into a one-mode network results in loss of information, both in terms of individual participation in events and overlapping patterns (Borgatti and Everett, 1997; Opsahl, 2013; Hollway and Koskinen, 2016). Another limitation refers to the lack of studies including the temporal dimension. Information on time is important for understanding how crime groups are shaped by individuals' criminal pathways (Morselli and Tremblay, 2004, p. 790; McGloin and Nguyen, 2014). Finally, the last limitation is due to the fact that this research has traditionally been confined to juvenile co-offending networks and street gangs, rather than other types of covert networks such as terrorist, Mafia and drug networks. Analysing people clustering in different types of covert networks can offer a better understanding of how the secrecy dimension affects structural properties and evolution trends in those networks. In the next sections, we analyse the effect of different type of links in different two-mode networks. With this work, we aim to offer a meaningful contribution to partially overcome some of the limitations described above.

3.3 Research questions and hypotheses

Do individuals change their accomplices or do they tend to co-offend with the same partner? Can the low presence of co-offending partnerships highlighted in previous research be dependent on the type of network data utilised? In other words, does the difference in co-offending partnerships among different covert networks (terrorist networks, criminal networks, co-arrests) depend on the nature of events considered?

Based on the previous discussion, we formulate the following hypotheses:

Hypothesis 1. The tendency to co-offend with the same partner over time is rare in all types of covert networks (e.g. two-mode terrorist, gang and co-arrest networks). Co-offending alliances are unstable because offenders are likely to change their accomplices, hoping to reduce their visibility, and by virtue of different tasks that need to be carried out.

Hypothesis 2. The type of events included in each dataset affects the results. We hypothesise that variations on co-offending partnerships are expected due to the nature of data. For example, two-mode covert networks in which events not only refer to illegal activities and violent acts but also include meetings and planning activities present higher levels of local clustering than networks with only violent attacks. This is because such events as operational meetings might capture other internal network processes, regarding, for example, the transmission of information.

3.4 Covert network datasets

The datasets for this study comprise four longitudinal real-world covert networks. All datasets are in the two-mode format with the events following the temporal order in which they occurred.

The datasets we utilise consist of:

1. Noordin Mohammed Top terrorist network. This dataset is related to Noordin Top, a Muslim extremist group related to Al Qaeda responsible for several terrorist attacks, such as the bombing at the Marriott Hotel in Jakarta in 2003, at the Australian Embassy in 2004 and in Bali in 2005. The dataset concerns 79 insurgents who took part in a total of 50 events, classified as either meetings, training camps or operations, such as bombing attacks and robberies, over 6 years from 1999 to 2005 (Everton, 2012b).
2. Abu Sayyaf Group (ASG) terrorist network in Southeast Asia. This network, referring to the Salafist extremist movement founded by Aburajak Janjalani in 1991, concerns 247 individuals who carried out 108 kidnappings in Malaysia and the Philippines over 19 years between 1992 and 2011 (Gerdes, Ringler and Autin, 2014). The kidnappings are considered the events.
3. UK Suffragettes network in Bristol and Bath. The dataset involves 52 individuals belonging to the Women's Social and Political Union (WSPU), a women's organisation in the UK during the 19th and early 20th century, which promoted women's suffrage. Forty events, including meetings, demonstrations, protests and vandalism acts, occurred in Bristol and Bath from 1907 until 1914. The data derive from historical sources of information, such as Suffragettes' diaries, autobiographies and local newspapers (Edwards, 2014).
4. UK Suffragettes network of co-arrests. This dataset identifies 1216 individuals, generally women, who appeared in 398 court sessions, between 1906 and 1920 (Crossley et al., 2012).

Those two last networks are an example of Covert Social Movement Networks (CSMN), characterised by a strong orientation toward a political and social change, and whose members stage protests and violent acts (Crossley et al., 2012).

Even if Suffragettes are not a criminal network as such, they can be considered as a covert organisation in the context of this chapter because the vertices of the organisations as well as some activities may have required a degree of secrecy. Since Suffragettes were exposed to violence and intimidations, meetings in preparation for open demonstrations tended to be secret for everyone with the exception of activists and organised in remote locations in order to be kept away from the public eye.

3.5 Methods of analysis (Hypothesis 1)

To test our first hypothesis, we used two strategies which allow the examination of bipartite graphs directly, without converting them into the one-mode format. We believe that our data can be better represented by using the two-mode format, which corresponds to an individual by event matrix of affiliations where rows and columns contain both individuals and events and only ties between individuals and events exist (Wasserman and Faust, 1994, pp. 29–30; Borgatti, Everett, and Johnson, 2013, pp. 20–21, 231). The first strategy adopted is bi-clique extraction and the second strategy uses conditional uniform distributions to determine whether the count of co-offending partnerships in real-world data is statistically significant. In what follows, we describe the two strategies in detail by also highlighting how they can offer an innovative contribution to the debate.

3.5.1 Bi-cliques extraction for bipartite networks

Recall the definition of 'bi-clique'. It refers to a subset of nodes where each node of a set is adjacent to all other nodes of the second set (Borgatti and Everett, 1997; Borgatti et al., 2013, p. 242). Traditionally, the smallest bi-clique is formed by at least two actors of each set (Borgatti and Everett, 1997, p. 264; Robins and Alexander, 2004, p. 76). In the case of individuals and events, a (2,2) bi-clique is composed of two individuals attending two events. However, the analysis of bi-cliques can also correspond to bigger configurations formed by more than two entities for each set of nodes. We searched for (3,3) bi-cliques, composed of three actors joining in three events, and (2,3) bi-cliques, involving, instead, two actors and three events. In order to capture the presence of subgroup structures in our networks, we used the *bi-clique* routine provided by the toolkit UCINET Version 6.600 (Borgatti, Everett and Freeman, 2002) by using the Command Line Interface.

In this case, we examine the underlying pattern of affiliations among co-offenders. For each observed network, we identify which individuals were more likely to carry out a task with the same accomplices and in relation to which events this happened. In addition, we represent the extracted bi-cliques graphically and we offer some narrative explanations about individuals' involvement in criminal activities over time.

Remark 1. This strategy helps in testing our first hypothesis by taking into account the two entities composing the networks, i.e. individuals and events and the time dimension. Since the bi-clique analysis is based on two-mode networks, it is possible to focus on both entities in their duality (Breiger, 1974) and to consider both as equally important (Everett and Borgatti, 2013). The emergence of bi-cliques configuration specifies to what extent co-offenders tended to commit a crime with the same accomplices.

3.5.2 Conditional uniform distributions for bipartite networks

The present research aims to examine counts of (2,2) and (2,3) bi-clique configurations in the networks by applying a more statistical approach, asking whether some patterns of linkages can be effectively considered as internal properties of the given network. This research strategy implies the comparison between the results observed in a real network and the results obtained when random networks with similar characteristics to the given one are simulated. Examples of the use of this approach include Moreno and Jennings (1938), Pattison and colleagues (2000) and Watts (1999), to name a few, for one-mode networks and, more recently, Robins and Alexander (2004) for bipartite graphs. Similarly to what Robins and Alexander did in their work, by comparing the given network against the simulations, we examine the statistical significance for the pattern of co-offending within the observed networks.

In particular, the simulation strategy adopted here corresponds to the conditional uniform distribution that simultaneously conditions on the indegree and the outdegree of the graph (see Wasserman, 1977; Wasserman and Faust, 1994, p. 550, for a more formal description of this approach). Since we have two different sets of ties, individuals and events, the application of this conditional uniform distribution allows controlling for the degree of each vertex for both entities to be equal to the observed bipartite graph before generating random graphs.[1] Broadly speaking, the process simulates a distribution of random graphs conditional on the constraints of the degree for controlling whether the tendency to co-offend in the observed graphs is statistically significant, meaning whether the observed count of co-offending partnerships is also likely to occur randomly.

Here we quantify the presence of (2,2) bi-cliques and (2,3) bi-cliques for the observed graphs and compared these with the same configurations within the

1 The strategy simulated 10,000 networks given the constraints for each graph. The algorithm is based on Markov chain Monte Carlo scheme with a thinning designed to reduce correlation between sample points. Here we thinned the resulting sample by keeping every two 200,000th graphs. We also initialised a burn-in of 200 full network samples for the co-arrests dataset.

simulated graphs. Bi-cliques (2,2) and (2,3) indicate the extent to which individuals tend to co-offend two or three times.

Then, we examine whether the number of bi-cliques in the observed graph is higher than the corresponding number obtained by calculating those configurations in the random simulations or, if, vice versa, the number of bi-cliques in the real networks is lower than the simulations. Either finding would support the idea that joint activities with same accomplices reflect some sort of internal mechanisms that might require further investigations. We report the standardised z-scores for the observed statistics based on the mean and the standard deviation from the simulated distributions for each given graph. Positive z-scores reflect the presence of high clustering within the observed graph. Conversely, negative z-scores mean a low clustering tendency.

High clustering reflects some collaboration mechanisms among individuals and suggests that they do tend to co-offend due to several reasons, e.g. role division, trust or a common aim. A significant presence of co-offending partnerships might also mean that individuals have the tendency to collaborate when carrying out criminal offences over time because the costs of co-offending with the same accomplice are lower than the costs of establishing new trust relationships. Low clustering, in turn, supports our first hypothesis that co-offences are less likely to occur than solo offences and might reflect different best practices among individuals. Finally, when the number of bi-cliques is close to the simulations (z-scores equals 0), it means that the bi-cliques configurations present in the given graph are actually similar to what would happen completely randomly, meaning the importance of bi-clique configurations for explaining the structural properties of the given network is negligible.

Remark 2. Since our networks are composed of individuals and events that follow a temporal order, bi-cliques are implicitly related to the temporal dimension. In line with our first hypothesis, through the use of conditional uniform distributions, it is possible to evaluate if the phenomenon of co-offending in our network is higher (or lower) than in random graphs so as to generalise if co-offending is rare or, on the contrary, a general tendency. In this way, we aim to test the idea that the presence of co-offending partnerships is a myth.

3.6 Comparison designs (Hypothesis 2)

This chapter adopts a 'most-similar systems' strategy of paired comparison (Tarrow, 2010). The method, borrowed from comparative politics, is used here for comparing pairs of networks which are similar in their characteristics. The advantage of comparing similar networks is that it focuses on the unique factor responsible for generating different outcomes in the networks. Using those paired comparisons, it is possible to see whether the network differences proved to be robust across those different networks. Only by looking closely at the type of data and especially at the type of events considered may we establish if the nature of data produces a certain discrepancy in the number of identified co-offending partnerships over time within those networks.

In this chapter, we compare the Noordin Mohammed Top terrorist network with the Abu Sayyaf Group (ASG) in the Southeast Asia and the Bristol and Bath branch of the Suffragettes with the UK Suffragettes network of co-arrests. The characteristics of the context, the type of individuals involved, the source of data and the nature of events considered that will affect the network are:

- *Context*: it refers to the fact that individuals are interacting in secrecy.
- *Type of individuals*: the first comparison refers to terrorists, whereas the second comparison concerns Suffragettes.
- *Source of data*: in the first case, network data is extracted from international reports and newspapers. In the second case, linkages are reconstructed by utilising archival data such as diaries and court documents.
- *Nature of event*: this is the independent variable that varies across the networks. The first comparison considers operational meetings, trainings and bombing attacks for the Noordin Top terrorist network, while it only refers to violent attacks (kidnappings) for the Abu Sayyaf Group (ASG). Similarly, the variable in the second comparison includes secret meetings as well as public protests and violent demonstrations for the Bristol and Bath branch of the Suffragettes, but only violence and vandalism for the UK Suffragettes network of co-arrests. The outcome of interest is the characterisation of the network topology in terms of the presence of bi-cliques. We consider as a 'dependent variable' the resulting z-scores, and, in particular, we expect those to be more consistent for the networks including different types of events, i.e. Abu Sayyaf Group (ASG) and UK Suffragette in Bristol and Bath.

Remark 3. The paired comparison strategy is used to test our Hypothesis 2. It allows an understanding of how the nature of events (meetings and violent attacks) affects the outcomes and whether adding meetings can result in stronger evidence of common participation in crimes.

3.7 Results and discussion

3.7.1 Results of (3,3) and (2,3) bi-clique analyses (Hypothesis 1)

In Figures 3.1 and 3.2, we present the results of the application of the bi-clique analysis for three of our four networks. Due to the big size of the Suffragette co-arrests dataset, UCINET was not able to extract the bi-cliques for this network. In the figures, the shapes of the nodes are presented as triangles (representing bi-cliques), squares (representing events) and circles (identifying individuals). The size of the nodes depends on the number of nodes that the node is adjacent to (degree) in those specific configurations, rather than the original two-mode networks. Bigger sizes of bi-cliques mean that they contain many individuals and/or many events. In turn, bigger sizes of individuals mean that those individuals are part of many bi-cliques – individuals who attended many events together with others – and identify who was more likely to co-offend. Similarly, bigger

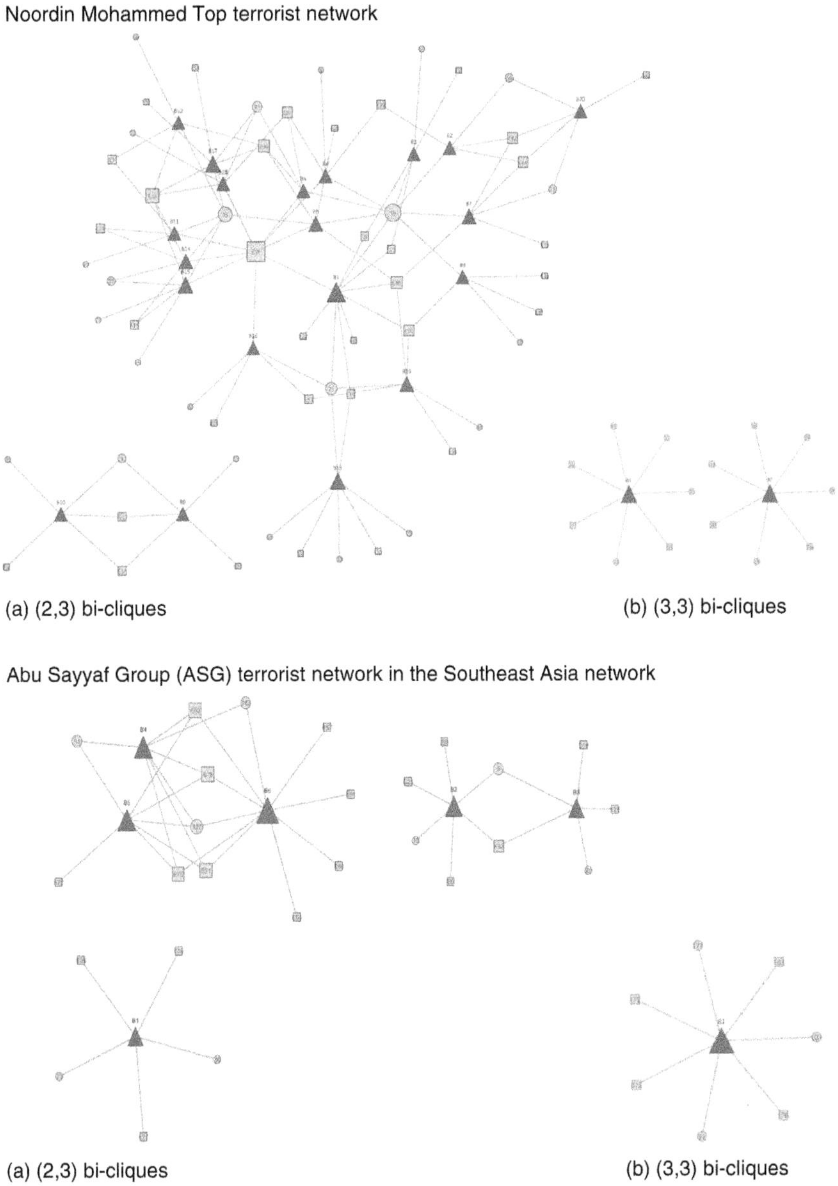

Figure 3.1 Representation of (2,3) and (3,3) bi-cliques for Noordin Mohammed Top terrorist network and Abu Sayyaf Group (ASG) terrorist network in the Southeast Asia network

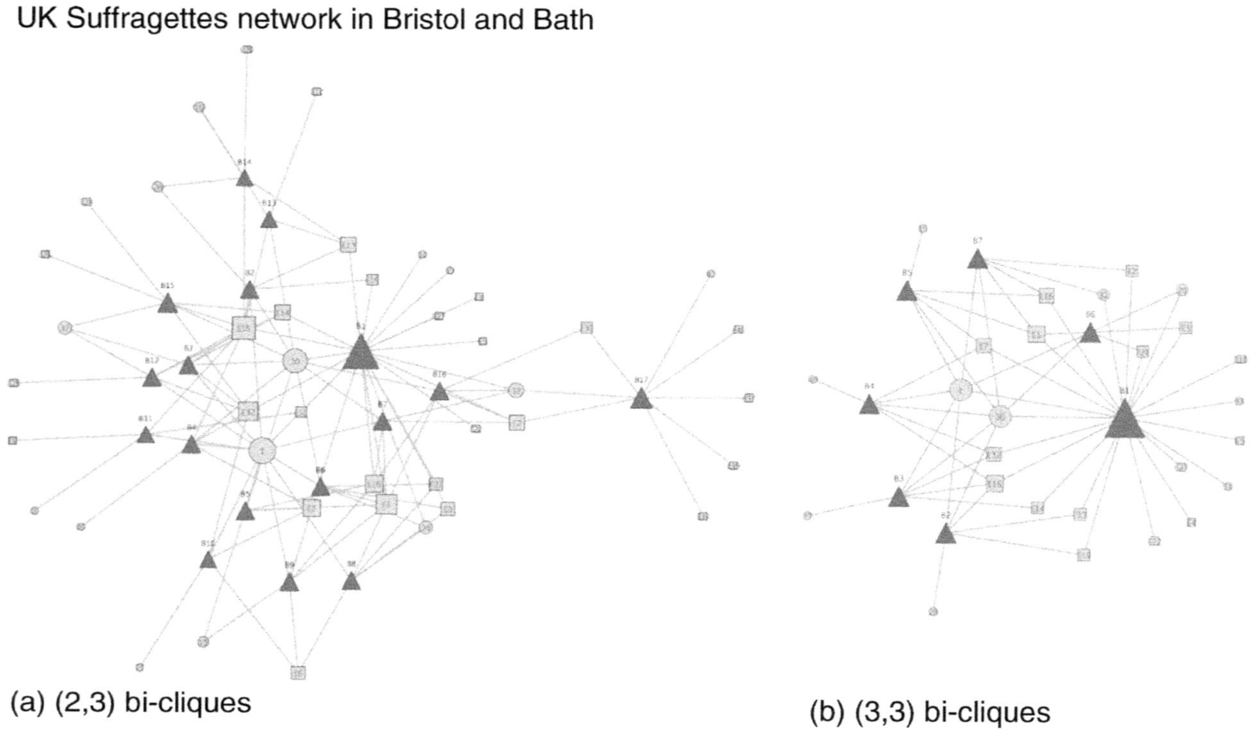

Figure 3.2 Representation of (2,3) and (3,3) bi-cliques for UK Suffragettes network in Bristol and Bath

sizes of events correspond to events that are part of many bi-cliques and show the most popular events that mobilised more individuals together. In what follows, we narrow our analysis by focusing on bi-cliques.

Overall, what can be deduced is that (2,3) bi-cliques are greater in number than (3,3) bi-cliques. The (3,3) bi-cliques routine for searching for at least three actors attending at least three events together revealed the presence of only two (3,3) bi-cliques in the Noordin Top network. The first one comprised the set {actor 23, actor 33, actor 51, actor 72, E6, E13, E19}, and the second one the set {actor 19, actor 37, actor 45, actor 74, E18, E32, E38}. These bi-cliques are overlapping neither in time nor with respect to individuals. Actors belonging to the first bi-clique were all operatives affiliated with the Jemaah Islamiah (JI) organisation such as the master bomb technician (23) and the explosives transporter (51). They took part together in three bombing attacks: the Christmas Eve bombing on December 2000 (event 6), the bombing in Bali on October 2002 (event 13) and the Marriott bombing attack on August 2003 (event 19). The second bi-clique concerns different actors and different types of events. Individuals belonging to this bi-clique were two suicide candidates, (19) and (37), a military trainer instructor (45) and a religious supporter (74). The events referred to two training camps (event 18 and event 32) that led up to the Austrian Embassy bombing attack in September 2004 (event 38). The fact that bi-cliques are not overlapping either through individuals or events can perhaps be explained by Noordin's strategy. After the Marriott bombing (bi-clique 1), Noordin suffered from a lack of monetary resources and followers due to the arrests of his close accomplices by the police. Therefore, he recruited new people to plan and carry out the Australian embassy bombing (bi-clique 2).

A different scenario presents itself when we look at the (2,3) bi-cliques. In total, 20 bi-cliques were detected. The central most consistent bi-clique refers to Noordin Top, who together with actor (23) attended eight events. Those events – meetings (E17, E20, E22, E40, E45) and bombing operations (E19, E38, E50) – revealed the close relationship between Noordin and one of his main partners (actor 23) in carrying out all attacks. By looking at the other bi-cliques we can identify other crucial alliances. For example, bi-clique 7 reveals the relationships between Noordin and a JI member (13) who became Noordin's assistant and used his personal network in order to find safe places to hide weapons and pass information. Bi-clique 18 refers to actors (73) and (77), both classmates at an-Nur University in Solo. They knew each other from the past and had a similar career. They attended a meeting (E27), through which they were recruited by their teacher, a following training camp (E32) and took part together at the Australian Embassy bombing (E38).

The bi-clique routine applied to the ASG terrorist network returned only one (3,3) bi-clique comprised by the actors (91), (103) and (127) and the events (E63), (E71), (E75) and (E78), and mainly occurred in Zamboanga City. From publicly available online sources (references available on request), we were only able to offer some basic explanations of individuals involved in this bi-clique. Actors were leaders of two different terrorist factions: the Abu Sayyaf Group (ASG) and the Moro Islamic Liberation Front (MILF). Events occurred at the end of the time window, between July 2008 and April 2009, meaning that those alliances emerged only at a later stage and between insurgents with an established delinquent reputation. The (2,3) overlapping bi-cliques depicted in panel (a) in Figure 3.1 brought to light additional connections, representing other leaders of small terrorist factions collaborating with each other simultaneously.

The UK Suffragette network yielded seven (3,3) bi-cliques and 17 (2,3) bi-cliques completely overlapping. The most consistent (3,3) bi-clique referred to the set {32, 20, 33, 31, 1, 30, E1, E2, E3, E4, E5, E10, E13, E14, E15, E16, E19, E22, E27, E32}. These events were mainly meetings, with the only exceptions being events 13, 19 and 27, which were processions and public demonstrations in Bristol and occurred between 1907 and 1914. This bi-clique concerns the two leaders of the Suffragette campaign in Bristol in Bath, Annie Kenney (1) and Mary Blathwayt (30), mobilising supporters in the campaign for female suffrage. The analysis of (2,3) bi-cliques expands the collaboration patterns by including in the picture other configurations. This result suggests that the most active individuals of the Suffragette movement in Bristol and Bath tended to carry out activities together as a group, despite a certain turnover of people. As a consequence of the imprisonments of Suffragettes that limited their actions, in fact, many of them were occasionally prevented from taking an active part in the campaign.

The search for (3,3) and (2,3) bi-cliques captured to what extent individuals tended to act together over time. We found that criminals are equally likely to choose the same accomplices to carry out a crime during the whole temporal window. Perhaps we might conclude that the idea following which co-offending partnerships are uncommon is true by looking at (3,3) bi-cliques output. However, the doubt that the reality is different remains if we consider the (2,3) search result. Not only does this result confirm the greater presence of dyads than triads (McGloin and Nguyen, 2014), but it also suggests that individuals tend to re-use their previous partners in crime and strengthen strategic alliances, notwithstanding the individuals' turnover. The tendency to co-offend also appears to be more likely by virtue of pre-existing ties and previous collaborations. Through relationships, individuals become aware of each other's skills and abilities. For example, the (2,3) bi-clique analysis applied to the Noordin network reveals that he maintained few stable partnerships along the entire time window, but also that he changed accomplices depending on the tasks and the bombing attacks he was planning. Finally, offenders prefer to reduce their risks by relying on the same persons over time. In other words, stable partnerships reduce the costs of changing accomplice and establishing new trust relationships. Therefore, our hypothesis does not appear entirely confirmed. Individuals do rely on the same co-offender over time and do not necessarily change their accomplices in order to reduce their visibility.

The bi-clique analysis not only reveals which individuals have been co-offending the most, but it also identifies relative to which events these partnerships were created and for how long they lasted. This is a particularly important aspect since it allows us to evaluate the stability of co-offending activity but also to reveal the events that incentivised collaboration. For example, consider the (2,3) bi-clique analysis for Noordin Top. It highlighted the importance of the Austrian Embassy bombing (E38) that involved the greatest number of people (18 individuals). This event is contained in several bi-cliques as the last intercourse among several pairs of individuals who were previously attending meetings and/or trainings leading up this attack. It can be concluded that the need to accomplish this attack fostered individual's partnerships more than other events.

3.7.2 Application of conditional uniform distributions for (2,3) and (3,3) bi-cliques (Hypothesis 1)

We now turn to the results of the conditional uniform distributions. Table 3.1 reports the observed distributions of (2,2) and (2,3) bi-cliques for the networks and reports the standardised z-scores for the observed values of bi-cliques based on the mean and the standard deviation from the simulated distributions. The observed covert networks differ from the conditional random distributions; all z-scores are statistically significant. In particular, this appears true for the (2,3) bi-clique configurations, with the only exception of the Noordin Top network where, in turn, (2,2) are higher. The results suggest that the observed bi-cliques are not only due to the constraints adopted by the simulation strategy, but they reflect other occurring social processes.

Since there are many more (2,2) and (2,3) bi-cliques than expected from the simulated graph distributions, we might infer that, at the global level, individuals tend to have the same partners in crime more frequently than what would occur by chance, given the popularity of events and activity of actors. Next, Figure 3.3 visually shows where the observed (2,2) and (2,3) bi-clique statistics are posited (black lines) compared to the simulated distributions.

The significant presence of partnerships composed of two individuals attending three events together seems to provide substantial evidence that individuals tend to co-offend with the same person consistently over time, rather than changing partners. This result seems to suggest that individuals tend to co-offend with the same accomplice no matter the possible consequences for accomplishing their criminal intents. These findings are in stark contrast to previous research. While it has been suggested that individuals tend to maximise their secrecy by reducing communication and avoiding consistent participation in events, here the opposite trend is evident. Individuals reduce their risks by relying on the same persons because maintaining stable partnerships of collaboration over time overcomes the costs of changing accomplices and activating new ties. To conclude, those results seem to not entirely confirm our first hypothesis. The present research seems to suggest that individuals do strengthen alliances over time and collaboration dynamics and that, overall, partnerships are not extremely rare and changeable over time as we expected.

These results can open up further possible theoretical explanations regarding co-offending. First, the observed bipartite clustering for the Philippine and the

Table 3.1 Graph statistics for the four covert networks (Counts of configurations in the observed networks, means and standard deviations for the simulations: standardised z-score for the observed values)

	Statistics	*Observed*	*Simulated distribution*	*Z-score*
Noordin Mohammed Top terrorist network	(2,2) bi-cliques 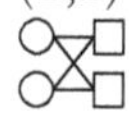	184	119.8 (19)	+3.34
	(2,3) bi-cliques 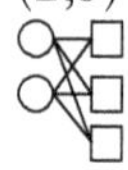	105	55.2 (27)	+1.82
Abu Sayyaf Group (ASG) terrorist network in Southeast Asia	(2,2) bi-cliques 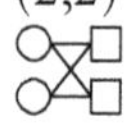	178	79.9 (19)	+5.77
	(2,3) bi-cliques 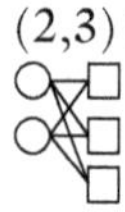	76	11.4 (8)	+9.61
UK Suffragettes network in Bristol and Bath	(2,2) bi-cliques 	228	142.6 (22)	+3.98
	(2,3) bi-cliques 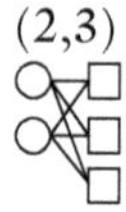	617	177.9 (69)	+6.49
UK Suffragette network of co-arrests	(2,2) bi-cliques 	1372	676 (128)	+14.94
	(2,3) bi-cliques 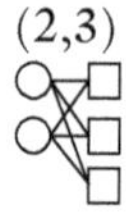	190	38 (23)	+15.28

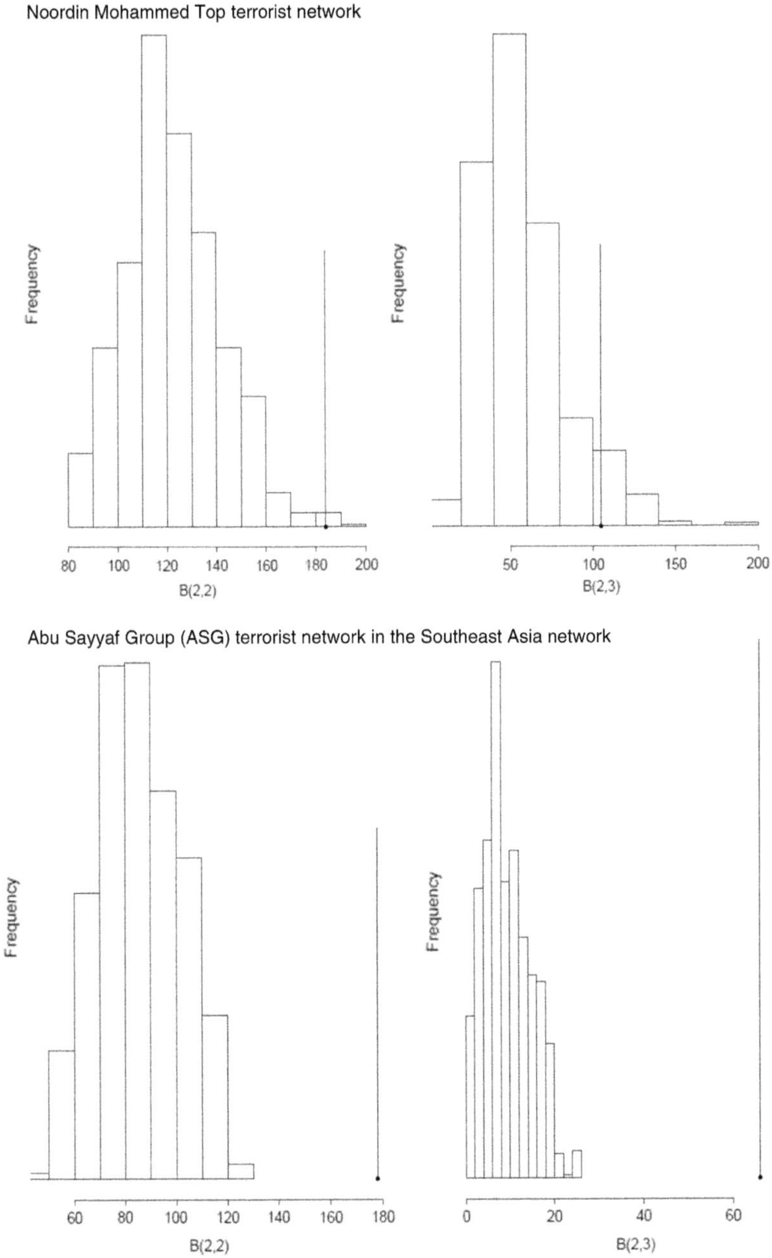

Figure 3.3 (2,2) and (2,3) Bi-clique distributions for the four covert networks

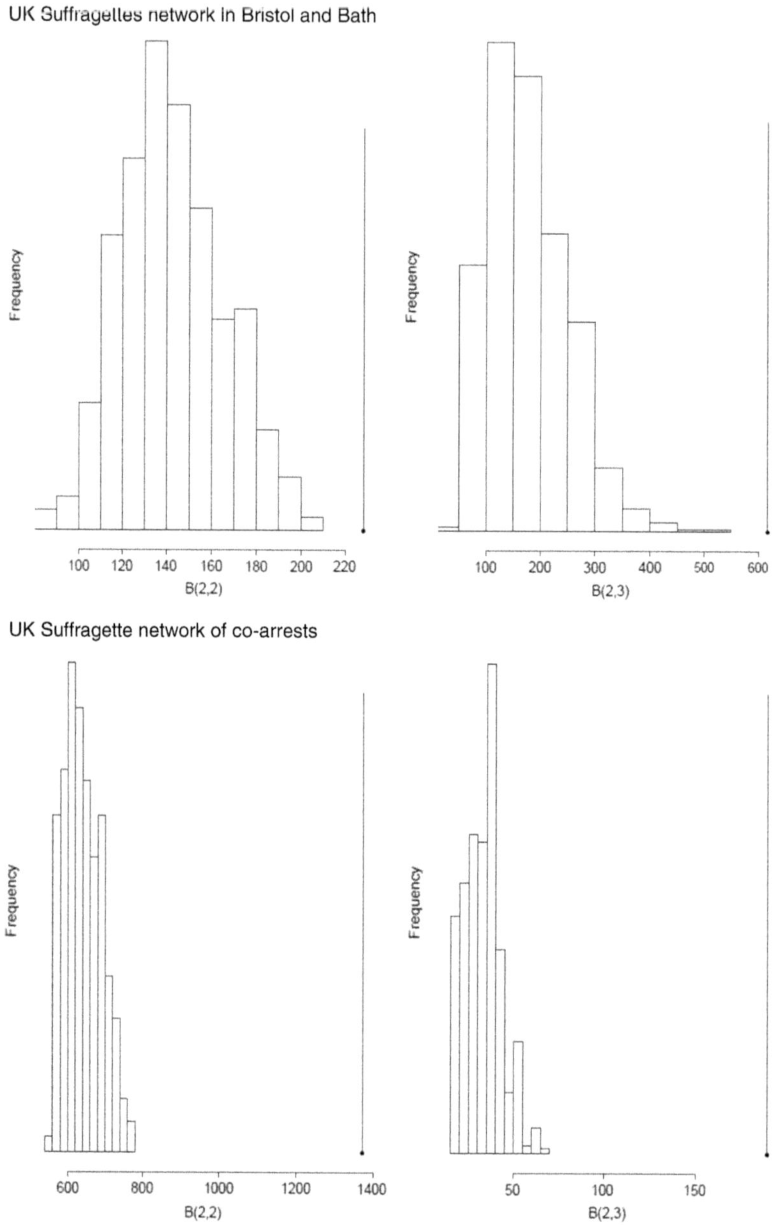

Figure 3.3 Continued

Suffragette co-arrests datasets might be derived from the tendency to localise geographically spread events. These two datasets, in fact, referred to events that occurred in very large areas compared to the Noordin Top network and the UK Suffragette two-mode networks in Bristol and Bath. Second, since the clustering seemed unrelated to the degree of events and individuals, the stability of co-offending can be explained by a range of other possible factors.

3.7.3 Paired comparisons (Hypothesis 2)

Table 3.2 summarises the two most-similar system designs for the paired comparisons adopted here and the results we expected to find based on our second hypothesis that co-offending partnerships depend on the nature of the events.

The z-scores capture the tendency of clustering over time in the observed criminal networks. In the previous section, we concluded that the co-partnerships do exist in covert networks and that individuals tend to co-offend, contrary to the first hypothesis. Here, we hypothesised that covert networks concerning a different range of events such as bombing attacks, violent protests and vandalism acts as well as planning and occasional meetings would result in more common participation in crimes, compared to criminal networks only concerning the most violent and brutal events.

The outcome seems to contradict our second hypothesis. The z-scores for the two different terrorist networks (Table 3.2, first comparison) reveal, in fact, a different trend. The networks exhibit a fair amount of bi-cliques, no matter the nature of events considered. Here, we find z-scores equal to +3.34 (Noordin Top) and +5.77 (ASG) for (2,2) bi-clique configurations, and +1.82 (Noordin Top) and +9.61 (ASG) for (2,3) bi-cliques. The z-scores for the ASG terrorist network (+5.77, +9.61), which only considered violent events, are even more consistent than the corresponding ones for Noordin Top (+3.34, +1.82), which, instead, concern different types of events, such as bombing attacks, training camps and planning meetings.

The comparison of the z-scores for the two UK Suffragette networks (Table 3.2, second comparison) also goes against our hypothesis. In this case, the z-scores for the UK Suffragette network in Bristol and Bath are higher than expected (+3.92 and +6.29) as well as the outcomes for the UK Suffragette co-arrests (+14.94 and +15.28). Even in this case, the observed number of partnerships in crime seems to be higher than what we could obtain by chance. One can interpret this outcome by suggesting that the tendency of clustering is relevant to the network of co-arrests, as well as to the Suffragette network in Bristol and Bath. This outcome is not surprising because both networks refer to the Women's Social and Political Union – the Suffragettes. However, since the data referring to the Suffragette branch in Bristol and Bath comprises also secret meetings, we were expecting stronger evidence of common participation in crimes compared to the co-arrest data. Our results do not confirm this hypothesis.

Table 3.2 Most-similar system designs for covert networks paired comparisons

	Independent variables				*Dependent variable*
	C1	*C2*	*C3*	*C4*	*E*
	Context	*Individuals/type of network*	*Source of data*	*Types of events considered*	*Co-offending partnerships (Z-scores)*
Noordin Mohammed Top network	A Under secrecy	B Terrorist network	C Social media (international crisis reports)	X Meetings and violent attacks	Y We hypothesise Z-scores higher than expected randomly
Abu Sayyaf Group (ASG) terrorist network	A Under secrecy	B Terrorist network	C Media (newspapers)	NON X Only violent attacks	NON Y We hypothesise Z-scores lower than expected randomly

	Independent variables				*Dependent variable*
	C1	*C2*	*C3*	*C4*	*E*
	Context	*Individuals/type of network*	*Source of data*	*Types of events*	*Co-offending partnerships(Z-scores)*
UK Suffragettes Bristol and Bath	A Under secrecy	B CSMN	C Archive data (diaries)	X Meetings and violent attacks	Y We hypothesise Z-scores higher than expected randomly
UK Suffragette co-arrests	A Under secrecy	B CSMN	C Archive data (home office document)	NON X Only violent attacks	NON Y We hypothesise Z-scores lower than expected randomly

Therefore, including different kinds of events in the analysis does not necessarily result in a higher estimation of the tendency of clustering within the observed networks. Yet, researchers might need to be aware of the limited impact that the nature of events considered can have on the results when interpreting outcomes.

3.8 Conclusion

It has long been thought that criminals involved in covert activities try to limit their overexposure by keeping lower levels of direct involvement in violent and illegal acts. In this study, we explored two hypotheses behind this assumption: 1) that covert networks necessarily present a rare tendency of co-offending partnerships in crimes over time, and 2) that the nature of events considered affects the resulting level of clustering. We addressed these hypotheses by investigating four different covert networks and by adopting two different strategies for quantifying the presence of co-offending patterns and comparing the results.

The investigation of co-offending patterns involved analysing the presence of (2,2), (2,3) and (3,3) bi-cliques by identifying to what extent two or three offenders attended at least two or three criminal events over time with the same accomplice. Our analyses do not find support for the first hypotheses we postulated. We concluded that co-offending partnerships are not extremely rare and that actors were likely to collaborate in order to carry out their intentions. The bi-cliques analyses helped in unpacking the presence of co-offending partnerships either among different network subgroups as in the Noordin Top and the Abu Sayyaf Group (ASG) terrorist networks or among the most active individuals as it occurred in the first Suffragette network. This analysis also assisted in drawing attention to individuals and events who had the higher impact on the evolution of the network structure. We have shown how individuals tended to co-attend events with the same accomplice due to previous collaborations, but also by virtue of individuals' commitment and shared aims. This result opens new perspectives for studying the formation of strategic alliances in co-offending networks since we suggest that stable partnerships are preferable in order to reduce the costs of changing accomplices and establishing trust. The results obtained by using conditional uniform distributions also support this claim and confirm that co-offending partnerships are an important aspect to take into account when explaining network structures. The observed graphs present a higher tendency of clustering compared to random ones.

To verify our second hypothesis, we adopted the most-similar comparison design in order to compare pairs of networks with similar characteristics. Findings brought to light the limited importance of the nature of the events. Contrary to what was expected, considering different types of crime events does not necessarily result in a stronger evidence of common participation in crimes.

In general, this research breaks away from the common thinking in the literature, which saw co-offending alliances as mainly a sporadic phenomenon, rather than a consistent and long-lasting one. This work develops the idea of examining co-offending partnerships over time in different types of two-mode covert networks. However, our study leaves unanswered the question of the extent to which co-offending partnerships influence network properties. Further research may assess the impact of alliances' formation over time in affecting the network structures by recreating the internal structure of a given network with exponential random graph models. This allows a better understanding of the network internal dynamics and can offer insights on the individual behaviours under secrecy.

Acknowledgements

The authors would like to thank Nick Crossley, Gemma Edwards and Luke M. Gerdes for sharing their datasets. The datasets used here have been collected within the research project at the University of Manchester 'Analysing and Collecting Secondary Covert Networks'.

Funding

This research is supported by the Leverhulme Trust Grant RPG-2013-140.

References

Borgatti, S. P. and Everett, M. G. (1997) 'Network Analysis of 2-Mode Data', *Social Networks*, 19(3), pp. 243–269.

Borgatti, S. P., Everett, M. G. and Freeman, L. C. (2002) *Ucinet for Windows: Software for Social Network Analysis.* Harvard, MA: Analytic Technologies.

Borgatti, S. P., Everett, M. G. and Johnson, J. C. (2013) *Analyzing Social Networks.* London: Sage Publications.

Breiger, R. L. (1974) 'The Duality of Persons and Groups', *Social Forces*, 53(2), pp. 181–190.

Brinton Milward, H. and Raab, J. (2006) 'Dark Networks as Organizational Problems: Elements of a Theory', *International Public Management Journal*, 9(3), pp. 333–360.

Bruinsma, G. and Bernasco, W. (2004) 'Criminal Groups and Transnational Illegal Markets', *Crime, Law and Social Change*, 41(1), pp. 79–94.

Campana, P. (2016) 'Explaining Criminal Networks: Strategies and Potential Pitfalls', *Methodological Innovations*, 9(0). doi: 10.1177/2059799115622748.

Carrington, P. J. (2009) 'Co-offending and the Development of the Delinquent Career', *Criminology*, 47(4), pp. 1295–1329.

Carrington, P. J. (2011) 'Crime and Social Network Analysis'. In: Scott, J. and Carrington, P. J. (Eds), *The SAGE Handbook of Social Network Analysis.* London: SAGE Publications, Inc., pp. 236–255.

Carrington, P. J. and van Mastrigt, S. B. (2013) 'Co-offending in Canada, England and the United States: A Cross-National Comparison', *Global Crime*, 14(2–3), pp. 123–140.

Crossley, N., Edwards, G., Harries, E. and Stevenson, R. (2012) 'Covert Social Movement Networks and the Secrecy-Efficiency Trade Off: The Case of the UK Suffragettes (1906–1914)', *Social Networks*, 34(4), pp. 634–644.

Edwards, G. (2014) 'Infectious Innovations? The Diffusion of Tactical Innovation in Social Movement Networks, the Case of Suffragette Militancy', *Social Movement Studies*, 13(1), pp. 48–69.

Eilstrup-Sangiovanni, M. and Jones, C. (2008) 'Assessing the Dangers of Illicit Networks', *Networks*, 32(1), pp. 7–44.

Enders, W. and Jindapon, P. (2010) 'Network Externalities and the Structure of Terror Networks', *Journal of Conflict Resolution*, 54(2), pp. 262–280.

Enders, W. and Su, X. (2007) 'Rational Terrorists and Optimal Network Structure', *Journal of Conflict Resolution*, 51(1), pp. 33–57.

Erickson, B. H. (1981) 'Secret Societies and Social Structure', *Social Forces*, 60(1), pp. 188–210. doi: 10.1017/CBO9781107415324.004.

Everett, M. G. and Borgatti, S. P. (2013) 'The Dual-Projection Approach for Two-Mode Networks', *Social Networks*, 35(2), pp. 204–210.

Everton, S. F. (2012a) 'Connections Network Topography , Key Players and Terrorist Networks', *Connections*, 32(1), pp. 12–19.

Everton, S. F. (2012b) *Disrupting Dark Networks.* New York: Cambridge University Press. Online publication date: April 2013 Print publication year: 2012 Online ISBN: 9781139136877 https://doi.org/10.1017/CBO9781139136877.

Gerdes, L. M., Ringler, K. and Autin, B. (2014) 'Assessing the Abu Sayyaf Group's Strategic and Learning Capacities', *Studies in Conflict and Terrorism*, 37(3), pp. 267–293.

Hollway, J. and Koskinen, J. (2016) 'Multilevel Embeddedness: The Case of the Global Fisheries Governance Complex', *Social Networks*, 44, pp. 281–294.

Iwanski, N. and Frank, R. (2014) 'The Evolution of a Drug Co-Arrest Network'. In: Morselli, C. (Ed.), *Crime and Networks.* New York, NY: Routledge.

Kirby, A. (2007) 'The London Bombers as 'Self-Starters': A Case Study in Indigenous Radicalization and the Emergence of Autonomous Cliques', *Studies in Conflict and Terrorism*, 30(5), pp. 415–428.

Koschade, S. (2006) 'A Social Network Analysis of Jemaah Islamiyah: The Applications to Counterterrorism and Intelligence', *Studies in Conflict and Terrorism*, 29(6), pp. 559–575.

Krebs, V. E. (2002) 'Mapping Networks of Terrorist Cells', *Connections*, 24(3), pp. 43–52.

Lauchs, M., Keast, R. L. and Le, V. (2012) 'Social Network Analysis of Terrorist Networks: Can It Add Value?', *Pakistan Journal of Criminology*, 3(3), pp. 21–32.

Lindelauf, R., Borm, P. and Hamers, H. (2009) 'The Influence of Secrecy on the Communication Structure of Covert Networks', *Social Networks*, 31(2), pp. 126–137.

Malm, A. and Bichler, G. (2011) 'Networks of Collaborating Criminals: Assessing the Structural Vulnerability of Drug Markets', *Journal of Research in Crime and Delinquency*, 48(2), pp. 271–297.

van Mastrigt, S. B. (2014) 'Co-offending and offender attributes'. In: Gerben Bruinsma and David Weisburd (Eds), *Encyclopedia of Criminology and Criminal Justice.* New York: Springer-Verlag, pp. 559–570.

McGloin, J. M. and Nguyen, H. (2014) 'The Importance of Studying Co-offending Networks for Criminological Theory and Policy'. In: Morselli, C. (Ed.), *Crime and Networks.* New York, NY: Routledge, pp. 13–27.

McGloin, J. M., Piquero, A. R. (2010) 'On the Relationship Between Co-offending Network Redundancy and Offending Versatility', *Journal of Research in Crime and Delinquency*, 47(1), pp. 63–90.

McGloin, Jean Marie, Christopher J. Sullivan, Alex R. Piquero and Sarah Bacon (2008) 'Investigating the stability of co-offending and co-offenders among a sample of youthful offenders', *Criminology*, 46(1), pp. 155–188.

Moreno, J. L. and Jennings, H. H. (1938) 'Statistics of Social Configurations', *Sociometry*, 1(3/4), pp. 342–374.

Morselli, C. (2009) *Inside Criminal Networks*. New York, NY: Springer New York (Studies of Organized Crime).

Morselli, C. (2010) 'Assessing Vulnerable and Strategic Positions in a Criminal Network', *Journal of Contemporary Criminal Justice*, 26(4), pp. 382–392.

Morselli, C. (2014) 'Introduction'. In: Morselli, C. (Ed.), *Crime and Networks*. New York, NY: Routledge.

Morselli, C. and Tremblay, P. (2004) 'Criminal Achievement, Offender Networks and the Benefits of Low Self-Control', *Criminology*, 42(3), pp. 773–804.

Opsahl, T. (2013) 'Triadic Closure in Two-Mode Networks: Redefining the Global and Local Clustering Coefficients', *Social Networks*, 35(2), pp. 159–167.

Papachristos, A. V. and Smith, C. M. (2014) 'The Embedded and Multiplex Nature of Al Capone'. In: Morselli, C. (Ed.), *Crime and Networks*. New York, NY: Routledge, pp. 97–115.

Pattison, P., Wasserman, S., Robins, G. and Kanfer, A. M. (2000) 'Statistical Evaluation of Algebraic Constraints for Social Networks', *Journal of Mathematical Psychology*, 44(4), pp. 536–568.

Pettersson, T. (2003) 'Ethnicity and Violent Crime: The Ethnic Structure of Networks of Youths Suspected of Violent Offences in Stockholm', *Journal of Scandinavian Studies in Criminology and Crime Prevention*, 4(2), pp. 143–161.

Raab, J. and Milward, H. B. (2003) 'Dark Networks as Problems', *Journal of Public Administration Research and Theory*, 13(4), pp. 413–439.

Robins, G. and Alexander, M. (2004) 'Small Worlds Among Interlocking Directors: Network Structure and Distance in Bipartite Graphs', *Computational and Mathematical Organization Theory*, 10(1), pp. 69–94.

Sarnecki, J. (1990) 'Delinquent Networks in Sweden', *Journal of Quantitative Criminology*, 6(1), pp. 31–50.

Sarnecki, J. (2001) *Delinquent Networks Youth Co-offending in Stockholm*. London: Cambridge University Press.

Sparrow, M. K. (1991) 'The Application of Network Analysis to Criminal Intelligence: An Assessment of the Prospects', *Social Networks*, 13(3), pp. 251–274.

Stevenson, R. and Crossley, N. (2013) 'Change in Covert Social Movement Networks: The 'Inner Circle' of the Provisional Irish Republican Army', *Social Movement Studies*, 13, pp. 70–91.

Tarrow, S. (2010) 'The Strategy of Paired Comparison: Toward a Theory of Practice', *Comparative Political Studies*, 43(2), pp. 230–259.

Tayebi, M. A. and Glasser, U. (2012) 'Investigating Organized Crime Groups: A Social Network Analysis Perspective'. In: *2012 IEEE/ACM International Conference on Advances in Social Networks Analysis and Mining*. Istanbul, Turkey: Kadir Has University, pp. 565–572.

Warr, M. (1996) 'Organization and Instigation in Delinquent Groups', *Criminology*, 34(1), pp. 11–37.

Wasserman, S. S. (1977) 'Random Directed Graph Distributions and the Triad Census in Social Networks', *The Journal of Mathematical Sociology*, 5(1), pp. 61–86.

Wasserman, S. and Faust, K. (1994) *Social Network Analysis: Methods and Applications.* New York: Cambridge University Press.

Watts, D. J. (1999) 'Networks, Dynamics, and the Small-World Phenomenon', *American Journal of Sociology*, 105(2), pp. 493–527.

Yablonsky, L. (1959) 'The Delinquent Gang as a Near-Group', *Social Problems*, 7(2), p. 108.

Part II

Management of criminal networks

4 'It's just business'

Leaders' strategies for risk management in criminal networks

Siobhan Lawler and David Bright

4.1 Criminal networks and leadership

Scholars now generally agree that most contemporary criminal organisations operate through decentralised networks (Adler, 1993; Block, 1978; Desroches, 2007; Klerks, 2001; Sparrow, 1991). These structures are ideal for increased security as there is no clear point of vulnerability at which disruption efforts should be targeted (Benson & Decker, 2010, p. 132; Desroches, 2007, p. 835). However, some research has demonstrated (e.g. Calderoni, 2014; Krebs, 2002) that a decentralised structure does not imply that leadership is absent. Few studies have analysed the role of leadership in criminal networks and those that have tend to focus on the 'bosses' in mafia-type organisations (Calderoni, 2014; Chung, 2008) although there are some exceptions (Cunningham et al., 2013; Dickenson, 2014; Enders & Su, 2007; Hofmann & Gallupe, 2015; Porter & Alison, 2006). One approach to studying leadership in criminal networks is to first identify key actors based on their network position comparative to other group members (Borgatti, 2006; Bright, 2015; Carley et al., 2002; Lindquist, 2014). These studies present important steps toward revealing actors who are powerful or influential in criminal and social networks. However, they are limited by a lack of attention to individual level attributes and behaviour. Simply analysing how an individual is positioned in a group at a particular point in time arguably holds limited explanatory power. Previous research on criminal networks generally supports the notion that individuals who are central in a network are important (e.g. more active, have more influence) and are therefore worthy of attention (e.g. Baker & Faulkner, 1993; Lu et al., 2010; Xu & Chen, 2003). Previous studies (Chung, 2008; Cunningham, 2013; Hofmann & Gallupe, 2015; Kenney, 2007) have also focused on the dynamics of the group as a whole, with the leaders' role analysed within this context. Rarely are individual and social-structural factors (e.g. network positioning) considered together in explanations of crime. Significantly, no studies to date have analysed the relationship between these characteristics in considering how criminal leaders manage risk.

Research that has examined strategies aimed at enhancing security in criminal networks has tended to focus on drug-trafficking networks (Cross, 2000; Desorches, 2005; Hofmann & Gallupe, 2015; Jacobs, 1996; Kenney, 2007; Knowles, 1999) with some exceptions (Holt, 2014, 2015; Johnson &

Natarajan, 1995; Molony & Hunt, 2015). However, few analyse the role of leadership (Hofmann & Gallupe, 2015), and those that do are limited by the failure to account for the relationship between individual and social context variables. In line with previous research, the case study examined here is a drug trafficking network; however, the novel aspect of this research is the focus on leadership in this context, taking into account both micro- and macro-level variables. Various behavioural and social-structural tactics (e.g. network position) have been observed and analysed (Calderoni, 2011; Cross, 2000; Kenney, 2007) though few applications of this knowledge have been administered in a case-study setting (Hofmann & Gallupe, 2015). The current chapter examines two main ways that actors in criminal networks ensure security, with a focus on organisational structure and personal risk-management strategies.

4.2 Ensuring security through organisational structure

Compartmentalising operations and information are risk management strategies commonly observed in criminal enterprises that operate at higher market levels (e.g. importation; Morselli et al., 2007, p. 152; Simmel, 1950; von Lampe, 2007, p. 148; Zaitch, 2002, p. 241). These require effective division of responsibility so that individuals know no more than they need to at any time and may not even know each other's true identities (Cohen, 1977, p. 106; von Lampe, 2015, p. 170). Knowledge and information is tightly controlled and norms prevent individuals from seeking detailed information from other group members (Gambetta, 2009, p. 170). Interviews with high-level traffickers have revealed that these individuals preferred only to associate with those who were direct superior or subordinate members (Desroches, 2005). This strategy serves to reduce redundant ties, and in doing so, minimises the threat these associations present. Inevitably, there are difficulties associated with compartmentalisation of operations and information (Desroches, 2005, p. 125). These issues relate to competing needs in the effective and efficient functioning of criminal networks with various organisational goals (Morselli et al., 2007). Similarly, while brokerage is akin to advantage in social networks, the associated benefits can become redundant if an individual also has many direct connections in the network (Bright, 2015, p. 74; Morselli, 2010). As the defining characteristic of criminal activity is covertness, the visibility associated with popularity is strategically undesirable. Strategic positioning as an associative style is indicated in social network measures by a high-betweenness/low-degree centrality score (Morselli, 2010). Leaders of criminal networks must strike a delicate balance across the need for concealment, the requirement to be visible enough to conduct business and the need to manage the greatest risk, human capital.

4.3 Ensuring security through risk-managing behaviours

Various behavioural strategies have been observed in the literature as key methods of managing risk in organised crime; in particular, trust, violence and corruption.

There are numerous barriers to studying the activities of criminal and other covert groups. Desroches (2005) examined how higher level traffickers manage risk (compiled through interviews with 70 incarcerated prisoners in Canada). He developed a risk-management framework which can be applied to the activities of organised criminal groups more generally (Desroches, 2005). Table 4.1 provides an overview of this framework including definitions of each strategy. Two particularly salient concepts raised by traffickers in Desroches' (2005) research and in the wider literature (Calderoni, 2012; Campana & Varese, 2013; Cohen, 1977; Gottschalk, 2010; Granovetter, 1985; von Lampe & Johansen, 2004) are trust and violence. Trust facilitates the social and organisational relationships in both criminal and non-criminal contexts. The ease with which we live among others who are not our kin 'depends upon our readiness to believe that others are in fact doing what they seem to be doing and doing it according to commonly understood rules' (Cohen, 1977, p. 102). Trust is influenced by a sense of shared habits, norms and values, which are intrinsically related to one's reputation (von Lampe, 2015; von Lampe & Johansen, 2004). A good reputation is a valuable asset, a type of social capital that encourages business dealings with others operating outside of the immediate group (Granovetter, 1985, p. 495). Because risk is at the forefront of operations, recruitment in criminal organisations tends to occur through already established relationships based on friendship, kinship, ethnicity and common experience, such as time spent together in prison (Arquilla & Ronfeldt, 2001, p. 72; Calderoni, 2011, 2012; Hofmann & Gallupe, 2015; Varese, 2013; von Lampe, 2015, p. 164; Zaitch, 2002). While giving some criminal networks 'a competitive advantage' (Paoli, 2002; von Lampe & Johansen, 2004, p. 2), a lack of trust towards outsiders can result in missed opportunities. This relates to Granovetter's theory of weak ties, whereby the relationships characterised by less intimacy entail higher risk but are valuable through the provision of access to resources not already shared within the close social network (Granovetter, 1973).

When considering the differences between the functioning of legitimate business and organised crime, few are as salient as the use of violence to ensure organisational security (Gottschalk, 2010, p. 68). Despite the common assumption that actors in illicit markets are subject to violence as a means of dispute settlement, research continues to observe that sophisticated criminal networks approach trade in illicit commodities from an organisational standpoint similar to that of legitimate corporations, whereby violence is seen as 'bad for business' (Arquilla & Ronfeldt, 2001, p. 90; Brownstein et al., 2010, p. 68; Calderoni, 2012, p. 323; Gambetta, 2009, p. 170; Hofmann & Gallupe, 2015; Morselli, 2010; Pearson & Hobbs, 2003). High levels of physical violence are perceived as an indicator of instability rather than standard operating procedure, one that deters buyers and attracts the unwanted attention of media and law enforcement (Calderoni, 2012, p. 323). Threats of violence and exchanging evidence of violence and other misdeeds are common themes in the literature, with some evidence to suggest that simply discussing violence can significantly influence compliance (Campana & Varese, 2013). Despite notions of violence and crime as congruent concepts, whereby violence can be a key feature of organised crime activity, it is more commonly one of many instruments used to manage disputes and collect debts (Brownstein et al., 2010, p. 68; Cross, 2000, p. 80; Goldstein, 1985; Kleemans, 2007, p. 180; May & Hough, 2004, p. 551). The corruption of legitimate business and government by criminal organisations is also a central protective factor in strengthening resilience in criminal networks and one that often provides strategic advantage to both parties involved (Arquilla & Ronfeldt, 2001, p. 76). Corruption facilitates organised crime by influencing government (i.e. police, judiciary, political officials) through bribery, coercion and social bonds (von Lampe, 2015, pp. 352–354). Legal professionals are particularly valuable in providing resources to individuals engaged in organised crime (Morselli & Giguere, 2006, p. 188) and the significance of these actors cannot be understated. Unfortunately, the involvement of corrupt officials tends to be 'particularly hard to detect, contact or research' (Dorn et al., 1998, p. 29; Lyman & Potter, 2000).

Previous research shows that threat of detection by law enforcement influences the operation of criminal network activities, greatly affecting the structure and functioning of these groups. Less is known about how individuals in leadership positions respond to this threat in contemporary organised criminal groups. In the current study, we explore the relationship between social structural and behavioural risk management strategies employed by leaders in criminal networks. Specifically, we address three research questions:

1 How does the position of leaders within a criminal network serve to reduce their level of risk?
2 What risk managing behaviours do leaders employ in criminal networks?
3 Is there a relationship between network position and the types of risk management behaviour used by leaders?

4.4 Method

This study employed a case study approach to examine leaders' behavioural and structural risk management strategies. The case study is a transnational drug trafficking syndicate operational in Australia in the 1970s, about which there is reasonably detailed information publicly available. The data for this study was drawn from two types of sources, two non-fiction books (Hall, 2010; Shepherd, 2010) written about the organisation and a Royal Commission of Inquiry (Stewart, 1983, pp. 119–325). Both non-fiction books were read in full. Given the scope of the Royal Commission, it was neither practical nor necessary to read this source in its entirety. There is a specific section dedicated to the activities of the group (Stewart, 1983, pp. 119–325) and this section was subject to content analysis in the present study. All sources were utilised for all study purposes including establishing ties between network members, extracting evidence of leaders' risk management behaviours and identifying leaders, who were each allocated alphanumeric codes N4, N8, N13, N26 and N27 for anonymity. It is important to note that 'leadership' within the organisation was determined by reports of both individuals who were part of the network and by law enforcement and judicial officers. Leadership status is unlikely to simply reflect biases introduced into the data due to the focus of the police investigation.

4.4.1 Social Network Analysis (SNA)

Data was collected from each source for the purposes of social network analysis. All individuals involved in the organisation's activities were entered into an Excel spreadsheet on two mirrored axes. Evidence of a relationship between two members was nominated as either absent (coded 0) or present (coded 1) in the spreadsheet. The Excel document was then exported to the social network analysis software programme UCINET (Borgatti et al., 2002) and a graphical representation of the social network was produced. UCINET was used to calculate SNA metrics (closeness, degree and betweenness centrality). Closeness centrality measures how close an actor is to others in the network. Degree centrality measures the number of direct associations an individual has within a network. Betweenness centrality measures brokerage capacity, or the extent to which an actor connects previously unconnected others in the network. Strategic positioning was measured by representing actors' degree and betweenness scores on a scatterplot and interpreting leaders' position in one of four quadrants (high betweenness/low degree, high betweenness/high degree, etc.)

4.4.2 Qualitative analysis

Content analysis was conducted to identify evidence of leaders' risk management behaviours. Both non-fiction books and the relevant section of the Royal Commission were subject to content analysis. Phrases relating to risk management criteria were selected and coded into the relevant categories based on the descriptions in Table 4.1. Desroches' (2005) framework was employed as a predefined guide for the selection of relevant information from each text. This framework is outlined in Table 4.1. The framework outlines six categories of risk management strategies including secrecy, information networks, violence, trust, redundancy, corruption, and diplomacy. Explicit in-text references to behavioural risk management methods used by leaders were coded without factoring in the frequency that these were employed (Carley, 1993). An example of how concepts were coded during analysis is illustrated in Table 4.2. The SNA metrics for leaders were then compared with the behavioural strategies they employed to manage risk.

Table 4.1 Example of coding framework

Page	*Leader*	*Behaviour*	*Details*
150	N4	Trust	History of close friendship with N2
243	N8	Violence	Reputation as a youth

Table 4.2 Descriptive statistics of social network measures (n = 124)

	Degree	*Betweenness*	*Closeness*
Mean	7.63	87.54	42.22
Median	4.00	7.19	42.56
Mode	2.00	0.00	36.83
Std. deviation	9.44	340.47	6.49
Minimum	1.00	0.00	29.71
Maximum	75.00	3445.89	71.51

4.5 Results

The network map in Figure 4.1 provides a representation of the patterns of associations between the 124 individuals in the drug trafficking syndicate case study. Each node is labelled with an alphanumeric identifier. The sources indicate that N8 is the primary leader and N4, N13, N26 and N27 hold supporting or secondary leadership positions. N8 is referred to as the principal leader in all sources (Hall, 2010, p. 2785; Stewart, 1983, p. 9; Shepherd, 2010, p. xv) and N27 is referred to as second-in-charge of the organisation (Stewart, 1983, p. 437). Three other actors (N4, N13, N26) are referred to in the sources as 'principals', 'executives' and 'leaders' (Stewart, 1983, p. 81, 102, 108; Shepherd, 2010, p. xv). In Figure 4.1, the primary leader (N8) is coloured yellow, secondary leaders (N4, N13, N26, N27) are red and non-leaders are blue.

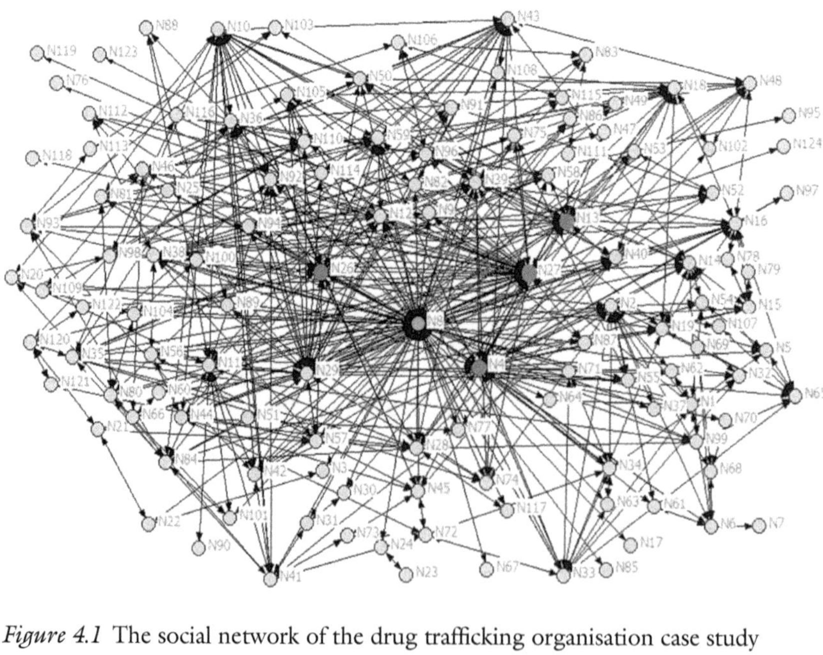

Figure 4.1 The social network of the drug trafficking organisation case study

4.5.1 *Strategic positioning*

Table 4.1 outlines the descriptive statistics for actors positioning styles across the case study criminal network. Table 4.2 displays each leader's score on the SNA measures. All individuals in leadership positions score well above the median score of 4.00 on degree centrality, above the median score of 7.18 on betweenness centrality and above the median score of 42.56 on closeness centrality. The median was chosen as a better metric for comparisons in order to prevent outliers skewing the data. N8 and N27 were the highest ranked of all actors on all measures.

Scores on degree and betweenness centrality are highly correlated across the network (r = 0.97), meaning that there is a strong relationship between these measures (Table 4.3). Figure 4.2 shows a scatterplot of the degree and betweenness centrality scores for all network members. The lines on both the x and y axes indicate the median score for each measure. Red circles indicate leaders and blue circles indicate non-leaders. Green circles indicate actors who are strategically positioned in the network. There were 124 actors in the data set. The majority (n = 113) of these actors fell into one of the four quadrants with the remaining eleven actors scoring on the median for degree or betweenness. These eleven actors were omitted from the analysis. The majority of actors fell within the lower left and top right hand quadrants. Individuals in the top right hand quadrant of the plot have high scores in both degree and betweenness centrality measures (n = 53). The majority of individuals fall into this category and all leaders fall into this category. Among leaders, N26 scores above, but closest to, the median score on degree centrality, followed by a gradual increase from N13, N4, N27 and lastly N8, whose score is far higher and removed from any other member. Individuals in the lower left quadrant score below the median on degree and betweenness centrality (n = 48). Individuals in the top left hand quadrant score below the median on betweenness but above the median on degree centrality (n = 6). Individuals in the bottom right hand side of the graph score above the median score in betweenness centrality and below the median score in degree centrality (n = 4). These individuals are the most strategically placed in the network. It is important to identify individuals who are strategically positioned in a covert network as it indicates reduced visibility (low score on degree centrality) in addition to control over activities through maintaining associations with a few non-redundant ties only, indicated by a high score on betweenness centrality

Table 4.3 Leader's scores on social network measures

Leader	*Degree*	*Betweenness*	*Closeness*
N8	75.00	3445.89	71.51
N27	45.00	1098.85	58.02
N4	33.00	843.43	55.90
N13	20.00	343.97	51.25
N26	15.00	88.89	48.06

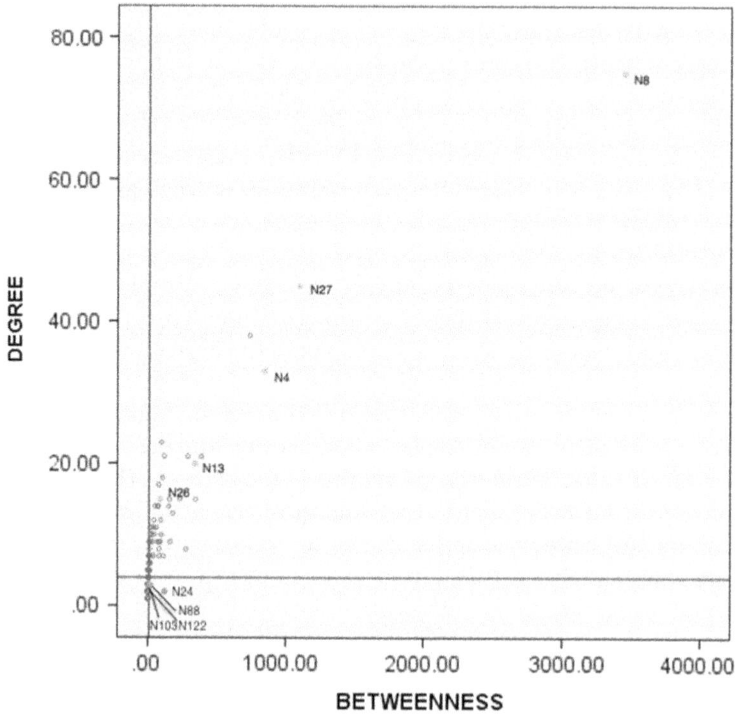

Figure 4.2 Scatterplot of degree centrality and betweenness centrality scores among individuals in the case study criminal network

(Morselli, 2010). None of the five individuals in leadership positions showed this positioning pattern. Four individuals who were not designated leaders were in this quadrant (N24, N88, N103, N122).

4.5.2 Risk management strategies

4.5.2.1 Secrecy

The compartmentalisation of information is indicated by the statement 'I was brought up to always honour a confidence. To never talk about anything told to me in secret' (N26 speaking to N27) (Shepherd, 2010, p. 277). N27 aimed to compartmentalise operations in a way that prioritised risk management, where 'The buyers never saw him [the delivery man] and he never had any physical contact with them. To help evade detection from honest cops, he never used the same street twice, or the same suburb. As I was the only person who knew who my delivery man was… the system worked very well' (Shepherd, 2010, p. 167).

Various rules, constituting a criminal 'code of conduct', were set out by N27 in one source as guidelines for managing risk. The primary focus of this 'code' was that one does not provide information to the authorities.

> Not questioning what other people did was simply the way I lived my life back then. I had been educated – both inside and outside prison – by older and more experienced criminals, who I respected, into some of the hard and fast rules they lived by. Rule number one, You never give anyone up or make a statement. Rule number two, you never rob or rip off any other crims. Rule number three, you never cooperate with the authorities, inside or outside prison. Rule number four, you always operate on a need to know only basis...
>
> (Shepherd, 2010, p. 252)

4.5.2.2 Redundancy

N8 also prioritised redundancy to increase security, evident by the use of multiple couriers to import product. In this context, redundancy helps to reduce the risks associated with any one courier being arrested. For example, 'The courier would have to spend at least 10 days in Singapore and Bangkok. In theory no courier should be used more than twice' (Hall, 2010, p. 1247).

Multiple companies were used by N4 for the laundering of syndicate proceeds and for the transport of product from source countries, i.e.:

> The... [various companies of N4] were mainly used as fronts for the export of drugs, chiefly heroin, to Australia and to a lesser extent NZ. Another important function of the companies was to launder moneys sent from Australia.
>
> (Stewart, 1983, p. 119)

N13 used multiple bank accounts and money launderers to receive payment from the proceeds of the organisation, i.e. 'The evidence establishes a clear intention... to launder this money so that the source was hidden and to pay the money to Mr and Mrs [N13] in Singapore, after a maze of transactions which would not normally be traceable' (Stewart, 1983, p. 147). N27 used multiple bank accounts and tax havens to launder money, i.e.:

> After setting up numerous bank accounts in Singapore and HK, as well as putting in place company structures to receive that money, I went a step further. Although it cost me close to 40,000, I had a lawyer fly over to the Netherlands and the Netherlands Antilles – a tax haven in the Caribbean – to set up tax structures so that I could move money freely around the world. I also used this company to send money back into Australia to help fund a land development project I was involved in... It became obvious to me at an early stage that the massive amounts of money we were accumulating could

> become a problem. Hence the numerous overseas bank accounts, the tax havens, the safe houses and even a bank vault.
>
> (Shepherd, 2010, pp. 160–161)

4.5.2.3 Corruption and information networks

N26 was significant to the functioning of the syndicate because he brokered access to police protection through his lawyer contact, N45. N8 heavily relied on his information networks for the purposes of recruitment, allowing existing couriers to recruit new couriers. For example, one of the syndicate's couriers allegedly reported, '[N8] told me to really always express the risks involved, that you could get 25 years if you were caught and for me to make sure that [N38] told that to her friend that she chose' (Stewart, 1983, p. 149).

N8 also used his contacts to gain introductions to a lawyer who could facilitate information from corrupt police and to arrange for the murder of various crewmembers, e.g. '[N8] asked [N26] if he could arrange the killings for 250,000. [N26] got the same team together to kill the two informers' (Hall, 2010, p. 1519). Access to the UK drug market may have been made possible for the organisation by N4 and his contacts there, 'The early stages of the UK connection were a [N4] operation' (Hall, 2010, pp. 773–780). N27 used his information networks to broker introductions between unconnected parties for a fee. His contacts were extremely valuable to the primary leader N8, who relied heavily on the corrupt lawyer that provided access to corrupt police, and N27 was able to provide this important commodity, for a price, 'It was agreed between us that I could go as high as $20,000 in getting a successful introduction' (Shepherd, 2010, p. 148). These contacts were extremely valuable to N27 as they provided information that could be brokered as well as used for his sole benefit, such as being tipped off when he became a person of interest and when to make himself scarce. This came at a high cost, as the excerpt below suggests:

> Other witnesses have claimed that [N27] was also given notice of police raids… he boasted of paying $50,000 to police every three months so that he would be advised beforehand if police were about to visit his dealers.
>
> (Stewart, 1983, p. 186)

N27 also used his contacts to access weapons for other members of the syndicate's leadership, 'I thanked [N26] for helping me acquire a weapon in London through his cousin' (Shepherd, 2010, p. 277). It is reported that N26 was able to provide resources such as false passports and police protection, through access to corrupt sources such as lawyers, allowing for syndicate members to travel undetected:

> He had an officer in the Passport Office, never exposed, who removed the paperwork from the file leaving a note saying 'Issued', and no other details. Thus the Organisation could create fictional people too.
>
> (Hall, 2010, p. 3314)

4.5.2.4 Violence and intimidation

The primary leader (N8) frequently employed violence, threats and intimidation to control and attempt to reduce risks. The violence assumed various forms, including physical violence, threats of violence to network members and their families and his notorious reputation. Physical violence was used systematically against associates who cooperated with police or posed a threat of informing, i.e. 'I made an example of him... broke every bone up to his neck... I left his face alone. I wanted him to live, just for an example' (Hall, 2010, p. 1025) and, 'If you are not prepared to kill... you should not be in the drug business. I have already killed six people' (Shepherd, 2010, p. 98). Threats were a common method employed by N8 to reduce the risk of betrayal. In particular, N8 regularly confided in his associates about some of the acts of violence he had committed as a 'constant means of intimidation' (Stewart, 1983, p. 141). Further, 'The involvement of associates in acts of violence compromised whatever independence they previously had, making it unlikely that they would ever be disloyal to [N8]' (Stewart, 1983, p. 200). The excerpt below indicates the importance of a violent reputation in organised crime:

> [N8] said they had been buried under cement construction work at Sydney's international airport. It has never been clear whether he did the job himself or contracted it out; but the Organisation members certainly believe that he was responsible. It was an eloquent testimony to his authority; it doesn't do a man any harm in the drug trade to have the reputation of one prepared to kill.
>
> (Hall, 2010, p. 728)

There is little evidence to suggest N4 was violent and indeed, some indication that he explicitly opted for non-violent tactics. N26 was able to rely on his reputation and association with the criminal underworld:

> They are growing grass down there by the truckload and [N26] is one of their top men. He handles most of the sales. They are all making fucking squillions, as they have the law on side. These boys are not the Mafia, but they are the closest thing to the Mafia in this country. Although the crew down there are all nice guys, they will not hesitate to have you killed. So beware my friend, if you ever do business with them.
>
> (Shepherd, 2010, p. 131)

While N26 did not need to make explicit threats of violence, he was able to trade on the violent reputation of groups with whom he associated.

All leaders managed risk through secrecy, information networks, redundancy and corruption. Information networks and corruption were the most commonly used strategies. Four out of five leaders demonstrated some evidence of using violence to manage risk, however, this was mainly through the use of intimidation rather than actual violence. N8 was the only leader to demonstrate evidence of using physical violence to reduce risk.

4.5.3 Relationship between network position and risk management behaviour

All leaders demonstrated high scores on betweenness centrality, however, there was no evidence of strategic positioning among leaders in this group (i.e. high betweenness combined with low centrality; see Morselli, 2010). All leaders fell into the high-degree/high-betweenness centrality quadrant, classifying them as among the most connected, visible and vulnerable of all network actors. The vulnerabilities associated with being highly visible tend to outweigh any benefit from being in brokerage positions.

Table 4.4 illustrates the relationship between network position and risk management strategies. For example, the table shows that while all leaders used multiple strategies, N8 demonstrated more protective behaviour than any other actor in this group and also scored highest on all measures of centrality. With respect to leaders' behaviour, N8 was the only leader to use physical violence to manage risk. N8 was the primary leader of the organisation as well as the highest scoring actor on all measures of centrality. All other leaders used non-violent methods of managing risk, particularly information networks, corruption, secrecy and redundancy. Specifically, reputation was a protective factor for N8, N26 and N27. Unlike N8, however, N26 and N27 did not engage in physical violence. The more extreme methods of reducing risk demonstrated by N8 may be partly associated with the particularly central, visible and therefore vulnerable position he held in the network. It is also possible that the violence demonstrated by N8 reduced the need for other leaders to engage in violence as a protection tactic. Whether intentional or not, by using violence as a self-preservation strategy, N8 also indirectly

Table 4.4 Relationship between network position and risk management behaviour

*Leader**	*N8*	*N27*	*N4*	*N13*	*N26*
Degree	75.0	45.0	33.0	20.0	15.0
Betweenness	3445.9	1098.9	843.4	344.0	88.9
Closeness	71.5	58.0	55.9	51.3	48.1
Risk management strategies	Information networks Intimidation and violence Trust Redundancy Corruption Reputation	Secrecy Information networks Corruption Reputation	Information networks Trust Corruption	Information networks Secrecy	Information networks Corruption Reputation

*All leaders scored above the median scores on measures of centrality, including degree (4.0), betweenness (7.2) and closeness (42.6).

protected other leaders in the network from the perceived threat. As the primary leader, N8 exercised systematic violence that clearly communicated the consequences of disloyalty to potential informants while also potentially reducing the need for other leaders to engage in violent means of protection.

4.6 Discussion

Actors engaging in criminal activities face distinct threats and challenges and none are more central than the threats from law enforcement (seizure of product, arrest of actors). Some scholars have suggested the 'more strategic participants in the network would, therefore, be more content in remaining peripheral, and not directly central, to the action taking place' (Morselli, 2010, p. 384). In the case study we analysed, the primary leader (N8) scored highest on all measures of centrality. This is consistent with past research associating degree centrality with power and influence in criminal networks (Krebs, 2002, p. 47; Xu & Chen, 2003, p. 235).

High scores on degree centrality can indicate influence and power, but may also reflect visibility and therefore vulnerability to detection (e.g. Morselli, 2010). In the current case study, leaders' scores on SNA metrics indicate they are among the most exposed and structurally unprotected of all actors in the network. While some syndicate members were positioned strategically within the network (i.e. N24, N88, N103, N122), none of these individuals were considered to be leaders. In contrast, all leaders fell in the high-degree/high-betweenness centrality group. Studies have demonstrated that such high-degree centrality/low-betweenness centrality combinations were more likely to receive a guilty verdict and a greater sentence than strategically positioned actors (85% compared to 25% arrested) (Baker & Faulkner, 1993; Morselli, 2010).

Past literature suggests that the goals of, and demands on, a particular group influence its organisational structure (Morselli et al., 2007). The centralised nature of the case study criminal network where leaders comprised the core is in line with studies suggesting criminal groups with 'high processing needs' require those co-ordinating operations to be more involved (Baker & Faulkner, 1993, p. 856). While leaders in the case study assumed high levels of power and control within the organisation, this also increased their likelihood of detection by law enforcement. The findings from the case study support the premise that degree centrality is associated with a guilty verdict, as three out of the five leaders (N8, N13 and N27) were arrested and sentenced to long prison terms for their involvement. Herein, the efficiency and security trade-off may explain why those controlling illicit activities sometimes position themselves in such a vulnerable position (Morselli et al., 2007). Profit-driven criminal networks (like drug trafficking networks) prioritise efficiency because there are short time periods within which decisive action must occur. All leaders demonstrated a need to be highly connected to other actors within the network, perhaps reflecting a desire for increased control and coordination over activities. In fact, there was no evidence of leaders employing structural risk management strategies to protect their position of power. If this finding applies to transnational drug trafficking organisations in the contemporary context, it suggests that actors centrally located in criminal networks may be important targets for surveillance. Further, this also highlights the benefit of employing complementary qualitative research approaches to enrich studies that employ SNA (Calderoni, 2011, 2012; Morselli, 2010). While no leaders were strategically positioned, the analysis allowed for identification of other network members who had assumed this type of social positioning strategy. These individuals may not have been considered significant players by law enforcement and there is little information available about the nature of their roles and level of involvement in the syndicate's day-to-day activities. While the qualitative analysis did not indicate they were significant players in the functioning of this particular criminal network, our network analyses reveal that they played important brokering roles that can be the structural glue that holds the network (and its activities) together. One of these actors (N24) was reportedly a wholesaler who acquired product from the primary leader in the case study (N8) but was associated with a separate criminal organisation. Despite a lack of further detail, together the data sources and this finding (significantly) suggest that early identification by law enforcement would have tied N24 and therefore N8 to a separate criminal enterprise and a significant figure in the prostitution industry (Hall, 2010, p. 632).

The use of information networks and corruption were interrelated strategies. The use of information networks refers to informal networking with the purpose of gathering and verifying information so as to keep informed about potential risks and rewards in the environment (Desroches, 2005, p. 128). Leaders networked with other criminals to arrange introductions to brokers who could facilitate access to resources such as law enforcement intelligence, couriers, suppliers and contract killers. The statement below provides an example of information networks in practice:

> That was the connection [N8] needed to operate in Sydney – access to corrupt police – and [N26] was able to facilitate that desire.
>
> (Shepherd, 2010, p. 131)

Information networks clearly benefited leaders by reducing risk in various ways. N8 used his contacts (i.e. N26, N13) to access lawyers, corrupt officials, suppliers and couriers, as well as to arrange the murder of problematic employees. While N8 had access to key resources (i.e. money, product, contacts), others (i.e. N27, N13, N26) benefited through the provision of that access, as outlined by the quote below:

> It was agreed between us that I could go as high as $20,000 in getting a successful introduction.
>
> (Shepherd, 2010, p. 148)

Individuals who can provide access to otherwise unavailable information or resources fill holes in the social structure and in doing so create competitive advantage (Burt, 1992; Granovetter, 1973, p. 1361). N26 became vital to the functioning of the syndicate through his capacity to broker between licit and illicit worlds. N26 was introduced to N8 by N27 through his own information network. Through his involvement in a separate criminal organisation, N26 was able to provide N8 access to novel and valuable resources that were not already being shared among N8's close ties. As Morselli (2001) explains, 'such entrepreneurial flexibility is indicated by the capacity to control the resources needed by others' (Morselli, 2001, p. 210). The multiple key criminal assets provided by N26 (i.e. access to police protection, false passports and hired assassins) constituted significant criminal capital (Burt, 1997, p. 340).

Most leaders in the case study did not use physical violence to manage risks. This is consistent with past research suggesting that higher-level traffickers avoid violence for the unwanted attention it brings (Arquilla & Ronfeldt, 2001, p. 90; Desroches, 2005, p. 119; Gambetta, 2009, p. 170; Hofmann & Gallupe, 2015; Morselli, 2010; Pearson & Hobbs, 2003). In contrast to this, the behaviour that most distinguished N8 from other leaders was his propensity towards physical violence, particularly murder, as a means of managing risk. This may reflect personal attributes and attitudes of this particular individual, or that he lacked the social skills to manage and/or manipulate others without recourse to violence. Physical violence was often the response to intelligence collected through information networks, particularly with regard to the threat of informants. The use of explicit and implicit threats of violence is consistently discussed throughout all sources as the key strategy that enabled N8 to control associates and eliminate threat. This behaviour distinguished N8 from the other leaders who demonstrated no evidence of physical violence to manage risk.

Despite efforts to reduce risk through threats and the use of violence to ensure compliance, leaders in the case study afforded little attention to the recruitment of less central members. Research examining contemporary criminal networks suggests that peripheral members tend to be recruited through looser relationships than those of core membership and they are generally less invested in the organisation as 'the bonding mechanisms are not as strong' (Williams, 1994, p. 155). This was found in the current study, where new and unfamiliar couriers were recruited by syndicate members who were relatively new themselves rather than through pre-existing trusted relationships. The issue with this has been highlighted in past research. A recent case study of a cocaine trafficking syndicate found the use of multiple smuggling routes resulted in a lack of central oversight over recruitment and screening processes (Hofmann & Gallupe, 2015). In their case study, as in the current case study, couriers recruited through weak ties led to the downfall of the criminal network as a whole. This is consistent with past research describing the heightened threat these individuals pose as informants (von Lampe & Johansen, 2004, p. 149). In both cases, attempts to increase efficiency proved detrimental to organisational security, consistent with the security/efficiency trade-off argument put forth by Morselli and colleagues (Morselli et al., 2007).

The findings here highlight that while SNA is an important tool in conceptualising criminal organisation and identifying important individuals in networks, it is limited in explaining criminal behaviour as it does not account for individual-level variables. On the other hand, interpreting behaviour from a solely individual-level perspective is also incomplete as behaviour is affected by social context variables (such as being highly connected). The case study demonstrates that the selection of any particular risk management strategy is also influenced by differences in individual learning experiences. As Robins (2009) notes, 'a richer description of individual action within a complex social system will require better knowledge about how personality, social identity and other psychological factors are distinct from, and yet may interact with, self-organising network processes' (Robins, 2009, p. 182). Individual differences in strategy selected and most relied on were observed and these tendencies are likely to be influenced by past learning experiences, adhered cultural norms and differences in personality. When applying these findings across other criminal contexts, it will be important to bear in mind that any strategy selected to reduce individual risk is to some extent a choice that will vary between agents.

4.6.1 Limitations

A primary limitation to studying criminal networks is difficulty locating reliable data. The bias of the criminal memoir account is acknowledged. While often rich and unique in perspective, the recall is subject to distortions, leans towards exaggerations and is ego-centric by nature (Morselli, 2001, p. 210). The use of historical case studies to make inferences about contemporary criminal activity is a common method employed in criminology but not without its confines. While the current case study criminal network was operational in the 1970s, it could be argued that the transnational nature of the organisation renders it relevant to the current context and the investigation of risk management involves examination of themes that remain prominent in the literature.

The issue of missing data is always at the forefront in studying covert groups. Law enforcement data, while often difficult to obtain, is the primary source of information used by researchers studying the organisational structure of criminal groups. A key issue associated with this approach is that the information is biased by the goals of the initial investigation (Berlusconi, 2013; Bright et al., 2012; Campana & Varese, 2013), ensuing that the boundaries of the criminal network are often not accurately reflected by the findings of the police investigation. This relates to the problem of 'fuzzy boundaries', where it is difficult to determine which individuals and relationships are pertinent to the analysis. The triangulation of alternate data sources attempts to increase the reliability and validity of the current research design. Detailed data from various perspectives that document the activities and strategies employed by a single criminal organisation are rare, and the wealth of information available on the case study allowed for detailed examination of criminal organisation and behaviour.

4.6.2 Implications for practice and policy

The findings from the current case study suggest that for the purposes of intelligence collection and designing intervention strategies, law enforcement should not only focus on 'leaders' but also on individuals who may seem less active in an organisation. SNA may be a particularly useful tool to identify such individuals. Results suggest that law enforcement should target not only leaders but strategically positioned actors, as such an approach may lead to identifying ties with other active criminal organisations and may be a more effective way of dismantling the network as a whole. Further, criminal leaders in the case study primarily employed behavioural methods of managing risk. A better understanding of how individuals involved in criminal activity assess and manage risks will assist in informing law enforcement initiatives aimed at identifying, infiltrating and disrupting these groups.

Acknowledgements

The data collection and analysis for this chapter was conducted while the first author was an Honours student at the School of Social Sciences, University of New South Wales, Australia.

References

Adler, P. A. (1993) *Wheeling and Dealing: An Ethnography of an Upper-Level Drug Dealing and Smuggling Community.* New York: Columbia University Press.

Arquilla, J., and D. Ronfeldt (2001) *Networks and Netwars: The Future of Terror, Crime, and Militancy.* Santa Monica, CA: Rand Corporation.

Baker, W. E., and R. R. Faulkner (1993) 'The social organization of conspiracy: Illegal networks in the heavy electrical equipment industry', *American Sociological Review*, 58(6), pp. 837–860.

Benson, J. S., and S. H. Decker (2010) 'The organizational structure of international drug smuggling', *Journal of Criminal Justice*, 38(2), pp. 130–138.

Berlusconi, G. (2013) 'Do all the pieces matter? Assessing the reliability of law enforcement data sources for the network analysis of wire taps', *Global Crime*, 14(1), pp. 61–81.

Borgatti, S. P. (2006) 'Identifying sets of key players in a social network', *Computational and Mathematical Organization Theory*, 12(1), pp. 21–34.

Borgatti, S. P., M. G. Everett, and L. C. Freeman (2002) *UCINET 6 for Windows.* Columbia, SC: Analytic Technologies.

Bright, D. A., C. Greenhill, A. Ritter, and C. Morselli (2015) 'Networks within networks: Using multiple link types to examine network structure and identify key actors in a drug trafficking operation', *Global Crime*, 16(3), pp. 219–237, DOI: 10.1080/17440572.2015.1039164.

Bright, D. A., C. E. Hughes, and J. Chalmers (2012) 'Illuminating dark networks: A social network analysis of an Australian drug trafficking syndicate', *Crime, Law and Social Change*, 57(2), pp. 151–176.

Brownstein, H. H., T. M. Mulcahy, J. Huessy, B. G. Taylor, and D. Woods (2010) 'The organization and operation of illicit retail methamphetamine markets', *Criminal Justice Policy Review*, 23(1), pp. 67–89.

Burt, R. (1992) *Structural Holes: The Social Structure of Competition.* Cambridge, MA: Harvard University Press.

Burt, R. S. (1997) 'The contingent value of social capital', *Administrative Science Quarterly*, 42(2), pp. 339–365.

Calderoni, F. (2011) Strategic positioning in mafia networks. Paper presented at the Third Annual Illicit Networks Workshop, Montreal.

Calderoni, F. (2012) 'The structure of drug trafficking mafias: The 'Ndrangheta and cocaine', *Crime, Law and Social Change*, 58(3), pp. 321–349.

Calderoni, F. (2014) 'Identifying mafia bosses from meeting attendance'. In: A. J. Masys (ed.), *Networks and Network Analysis for Defence and Security.* Switzerland: Springer International Publishing, pp. 27–48.

Campana, P., and F. Varese (2013) 'Cooperation in criminal organizations: Kinship and violence as credible commitments', *Rationality and Society*, 25(3), pp. 263–289.

Carley, K. (1993) 'Coding choices for textual analysis: A comparison of content analysis and map analysis', *Sociological Methodology*, 23, pp. 75–126.

Carley, K. M., J.-S. Lee, and D. Krackhardt (2002) 'Destabilizing networks', *Connections*, 24(3), pp. 79–92.

Chung, A. (2008) 'The big circle boys: Revisiting the case of the flaming eagles', *Global Crime*, 9(4), pp. 306–331.

Cohen, A. K. (1977) 'The concept of criminal organisation', *The British Journal of Criminology*, 17(2), pp. 97–111.

Cross, J. C. (2000) 'Passing the buck: Risk avoidance and risk management in the illegal/informal drug trade', *International Journal of Sociology and Social Policy*, 20(9/10), pp. 68–94.

Cunningham, D., S. Everton, G. Wilson, C. Padilla, and D. Zimmerman (2013) 'Brokers and key players in the internationalization of the FARC', *Studies in Conflict and Terrorism*, 36(6), pp. 477–502.

Desroches, F. (2005) *The Crime That Pays: Drug Trafficking and Organized Crime in Canada.* Ontario: Canadian Scholars' Press Inc.

Desroches, F. (2007) 'Research on upper level drug trafficking: A review', *Journal of Drug Issues*, 37(4), pp. 827–844.

Dickenson, M. (2014) 'The impact of leadership removal on Mexican drug trafficking organizations', *Journal of Quantitative Criminology*, 30(4), pp. 651–676.

Dorn, N., L. Oette, and S. White (1998) 'Drugs importation and the bifurcation of risk: Capitalization, cut outs and organized crime', *British Journal of Criminology*, 38(4), pp. 537–560.

Enders, W., and X. Su (2007) 'Rational terrorists and optimal network structure', *Journal of Conflict Resolution*, 51(1), pp. 33–57.

Gambetta, D. (2009) *Codes of the Underworld: How Criminals Communicate.* Princeton, NJ: Princeton University Press.

Goldstein, P. J. (1985) 'The drugs/violence nexus: A tripartite conceptual framework', *Journal of Drug Issues*, 15(4), pp. 493–506.

Gottschalk, P. (2010) 'Criminal entrepreneurial behaviour', *Journal for International Business and Entrepreneurship Development*, 5(1), pp. 63–76.

Granovetter, M. S. (1973) 'The strength of weak ties', *American Journal of Sociology*, 78(6), pp. 1360–1380.

Granovetter, M. (1985) 'Economic action and social structure: The problem of embeddedness', *American Journal of Sociology*, 91(3), pp. 481–510.

Hall, R. (2010) Greed: The 'Mr Asia' connection, *Kindle Edition*, accessed 15 May 2015 from Amazon.com.

Hofmann, D. C., and O. Gallupe (2015) 'Leadership protection in drug-trafficking networks', *Global Crime*, 16(2), pp. 123–138.

Holt, T. J., K. R. Blevins, and J. B. Kuhns (2014) 'Examining diffusion and arrest avoidance practises among johns', *Crime and Delinquency*, 60(2), pp. 261–283.

Jacobs, B. A. (1996) 'Crack dealers and restrictive deterrence: Identifying narcs', *Criminology*, 34(3), pp. 409–431.

Johnson, B. D., and M. Natarajan (1995) 'Strategies to avoid arrest: Crack sellers' response to intensified policing', *American Journal of Police*, 14(3/4), pp. 49–69.

Kenney, M. (2007) 'The architecture of drug trafficking: Network forms of organisation in the Colombian cocaine trade', *Global Crime*, 8(3), pp. 233–259.

Kleemans, E. R. (2007) 'Organized crime, transit crime, and racketeering', *Crime and Justice*, 35(1), pp. 163–215.

Klerks, P. (2001) 'The network paradigm applied to criminal organizations: Theoretical nitpicking or a relevant doctrine for investigators? Recent developments in the Netherlands', *Connections*, 24(3), pp. 53–65.

Knowles, G. J. (1999) 'Deception, detection and evasion: A trade craft analysis of Honolulu, Hawaii's street crack-cocaine traffickers', *Journal of Criminal Justice*, 27(5), pp. 443–455.

Krebs, V. E. (2002) 'Mapping networks of terrorist cells', *Connections*, 24(3), pp. 43–52.

Lindquist, M. J., and Y. Zenou (2014) *Key Players in Co-offending Networks*. IZA Discussion Paper, No. 8012.

Lyman, M., and G. Potter (2004) *Organized Crime*. Upper Saddle River, NJ: Prentice Hall.

May, T., and M. Hough (2004) 'Drug markets and distribution systems', *Addiction Research and Theory*, 12(6), pp. 549–563.

Morselli, C. (2001) 'Structuring Mr. Nice: Entrepreneurial opportunities and brokerage positioning in the cannabis trade', *Crime, Law and Social Change*, 35(3), pp. 203–244.

Morselli, C. (2010) 'Assessing vulnerable and strategic positions in a criminal network', *Journal of Contemporary Criminal Justice*, 26(4), pp. 382–392.

Morselli, C., and C. Giguere (2006) 'Legitimate strengths in criminal networks', *Crime, Law and Social Change*, 45(3), pp. 185–200.

Morselli, C., C. Giguère, and K. Petit (2007) 'The efficiency/security trade-off in criminal networks', *Social Networks*, 29(1), pp. 143–153.

Paoli, L. (2002) 'The paradoxes of organized crime', *Crime, Law and Social Change*, 37(1), pp. 51–97.

Pearson, G., and D. Hobbs (2003) 'King pin? A case study of a middle market drug broker', *The Howard Journal of Criminal Justice*, 42(4), pp. 335–347.

Porter, L. E., and L. J. Alison (2006) 'Behavioural coherence in group robbery: A circumplex model of offender and victim interactions', *Aggressive Behavior*, 32(4), pp. 330–342.

Robins, G. (2009) 'Understanding individual behaviors within covert networks: The interplay of individual qualities, psychological predispositions, and network effects', *Trends in Organized Crime*, 12(2), pp. 166–187.

Shepherd, J. (2010) *Mr Asia: The Last Man Standing: Inside Australia's Most Notorious Drug Syndicate*. Sydney: Macmillan.

Simmel, G. (1950) *The Sociology of Georg Simmel.* IL, New York: The Free Press.

Sparrow, M. K. (1991) 'The application of network analysis to criminal intelligence: An assessment of the prospects', *Social Networks*, 13(3), pp. 251–274.

Stewart, D.G. (1983). 'Royal Commission of Inquiry into Drug Trafficking', AGPS: Canberra.

Varese, F. (2013) 'The structure and the content of criminal connections: The Russian Mafia in Italy', *European Sociological Review*, 29(5), pp. 899–909.

von Lampe, K. (2007) 'Criminals are not alone: Some observations on the social microcosm of illegal entrepreneurs'. In: P. C. van Duyne, A. Maljevic, M. van Dijck, K. von Lampe, and J. Harvey (eds.), *Crime Business and Crime Money in Europe: The Dirty Linen of Illegal Enterprise.* Netherlands: Wolf Legal Publishers, pp. 131–156.

von Lampe, K. (2015) *Organized Crime: Analysing Illegal Activities, Criminal Structures, and Extra-Legal Governance.* Thousand Oaks, CA: Sage Publishing.

von Lampe, K., and P. Ole Johansen (2004) 'Organized crime and trust: On the conceptualization and empirical relevance of trust in the context of criminal networks', *Global Crime*, 6(2), pp. 159–184.

Williams, P. (1994) 'Transnational criminal organisations and international security', *Survival*, 36(1), pp. 96–113.

Xu, J., and H. Chen (2003) 'Untangling criminal networks: A case study'. In: H. Chen, R. Miranda, D. D. Zeng, C. Demchak, J. Schroeder, and T. Madhusudan (eds.), *Lecture Notes in Computer Science, Vol. 2665: Proceedings of the ISI 2003 Symposium on Intelligence and Security Informatics.* Berlin, Germany: Springer, pp. 232–248.

Zaitch, D. (2002) 'From Cali to Rotterdam: Perceptions of Columbian cocaine traffickers on the Dutch port', *Crime, Law and Social Change*, 38(3), pp. 239–266.

5 Cybercrime, money mules and situational crime prevention

Recruitment, motives and involvement mechanisms

E.R. (Rutger) Leukfeldt and E.R. (Edward) Kleemans

5.1 Introduction

> OK, I will tell you the truth. I don't want to lie about it. I was contacted several times a day by a guy asking for my cash card and PIN-code. I was supposed to get something in return. At that time, I had serious problems. Although I refused several times, eventually I gave him my cash card. After all, there was no money in my bank account and I would get some money in return.

This quote from an interrogation shows how a money mule was recruited for a cybercriminal network. The offenders put money, stolen from victims of phishing or banking malware, into this bank account. The money trail to the offenders is interrupted by withdrawing the money from the account of the money mule directly after the money has been transferred to this bank account. Therefore, money mules are an important part of the crime script of criminal networks involved in committing financial cybercrimes, such as phishing and malware. However, as this section shows, little empirical research on money mules has been carried out. This chapter, therefore, adds to the literature by providing insight into recruitment processes of money mules and the motives and neutralisation techniques of money mules.

Phishing is the process aimed at tracing users' personal information by criminals posing as a trusted authority and thereby using digital means, such as e-mail (see, e.g. Lastdrager, 2014, who analysed 113 definitions of phishing). Crime scripts of phishers differ, but phishers usually use e-mails that appear to be sent by a bank to gain login credentials of victims (see, for various examples, Leukfeldt et al. 2017a, 2017b). The e-mail is, for example, about the security of the online bank account of the victim and immediate action is required. The victim is persuaded to click on a link in the e-mail to solve the security problem. The link leads to a phishing website which appears to be from the bank. Once the victim logs on to the website, the criminals obtain his or her credentials. In order to transfer money from the victim's account, the criminals have to obtain transaction authentication codes. The next step, therefore, is to telephone the victim.

A criminal calls the victim and poses as a bank employee who wants to finalise the security update of the online bank account and needs security codes to do so. Depending on the bank of the victim and type of transaction authentication method used by the bank, the victim has to generate a code, which is abused by the criminals to transfer money. The money is not transferred to members of the criminal network, but to money mules. Money from the money mule accounts is cashed as soon as possible. These money mules are not directly linked to the members of the criminal network and are used to obscure the trail to the criminal network.

The crime script of networks using malware is slightly different. Malware is short for malicious software. This software is used by criminals to intercept users' personal information in an automated way. Once the computer of the user is infected with the malware, the criminal gains control over this computer. An infection is started, for example, by opening an infected attachment of an e-mail. Once the criminals control the victim's computer, criminals are able to manipulate online banking sessions and send money to accounts of money mules. Again, money mules play an important part in this crime script.

Money mules, therefore, are not part of the group of core offenders coordinating the illicit activities. Nevertheless, they are a crucial part of the crime script, as they interrupt the money trail while at the same time the core offenders are able to reap their profits anonymously. They take a high risk for a relatively low reward and enable cybercriminal networks to operate smoothly. Surprisingly, hardly any empirical research has been done into money mules. Scholars acknowledged decades ago that criminals abuse Information and Communication Technology (ICT) to commit crimes (for example, Aston et al. 2009; Loch et al., 1992; Akdeniz, 1996; Wall, 1997; Mann and Sutton, 1998; Gattiker and Kelley, 1999; Capeller, 2001; Grabosky, 2001; Grabosky and Smith, 2001) and more recently the nature and functioning of cybercriminal networks are gaining more and more attention (for example, Peretti, 2008; Holt and Lampke, 2010; Lu et al., 2010; Décary-Hetú and Dupont, 2012; Lusthaus, 2012; Soudijn and Monsma, 2012; Yip et al., 2012; Afroz, 2013; Leukfeldt, 2014; Leukfeldt et al., 2017a, 2017b, 2017c, 2017d). Furthermore, several studies acknowledge the important role of money mules in the diversion of money stolen by cybercriminals who are engaged in financial cybercrimes (Choo, 2008; Moore and Clayton, 2007; Aston et al., 2009; McCombie, 2011; Soudijn and Zegers, 2012; Leukfeldt, 2014; Leukfeldt et al. 2017a, 2017b, 2017c, 2017d). These studies, however, concentrate primarily on the core of criminal networks and the role of money mules within these cybercriminal networks remains underexposed.

The crucial function of money mules in the crime scripts of phishing and malware networks makes this specific group extremely relevant for situational crime prevention. If it is hard to carry out these illicit activities without money mules, they are an obvious target for situational crime prevention, e.g. by making it harder to recruit money mules, by making it less attractive to be a money mule or by removing excuses. Removing excuses is one of the strategies of situational crime prevention (e.g. Cornish and Clarke, 2003), but can also be traced back to the techniques of neutralisation (Sykes and Matza, 1957; for a review of empirical research see Maruna and Copes, 2005). The interrogation we mentioned in the introduction illustrates various excuses for cooperating as a money mule: he only agreed after several refusals, he had serious problems and needed extra money, and after all, there was no money in his bank account. More insight into the nature of these excuses could help design effective intervention strategies.

This chapter explores the possibilities for situational crime prevention regarding the recruitment of money mules. Section 5.2 contains a brief description of situational crime prevention, the theoretical angle of this chapter. Section 5.3 analysed the data and methods of 14 Dutch criminal investigations into cybercriminal networks to get insight into the motives and techniques of neutralisation of money mules. Section 5.4 takes the perspective of the recruiters and answers the question of how recruiters find money mules, e.g. by using social contacts and/or specific offender convergence settings. Section 5.5 focuses on the motives and techniques of neutralisation used by money mules. Section 5.6 presents the main conclusions and opportunities for situational crime prevention.

5.2 Strategies for situational crime prevention

Situational crime prevention strategies encompass a wide range of opportunity-reducing measures aimed at hindering or preventing crime. Originally, Clarke (1980) distinguished two potential strategies: reducing the physical opportunities for offending and increasing the chances of an offender being caught. Over the years, strategies and methods were elaborated and adapted in response to new empirical research (see, e.g. Clarke, 1997; Clarke and Homel, 1997; Cornish and Clarke, 2003). At this moment, five different strategies for situational crime prevention are recognised:

- Increase the effort of crime (e.g. target hardening by installing better locks);
- Increase the risk of crime (e.g. extend guardianship by neighbourhood watch);
- Reduce the rewards of crime (e.g. remove targets or identify property);
- Reduce provocations that invite criminal behaviour (e.g. neutralise peer pressure);
- Remove excuses for criminal behaviour (e.g. set rules about (un)wanted behaviour).

Based on these five strategies for situational crime prevention, Cornish and Clarke distinguish 25 techniques for situational crime prevention. According to these authors, this 'classification of crime prevention techniques is designed to provide a conceptual analysis of situational strategies, and to offer practical guidance on their use in reducing criminal opportunities' (Cornish and Clarke, 2003, p. 41).

The primary focus of these 25 techniques for situational crime prevention was opportunistic street-level crime. Only later on was the situational crime prevention theory transplanted to other, more serious types of 'organized crimes' (e.g. Cornish and Clarke, 2002; Bullock et al., 2010; Kleemans and Soudijn, 2017). However, situational crime prevention cannot only be applied to offline crime, but also to online crime. Hartel et al. (2011) review the literature and show that principally these techniques are equally applicable to cybercrime. Examples include increasing the effort of crime by using password-protected files, increasing the risk of crime through extended guardianship by Internet service providers who filter e-mails, reduce the rewards of crime by encrypting valuable data, reduce provocations that invite criminal behaviour by discouraging imitation by prompting software patching, and remove excuses for criminal behaviour by posting instructions and making the general public aware of the consequences of crime.

When we focus on money mules, we might interpret them as 'facilitators' or 'enablers,' as these persons carry out three essential functions: they make it possible to transfer the stolen money to a bank account, they make it impossible to trace the core members of the criminal network and they enable these offenders to withdraw the cash from the bank account. At the same time, they run a high risk to be caught and they receive a relatively low reward. How do core members recruit these money mules? Do they use traditional offline social contacts, online contacts, digital offender convergence settings such as forums, et cetera (e.g. Leukfeldt, 2014; Leukfeldt et al. 2017a, 2017b)? And what are the motives and techniques of neutralisation of these money mules? These questions will be answered in Sections 5.4 and 5.5.

5.3 Data and methods

Fourteen Dutch criminal investigations into cybercriminal networks were analysed to get insight into motives and techniques of neutralisation of money mules. The investigations lasted six months to three years and were carried out in the period 2004–2014. The investigations show that often hundreds of money mules are used by these cybercriminal networks (for example, because the investigations show to which money mules the money is transferred from the victims' bank accounts). However, the number of interrogated money mules is much lower. One reason for this is that investigations are not always focused on money mules, but on core members or important enablers. Another reason is that tracing and interrogating all money mules is too time-consuming. Therefore, the number of interrogated money mules varies for each investigation.

The 14 analysed investigations contained interrogations of 211 money mules. Four investigations included two to 10 interrogated money mules, six investigations included 11 to 20 interrogated money mules, and three investigations contained 20 or more interrogated money mules. Not all interrogations of these 211 money mules yielded enough information for this analysis: 69 suspects did not cooperate during the interrogation ('no comment') and 30 claimed to be innocent. The other 112 money mules admitted to having assisted in cashing the money that was stolen by phishing or malware attacks. The analysis of this chapter focuses on these 112 interrogations.

This chapter does not include all forms of cybercrime. There are simply too many types of cybercriminal networks with major differences between them, ranging, e.g. from networks that threaten banks or major online retailers to shut down their websites or online systems to groups engaged in producing and distributing child pornography. This study is part of the Research Programme on Safety and Security of Online Banking. Therefore, this study only includes money mules which are used by groups carrying out attacks on online banking. That boils down to phishing attacks and malware attacks. In literature, different definitions for phishing are presented (see, for example, Lastdrager, 2014). The scope of these definitions is as follows: Phishing is the process aimed at retrieving users' personal information by criminals posing as a trusted authority and thereby using digital means, such as e-mail. As mentioned before, a criminal, for example, sends an e-mail that seems to come from a trusted third party such as a bank. The e-mail refers to a problem with the online bank account of the user (e.g. 'A security upgrade is needed') coupled with the request to take immediate action to resolve the issue (e.g. 'Log in using the link in the e-mail to update the security of your account'). The aim of the attack is to intercept user credentials. User credentials can also be intercepted in a more technological way. Criminals use malware – or malicious software – such as viruses, worms, Trojan horses and spyware, to intercept credentials or manipulate entire online banking sessions.

The 14 police investigations are not publicly available. The Public Prosecution Office ('College van PG's') must give permission for the scientific analysis of a police investigation, and the research proposal must first be assessed by the Research and Documentation Centre (WODC) of the Dutch Ministry of Security and Justice. WODC gives advice on the (scientific) quality of the research proposal and the research topic (e.g. added value regarding current research projects).

It was decided to use investigations into criminal networks which had been completed by the police. Completed means that the investigation team has collected enough evidence for the public prosecutor to decide to prosecute the suspects. There may not necessarily have been a ruling by a judge yet. Excluding cases where no judgment is yet available would mean that only a few cases would remain because it may take years before suspects are convicted (after appeal) (Kleemans, 2014).

There is no central registration system in the Netherlands that allows for a quick overview of all criminal investigations into phishing networks. The selection of cases was, therefore, carried out by using the snowball method. Starting points were cybercrime and fraud teams on a national and (inter)regional level. Using existing contacts within the Dutch police, the Police Academy and Public Prosecutors, team leaders and senior investigators of these teams were asked whether they knew any investigations into networks using phishing or malware to attack users of online banking. Furthermore, an online database in which court documents are published was used and a media analysis was done to find news reports about relevant cases. During the file study, law enforcement officers and public prosecutors involved in the criminal investigation were asked whether they knew of any other phishing cases.

5.4 The recruitment of new money mules

Although not all interrogations of money mules have detailed information about their financial situation – sometimes police officers simply do not ask any questions about this – the majority of the 112 money mules seem to have limited financial funds. At least 40 money mules are still in high school or university and only have part-time jobs, five others quit school and have a part-time job, 35 money mules are out of work and rely on benefits and 58 claim to be in debt. Recruiters seem to make use of this vulnerability. They promise potential money mules a financial reward for little effort, namely offering their bank accounts for a fee.

In 13 out of 14 investigations into phishing and banking malware networks, money mules are recruited through existing social contacts. Core members or recruiters (used by these networks) contact people they know from their own neighbourhoods, schools or sports clubs. They ask questions about the financial situation of potential money mules, or they ask frankly if they want to earn easy money. Box 1 includes some examples.

Box 1 Recruitment through social contacts

'I knew the recruiter from soccer. I played soccer against his team once in a while. I also know him from nightlife, apart from that I did not meet him on a regular basis. He's not a friend of mine, but I do occasionally meet him. I didn't have too bad an impression of him. I've also never met him at home. He asked several times for a cash card. Eventually, I just gave it to him.'

'I knew her through my niece, she attended the same school. She's not really my niece. I know her all my life, so she's just like a niece to me. We originate from the same country and our parents also know each other. This way, I actually came into contact with them. And, as a result, I was introduced to other people again and again. This all happened at a school in the Bijlmer-neighbourhood in Amsterdam.'

The networks that do not recruit through direct social contacts have to find potential money mules through other ways. An example is posting advertisements on job websites, as described in studies by Aston et al. (2009) and McCombie (2011). On these websites, recruiters are able to target people looking for work. In one of the analysed investigations, money mules are recruited in a similar way (see Box 2). In this case, money mules are recruited through e-mails that were sent on a massive scale. These e-mails asked for employees for a financial company. This company also wants to service Dutch clients and is, therefore, looking for a new employee who wants to offer his or her bank account to put money into. These payments need to be transferred to a third party. The 'employees' are allowed to keep a commission regarding this payment.

Box 2 Recruitment through spam

The e-mail with a fake job description promises a guaranteed salary of 2000 US dollars. A police agent enrols as a new employee through the website mentioned in this e-mail. The next e-mail by this 'company' includes a labour contract that needs to be filled out and sent back to the company. Furthermore, the e-mail explains again the earnings (5% of the transferred money) and that the money needs to be transferred through Western Union. After the signed contract has been sent back, a second e-mail follows asking for the bank account number, type of account (business or private), transfer limits, and IBAN and SWIFT numbers. After answering this e-mail, a third e-mail follows stating that 9,447 Euro has been transferred. The employee is entitled to keep 473 Euro. The rest has to be transferred to two persons in Russia through Western Union. Furthermore, the e-mail mentions that after the transfer, specific data of this transaction need to be e-mailed to this company. If any travel costs are involved because the Western Union office is not nearby, employees get 100 Euro per 100 kilometres.

5.5 Motives and techniques of neutralisation

During interrogations, money mules make different statements about why they assisted in transferring money. Not all suspects admit to having participated deliberately, and others refuse to cooperate with the interrogators. Interrogations yielding information about motives of money mules, however, show various motives and techniques of neutralisation that will be described below. They are described separately, but in reality, they can appear in various combinations.

One group of money mules admits to having cooperated knowingly and deliberately with the fraudulent money transfers and that they couldn't resist the lure of earning easy money. Many of these money mules are part of a subculture in which it is normal to cooperate with these kinds of fraudulent activities and say they feel pressured by recruiters to collaborate. Next to that, there are various money mules who admit to having cooperated, yet state as an excuse that they were not aware that these activities were fraudulent. For example, because they thought that the money transfers have a legitimate purpose or that virtual money would not imply real victims. A third group blames the victims. Examples of these motives of money mules will be described below.

5.5.1 Subculture

Statements of 26 money mules show they are part of a subculture in which it is normal to cooperate with such fraudulent activities. Several money mules claim during interrogations that it is relatively normal that they were approached by people who asked them to lend them their cash card (see Box 3).

Box 3 Subculture

During an interrogation, Suspect 38 states: 'I get text messages on a regular basis from several guys. These guys ask me if I know anyone who wants to make money. They simply ask you if you have cash cards.' Suspect 38 shows a text message that she got that morning from F: 'Don't you know a girl who wants booty?'

'Since about 2 years rumour has it that you can earn easy money by providing your bank account. Also through the Internet messages are sent that you can earn money by offering your bank account. I didn't want to cooperate, I am not a money mule or errand-boy. Some months ago I changed my mind. I really could use the money. I ran into a Surinamese boy and he introduced me to S1.'

Suspect 9 states: 'This is general knowledge in Amsterdam. It's a big hit. They do it with everything. They earn a lot of money with fraud.' About the person to whom she would have offered her cash card, she states: 'They call him Prince. It's from the streets. Really, everybody knows him. He's from Ghana. Together with his uncle he commits fraud (…) I said already that everybody in the Netherlands is involved. Many people do it. Especially youngsters. You can earn easy money and many want to do that. Many youngsters or junkies who have nothing to lose.'

5.5.2 *Earning easy money*

Thirty-one money mules state they simply wanted to earn easy money. Examples are described in Box 4.

Box 4 Earning easy money

Suspect 4: 'About two weeks later I went to S15 and he talked about money. He thought his student benefits were too low. He asked if I knew a way to get more money. S15 wanted more money for shoes, caps, and so on. I then told him that you could earn 800 or 900 Euro by offering your cash card. S15 stated that he knew who S9 was, he knew his face. I explained everything about the cash card. S15 asked about problems he might run into. I told him that S9 had communicated that you wouldn't run into problems and that otherwise, you could tell S9's name. S15 wanted to offer his cash card. However, he wanted to be sure he would get that 800 or 900 Euro.'

5.5.3 Looking up to the lifestyle of criminals

Furthermore, the interrogations of 15 money mules make clear that they look up to the lifestyle of core members and recruiters (see Box 5). The members of criminal networks carrying out phishing and malware attacks have a high prestige among local youngsters, and youngsters starting as recruiters suddenly turn out to be able to spend considerable sums of money. They drive luxurious cars, wear fancy clothes and spend lots of money on nightlife. Youngsters fancy earning easy money themselves. They are approached regularly on the streets, at hangouts, during nightlife or at school. Subsequently, contact details are exchanged and the Internet and mobile phones make it easy to maintain contact. Furthermore, other persons are actively approached via text messages on mobile phones. Youngsters get messages asking for cash cards from friends of vague acquaintances ('who wants to earn easy money').

Box 5 Looking up to the lifestyle of criminals

'Not a normal car, a fancy car. It was a dark car, it had been made lower. Sometimes Mercedes and sometimes BMW. The clothes of this guy were from Gucci, they also frequented a club. They were in the secured VIP-area, we were in the crowd. The two of them often were together. One was wearing a Moncler. That's an expensive coat. I've always wanted to have such a coat. Both had golden teeth.'

'In June or July 2012, I became acquainted with a guy (recruiter G). He is a nephew of a friend of my ex-boyfriend. This guy took me out for dinner several times and gave me expensive clothes, for example, a jacket of 500 Euro and shoes of 250 Euro. He also offered me money once in a while to buy something for my son. Recruiter G heard about my financial problems and knew a way to earn easy money. I knew it was about fraud. I had to register as nail stylist at the Chamber of Commerce. First, I didn't want to, but after some encouragement, I eventually agreed to do it.'

5.5.4 Money mules offer their services

One of the consequences of a subculture of youngsters in which core members and recruiters can show off their expensive lifestyle is that new money mules do not always have to be recruited. Potential money mules take the initiative and offer their services because they know they can earn money by providing their cash card and codes (see Box 6). During interrogations, seven money mules admitted to having taken the initiative to offer their services.

Box 6 Money mules offer their services

'I don't remember exactly. I was talking to X and she said that her mother wanted to make money. Apparently, because she went on a holiday, so it should have been before October. (…).With making money, I mean fraud with a cash card. After that talk I asked X if he knew such people. X said that he actually knew such people. I told this to her and she communicated that with her mother.'

5.5.5 *Pressure from recruiters*

Five other money mules state that in the end they couldn't stand the pressure from recruiters, they knew they could earn easy money by providing their bank accounts and they were frequently approached to collaborate. They claim they refused at first, but after some time they gave in due to the pressure of recruiters (see, for example, Box 7).

Box 7 Pressure from recruiters

'Actually, I hardly ever saw these guys. I had never seen them before. Suddenly, I saw them more frequently. Every time I was in the city, I ran into them. They often hang out with their cars near the Hema [a department store]. There I ran into them when I was walking to the train station. Nine out of ten times they approached me. They asked me if I still hadn't fixed it. That small guy asked me that and he told me I could earn a lot. I noticed that he took a pile of banknotes out of his pocket. Most banknotes were 50 Euro and some 100 Euro.'

5.5.6 *Excuses: Legitimate transactions*

Several money mules claim to be unaware that they were collaborating with crimes victimising other people. Thirty money mules state that they thought the money transactions served a legitimate goal (Box 8).

Box 8 Legitimate transactions

'I ran into him by coincidence. This was close to the Bijenkorf [a luxurious department store] in the city centre of Amsterdam. I saw that he was with S9. I heard that S11 asked me if he could use my account to transfer money from Congo. This would be from his family. I asked him why he didn't take care of that himself. He told me then that he had lost his cash card and that he needed it already today or tomorrow. I asked him how much it was.

He said he wasn't sure, possibly 2000 Euro. His family in Congo was rich according to him.'

'About March 2013, I met S1. I met him at C1000 [a supermarket] … I knew S1 from the McDonalds where I used to work in the past. S1 asked me if I could help him. S1 had lost his identity papers and therefore could not apply for a new cash card. He now had a problem, as his uncle in Turkey would transfer 5000 Euro to his bank account. Because he didn't have a cash card, he could not withdraw this money. S1 now wanted to transfer the money to my account, so I could withdraw it for him. I asked S1 to call this uncle in Turkey and spoke to him myself. The man told me indeed that he would transfer money from Turkey to my account. I trusted S1 and agreed. After we had agreed that his uncle would transfer the money, we went our own ways.'

5.5.7 *Excuses: Victimless crimes*

Other excuses comprise statements that money mules thought that the activities would be victimless. The statements of two money mules point in this direction. One of these statements is described in Box 9.

Box 9 Victimless crimes

'Subsequently, I got a message from recruiter 2 with the text: "I know somebody who works at the breakdown service of bank X and he could organise some kind of breakdown that makes it possible that virtual money, that is money being circulated around bank accounts in order to earn as much interest as possible, so to say pops up as your balance and we could nibble off a bit discretely which would yield me and you something nice." I thought OK, I can make some money. I didn't have the impression that this was fraud or crime.'

5.5.8 *Excuses: Blaming victims*

Thirteen money mules blame victims as an excuse. This involves only money mules recruited through spam (see Section 5.7). Box 10 gives an example of such a statement.

Box 10 Blaming victims

'I don't feel responsible because I think the companies are to blame.' This money mule points to the companies from which money was transferred. 'They apparently have bad security that this can happen.'

5.6 Conclusion and possibilities for situational crime prevention

This section focuses on the possibilities for situational crime prevention. The introduction shows that money mules are an important part of the crime script of phishing and malware networks. They interrupt the money trail while at the same time the core offenders are able to reap their profits anonymously. They take a high risk for a relatively low reward and enable cybercriminal networks to operate smoothly. Therefore, we will first present the main conclusions regarding the reasons mentioned by money mules to get involved in money transfers. Subsequently, opportunities for situational crime prevention will be discussed.

Motives and techniques of neutralisation can be distinguished into two categories. The first category comprises money mules who are part of a subculture in which it is normal to collaborate with fraudulent money transfers. Factors that stand out are earning easy money, looking up to the lifestyle of criminals, money mules offering their services and pressure from recruiters. Various motives contribute to the decision to facilitate activities that are obviously fraudulent. The second category refers to techniques of neutralisation and refers to money mules pointing to excuses for their behaviour: the money transfers had a legitimate goal, there were no real victims (as it relates to virtual money) or victims themselves are to blame (as they should have invested more in their own security).

Two situational crime prevention strategies might be suited for making recruitment of money mules more difficult. The first one is to reduce provocations that invite criminal behaviour, especially the measures of reducing peer pressure and imitation. The analysis shows that social ties and peer pressure are important for the recruitment of money mules. Criminal networks recruit new money mules via their own social networks. Potential money mules are, for example, approached on the streets, in hangouts, during nightlife, at sport clubs and in schools. Money mules often claim that everybody in their community knows about frauds being committed, that it is normal to be asked to cooperate, that they are approached to cooperate frequently and that criminals who are involved in phishing and malware have an enviable lifestyle. After a while, money mules offer themselves to the criminal network, as they have heard the stories of earning easy money and don't want to miss the boat.

The second situational crime prevention strategy is removing excuses for criminal behaviour, especially the measure of making potential money mules aware of criminal behaviour. Some money mules claim that they thought they were facilitating a legitimate transaction. Others think that there are no victims, or that the victims are to be blamed, as they have exposed themselves to these risks.

With regard to both strategies, awareness campaigns aimed at potential money mules can be developed. First, potential money mules have to be made aware that they are cooperating with criminals who steal money from innocent people. Second, it should be communicated clearly that money mules are used by criminals to lead law enforcement away from the criminals and towards the money mules. In a way, money mules are victims too. The consequences for money mules go beyond getting arrested; banks hold the money mules responsible for the money that was stolen from victims. Money mules, therefore, have to pay back the money to the bank, leaving them with the consequences of the crime instead of the core members of criminal networks.

5.7 Limitations

This is a first exploratory study into possibilities to counter the recruitment of money mules, based on 112 statements of money mules from 14 Dutch criminal investigations into phishing and malware networks. This provides unique insights into motives and techniques of neutralisation. However, there are also several limitations.

The analysed statements do not refer to a representative group of money mules. The data relate to suspects that were identified during these investigations and who were interrogated. As investigating money mules is not a high priority, not all money mules have been interrogated. According to police respondents, this is simply impossible as it would take too much time. Furthermore, not all money mules cooperated with the police, so we could only analyse 112 statements of the 211 interrogated money mules, as the other interrogations provided no information about motives.

It is important to note that we cannot fully judge the suspects' statements about motives. Suspects may speak the truth and the police check answers (by cross-examinations and verification questions), but this method also has its flaws. For this study, we put the statements in context, but we had to take the information about motives at face value.

The results of this study may be regarded as a first step in research into money mules. In future research, offender interviews might shed more light on the recruitment processes of money mules and their motives for cooperating with these activities. Furthermore, data from financial institutions might provide quantitative information about background characteristics of money mules. This might also be important to target awareness campaigns.

Acknowledgements

Data for this chapter was collected during the PhD study of the first author. This PhD study was part of the Dutch Research Program on Safety and Security of Online Banking and was funded by the Dutch banking sector, represented by the Dutch Banking Association (NVB), the Police Academy and the Cybercrime Program of the Dutch police.

References

Afroz, S., Garg, V., McCoy, D. & Greenstadt, R. (2013) *Honor Among Thieves: A Common's Analysis of Cybercrime Economies.* San Francisco, CA: IEEE Ecrime Research Summit.

Akdeniz, Y. (1996) Computer pornography: A comparative study of the US and the UK obscenity laws and child pornography laws in relation to the internet. *International Review of Law, Computers and Technology* 10(2), pp. 235–261.

Aston, M., McCombie, S., Reardon, B. & Watters, P. (2009) A preliminary profiling of internet money mules: An Australian perspective. In: *Proceedings of the 2009 Symposia and Workshops on Ubiquitous, Autonomic and Trusted Computing*. IEEE Computer Society, pp. 482–487.

Bullock, K., Clarke, R.V. & Tilley, N. (eds.) (2010) *Situational Prevention of Organised Crimes*. Cullompton, UK: Willan Publishing.

Capeller, W. (2001) Not such a neat net: Some comments on virtual criminality. *Social and Legal Studies* 10(2), pp. 229–242.

Choo, K.R. (2008) Organised crime groups in cyberspace: A typology. *Trends in Organized Crime* 11(3), pp. 270–295.

Clarke, R.V. (1997) Introduction. In: R.V. Clarke (ed.), *Situational Crime Prevention: Successful Case Studies*. Guilderland, NY: Harrow and Heston, pp. 1–43.

Clarke, R.V. & Homel, R. (1997) A revised classification of situational crime prevention techniques. In: S.P. Lab (ed.), *Crime Prevention at a Crossroads*. Cincinnati, OH: Anderson, pp. 17–27.

Clarke, R.V.G. (1980) Situational crime prevention: Theory and practice. *British Journal of Criminology* 20(2), pp. 136–147.

Cornish, D.B. & Clarke, R.V. (2002) Analyzing organized crimes. In: A.R. Piquero & S.G. Tibbetts (eds.), *Rational Choice and Criminal Behavior: Recent Research and Future Challenges*. New York: Garland, pp. 41–64.

Cornish, D.B. & Clarke, R.V. (2003) Opportunities, precipitators and criminal decisions: A reply to Wortley's critique of situational crime prevention. *Crime Prevention Studies* 16, pp. 41–96.

Décary-Hetú, D. & Dupont, B. (2012) The social network of hackers. *Global Crime* 13(3), pp. 160–175.

Gattiker, U.E. & Kelley, H. (1999) Morality and computers: Attitudes and differences in judgments. *Information Systems Research* 10(3), pp. 233–254.

Grabosky, P.N. (2001) Virtual criminality: Old wine in new bottles? *Social and Legal Studies* 10(2), pp. 243–249.

Grabosky, P.N. & Smith, R.G. (2001) Digital crime in the twenty-first century. *Journal of Information Ethics* 10, pp. 8–26.

Hartel, P., Junger, M. & Wieringa, R. (2011) *Cyber-Crime Science = Crime Science + Information Security*. (report) University of Twente.

Holt, T.J. & Lampke, E. (2010) Exploring stolen data markets online: Products and market forces. *Criminal Justice Studies* 23(1), pp. 33–50.

Kleemans, E.R. (2014) Organized crime research: Challenging assumptions and informing policy. In: E. Cockbain & J. Knutsson (eds.), *Applied Police Research. Challenges and Opportunities*. New York: Routledge, pp. 57–67.

Kleemans, E.R. & Soudijn, M.R.J. (2017) Organised crime. In: N. Tilley & A. Sidebottom (eds.), *Handbook of Crime Prevention and Community Safety*. Cullompton, UK: Willan Publishing, pp. 394–406.

Lastdrager, E.E. (2014) Achieving a consensual definition of phishing based on a systematic review of the literature. *Crime Science* 3(1), pp. 1–10.

Leukfeldt, E.R. (2014) Cybercrime and social ties. Phishing in Amsterdam. *Trends in Organized Crime* 17(4), pp. 231–249.

Leukfeldt, E.R., Kleemans, E.R. & Stol, W.P. (2017a) A typology of cybercriminal networks: From low tech locals to high tech specialists. *Crime, Law and Social Change* 67(1), pp. 21–37.

Leukfeldt, E.R., Kleemans, E.R. & Stol, W.P. (2017b) Cybercriminal networks, social ties and online forums: Social ties versus digital ties within phishing and malware networks. *British Journal of Criminology* 57(3), pp. 704–722.

Leukfeldt, E.R., Kleemans, E.R. & Stol, W.P. (2017c) Origin, growth and criminal capabilities of cybercriminal networks. An international empirical analysis. *Crime, Law and Social Change* 67(1), pp. 39–53.

Leukfeldt, R., Kleemans, E.R. & Stol, W.P. (2017d) The use of online crime markets by cybercriminal networks: A view from within. *American Behavioral Scientist* 61(11), pp. 1387–1402.

Loch, K.D., Carr, H.H. & Warkentin, M.E. (1992) Threats to information systems: Today's reality, yesterday's understanding. *MIS Quarterly* 16(2), pp. 173–186.

Lu, Y., Luo, X., Polgar, M. & Cao, Y. (2010) Social network analysis of a criminal hacker community. *Journal of Computer Information Systems* 51(2), pp. 31–41.

Lusthaus, J. (2012) Trust in the world of cybercrime. *Global Crime* 13(2), pp. 71–94.

Mann, D. & Sutton, M. (1998) Netcrime: More change in the organization of thieving. *British Journal of Criminology* 38(2), pp. 201–229.

Maruna, S. & Copes, H. (2005) Excuses, excuses: What have we learned from five decades of neutralisation research? *Crime and Justice* 32, pp. 221–320.

McCombie, S.J. (2011) Phishing the long line. Transnational cybercrime from Eastern Europe to Australia. PhD thesis. Macquarie University, Department of Computing.

Moore, T. & Clayton, R. (2007) Examining the impact of website take-down on phishing. In: *Proceedings of the Anti-Phishing Working Groups 2nd Annual eCrime Researchers Summit*. Pittsburgh, PA: ACM, pp. 1–13.

Peretti, K.K. (2008) Data breaches: What the underground world of "carding" reveals. *Santa Clara Computer and High-Technology Law Journal* 25(2), pp. 345–414.

Soudijn, M.R.J. & Monsma, E. (2012) Virtuele ontmoetingsuimtes voor cybercriminelen. (Virtual meeting places for cyber criminals). *Tijdschrift voor Criminologie* 54(4), pp. 349–360.

Sykes, G.M. & Matza, D. (1957) Techniques of neutralisation: A theory of delinquency. *American Sociological Review* 22(6), pp. 664–670.

Wall, D.S. (1997) Policing the virtual community: The Internet, cyber crimes and the policing of cyberspace. In: P. Francis, P. Davies & V. Jupp (eds.), *Policing Futures, the Police, Law Enforcement and the Twenty-First Century*. London: Macmillan, pp. 208–236.

Yip, M., Shadbolt, N. & Webber, C. (2012) *Structural Analysis of Online Criminal Social Networks*. ISI 2012, June 11–14, 2012, Washington.

Part III

Illicit trafficking networks

6 To get a good price, 'you have to sell in international bidding sites'

Trafficking of metal-detected cultural goods from South Asia

Samuel Hardy

6.1 Introduction

South Asia is a prestigious target for institutions and individuals who collect cultural property, who thus not only underwrite lucrative criminal markets, but also finance sophisticated criminal enterprises. Antiquities trafficking boss Subhash Kapoor ran a USD 100,000,000 business empire, which spanned South Asia and South-East Asia and reached from India to the United States (Mashberg and Bearak, 2015, AR1).

As the simplest identifier of *potential* producers in the illicit trade, this chapter targets non-archaeologists who use metal detectors to search for cultural objects (whether they identify, or are identified as, metal-detectorists or treasure-hunters). It can be difficult to categorise the legality of their activity, as some follow legal and ethical codes; some respect the law but disregard any ethical code that has been written by cultural heritage professionals; some respect the law but disregard any ethical code at all, even one that has been written by more socially responsible detectorists; some violate the law but respect some kind of ethical code, for example, by fraudulently recording their illegal finds in public registers of legal finds, wherein experts can study the objects, although it might be suspected that the primary motivation for such recording would be to launder illegal finds with paperwork that is offered for legal finds; and some disregard every legal and ethical code. Obviously, citation of metal-detectorists does not imply any wrongdoing on their part. But, assuming illicit detectorists have the same interests and serve the same markets as licit detectorists, the activity of licit detectorists may help to understand the activities of illicit detectorists.

This chapter analyses open-source evidence to advance understanding of the trafficking of cultural goods in South Asia. While this region also encompasses Bangladesh, Bhutan, the Maldives and Nepal, this chapter concentrates on Afghanistan; India, including India-administered Jammu and Kashmir; Pakistan, including Pakistan-administered Azad-Kashmir and Gilgit-Baltistan; and Sri Lanka. It excludes China-administered Aksai-Chin and the Trans-Karakoram Tract in Kashmir.

6.2 Method

This study is part of a global review of open-source evidence on the hobby, business and/or crime of metal-detecting for cultural objects. Any such research is limited by three primary obstacles: first, the capacity of detectorists to manage activity online; second, the enthusiasm of detectorists to manage activity online; and third, the capacity of researchers to find evidence of online management and offline activity.

Capacity to manage activity online varies according to infrastructure and cost. Enthusiasm to manage activity online varies according to 'detecting cultures' as well as legal risks. Theoretically, there might be more online activity where offline activity is criminalised (yet detectorists are unpoliced) than where offline activity is legalised (yet detectorists are unsociable). And capacity to find evidence of online organisation and offline activity varies according to the limits of language skill, machine translation and/or community terminology. It also varies according to the availability of automatically-generated online data from community activity, netnographic evidence of community activity and documentation by law enforcement agents, cultural heritage workers and others, such as journalists.

6.2.1 Markets

Nonetheless, as is observed by experts ranging from law enforcement agents in India (cf. Burke, 2015) to cultural property dealers in Nepal (cf. discussion under Buda, 2015), there is very little internal demand for cultural goods in local markets, as opposed to global markets. The large markets and high prices are abroad.

When cultural objects are intercepted during smuggling, major markets may be politely euphemised with characterisations such as 'some Far Eastern country' (e.g. Channa, 2015). And backward flows through restitution may be misleading indicators of outward flows through smuggling, as they reflect law, law enforcement capacity and public reporting standards in every jurisdiction from extraction to collection (Hardy, 2016a, pp. 3–4), particularly as cultural objects may be intercepted at points of trade or transit, instead of points of consumption.

Still, *typically*, sacred Buddhist and Hindu objects are consumed by non-Buddhist, non-Hindu markets for 'exotica'. According to the head of the Idol Wing of Tamil Nadu Police, Additional Director General of Police Prateep V Philip, cultural objects from India are consumed throughout the dominant Western markets, the growing Chinese market and the rising Middle Eastern market (cited by Burke, 2015). The United States, the United Kingdom, Italy and France are *some of* the markets that consume 'large numbers' of cultural objects from Pakistan (Khattak, 2015). Significant numbers of cultural objects that are exported from Bangladesh are transferred to France, Italy, Japan and South Korea (Blitz, 2012). And cultural objects from Nepal tend to go to Europe and the United States (cf. Davis and Capron, 2015), though those goods may then flow onwards to other markets such as China (cf. Fanelli, 2015).

In South Asia, due to flows and markets – and perhaps particularly due to the linguistic legacy of British colonialism and imperialism – much instructive material is in English (or contains enough English for the source to be found, then translated).

6.2.2 Open-source analysis

In English, Facebook, Google Scholar and Google Web were searched for 'metal detecting' or 'treasure hunting' plus 'territory name'. In Bengali, Farsi/Dari, Gujarati, Hindi, Kannada, Marathi, Nepali, Pashto/Pakhto, Punjabi, Sinhala, Sindhi, Tamil, Telugu and Urdu, Facebook and (albeit cursorily) Google Web were searched for 'metal' and 'detecting' plus 'territory name', then 'treasure' and 'hunting' plus 'territory name'. Searches on Google Web were augmented with 'forum' to exclude content on metal-detectors for security.

6.3 Evidence

While such searches almost exclusively found irrelevant results, they did find some relevant results, such as news reports that 'treasure hunters [had been] arrested [nidhan horu koṭuveyi]' in Sri Lanka (Live at 7 News, 2016). So, whether there were few relevant results or whether relevant results were obscured by more prominent irrelevant ones, the keywords were appropriate.

There was extremely little evidence in relation to Bangladesh, Bhutan, the Maldives and Nepal. Still, there was evidence of activity and the implication of more in the neglected territories. The Maldives, for example, attract at least a few metal-detecting tourists from around the world (e.g. welsh john, 2014, who was based in the United Kingdom; Docekal, 2014, who was based in the United States). There, it is illegal to conduct unauthorised 'research work on cultural or historical objects' or otherwise to 'damage[,] destroy or dismantle' historically informative 'objects and places that were used by the inhabitants' of the Republic of Maldives (RoM, 1979) 'or foreigners'. One Russia-based metal-detectorist explained that he had imported his detector to the Maldives by 'transport[ing it] in parts, in different suitcases [provez po chastyam, v raznikh chemodanakh]' (Serii Kopatel v Poiskakh Klada, 2016), which demonstrates remarkable dedication to finding keys and coins that have been lost by holidaymakers at the seaside.

Since such searches have been successful in identifying online communities of metal-detectorists/treasure-hunters in North America, Western Europe, Eastern Europe and beyond (Hardy, 2016b, 2017), it *seems* that such communities in South Asia are neither significantly large nor significantly active. Nevertheless, that is not a direct indication of offline activity, let alone any measure of the true scale of offline activity; it is only an indication of the scale of online social organisation of detecting, which thereby establishes a minimal level of offline activity.

At least in some places, 'metal-detecting', like 'digging', appears to be perceived as an action that is performed as part of an activity ('treasure-hunting'), rather than as an activity in itself. In Sri Lanka, for instance, metal-detector dealers are rigorously monitored, yet the country's embassies have 'no idea what metal detecting is', give 'no answer[,] yes or no', to the question of whether it is legal (Alejandro, 2013). As it will be demonstrated in the discussion through a consideration of law and diplomacy, this helps – in those cases, transnational criminals – to feign ignorance of laws against unlicensed excavation or other treasure-hunting. Sometimes, it enables them to acquire official documentation with incorrect information from one governmental institution or another. In these ways, official ignorance helps criminals to deter or sabotage prosecution. Furthermore, due to a lack of knowledge of these details, many reports on treasure-hunting do not itemise the tools, so it is not known whether looters have used detectors to find targets. Although, *technically*, then, it is also not known whether the looters have used shovels to extract targets. Likewise, due to a lack of interest in such details, many communities for treasure-hunting do not distinguish between the use of metal detectors and the interpretation of legends. This can skew potential data on the scale, intensity and organisation of unscientific excavation. So, those sources are excluded as inconclusive. Despite the limitations of the identifiable sources, the evidence is still instructive in understanding who is doing what, where and how.

6.4 Afghanistan

6.4.1 Conflict antiquities trafficking

In the past thirty years, antiquities have been looted/stolen and/or traffickers have been racketeered by Soviets (Richardson, 2012); Communists, Mujahideen, the Northern Alliance, the Taliban (Col, 1223–1224; Dupree, 1998; McGirk, 1996; Peters, 2010, p. 36; SPACH, 2004; UKHC, 2003; USICE, 2013); warlords, Islamic Party militia and Haqqani insurgents (Campbell, 2013, p. 121). Furthermore, al-Qaeda operative Mohamed Atta tried to sell looted antiquities from Afghanistan in Germany to subsidise his participation in the 9/11 terrorist attacks in the United States (Ruiz, 2010). Such illicit antiquities constitute 'conflict antiquities', which are used to finance political violence, including repression and terrorism as well as warfare. Thus, dealers and collectors cannot excuse illicit purchase as 'rescue' of cultural property from destruction, since it may finance more serious human rights violations (cf. Hardy, under review).

6.4.2 Metal-detecting/treasure-hunting

Under the Islamic State of Afghanistan (ISA, 2004, Article 8), although illicit excavators may skirt around the letter of the law, all 'historical and cultural properties' are 'the property of the State'. Unlicensed metal-detecting for cultural objects is an illegal activity, as 'excavation for the discovery of historical and cultural properties' may only be conducted by the Institute of Archaeology and licensed scientific institutions (ISA, 2004: Article 34; see also ISA, 2004, Article 35). Unlicensed trading, or other unlicensed transfer, of historical and cultural properties is also illegal (ISA, 2004, Article 57; see also ISA, 2004, Article 8).

Whether they use detectors or not, whether they are entrepreneurs or employees, some illicit excavations are mass endeavours, where 'a few hundred' villagers dig at once (according to Commander Bushire, cited by Stewart, 2005, p. 170) or 'hundreds of workmen' are put to work (according to a curator of Middle Eastern archaeology, St. John Simpson, cited by Wendle, 2013). Despite the scale of the plunder, very little revenue flows back to the source: 'one or two American dollars [per object] – good money' – for some, one or two dollars per day for others, according to Commander Bushire (cited by Stewart, 2005, p. 171). This keeps the illicit diggers in poverty and thus maintains the supply of illicit antiquities. One illicit digger, Ustaad Nasrullah, looted for at least forty years (Ferguson, 2009). As reported by the Killid Group (TKG, 2016), according to the Head of Culture and Information for Ghor Province, Ahmad Ehsan Ahmadyar, organised enterprises are exporting cultural objects through Iran and Pakistan.

Detectors are acquired from a variety of sources. Seemingly from 1992 onwards (cf. Curtis, 2011, p. 59), looters used detectors, which had 'originally [been] brought' into Afghanistan 'to detect Russian land mines', to detect antiquities at the Greco-Bactrian city of Aï Khanoum; it has since been looted to the point that it 'no longer exists' (Bopearachchi, 2006, p. 270). Demonstrating the organisation of the illicit trade, in 1993, all of the coins that had been excavated before the site was looted were then stolen from the National Museum in Kabul and, within 'days', sold through the bazaar in Peshawar, Pakistan, to private collectors (Bopearachchi, 2006, p. 267).

Around 2001–2002, one well-connected looter casually asked a foreign acquaintance who was interviewing a group about looting, 'do you think you could bring us a metal detector[,] next time you visit?' (Commander Bushire's son, Abdullah, cited by Stewart, 2005, p. 169). However, since then, the supply of metal-detectors appears to have become more organised. According to the Head of Culture and Information for Herat Province, Arya Rawoofian (cited by TKG, 2016), metal-detectors are being imported from or through 'neighbouring countries'. And, according to the Governor of Bamiyan Province, Mohammad Tahir Zahir, in 2016, the National Directorate of Security arrested looters and seized 'state of the art', 'treasure hunting equipment' that was capable of identifying 'buried historic monuments and other precious earth materials' – in other words, metal-detectors – which had been imported from Iran (cited by Khaama Press, 2016). Considering the albeit limited evidence for the sources of the equipment, it seems likely that metal-detectors are being illicitly imported by the same routes as metal-detected cultural objects are being illicitly exported.

Apparently, according to the Head of Culture and Information for Ghor Province, Fakhrudin Aryapoor, 'most' looting is conducted in Taliban-controlled territory (cited by TKG, 2016). The scale of looting increased between the 2000s and the 2010s (Stein, 2015, p. 188) and has continued to increase (TKG, 2016).

Despite the evidence of the use of detectors and the impunity of the users, there do not appear to be significant online communities of detectorists. Whether detectors are redeployed from mine clearance, bought indirectly through networks of acquaintances or bought directly in commerce, acquisition of metal-detectors, training in metal-detecting and trading in metal-detected cultural objects may remain primarily offline affairs. According to Miniwatts Marketing Group (MMG, 2017), only around 11.7 per cent of the population have access to the internet. Otherwise, those activities may have leapfrogged to encrypted communications and private online trading via WhatsApp, Telegram and other such apps. Furthermore, Farsi/Dari-speaking detectorists may learn from or participate in Farsi-speaking online communities that primarily serve those in Iran; Uzbek-speaking and Turkmen-speaking detectorists may use Turkish-speaking online communities that primarily serve those in Turkey.

Still, there is some evidence of detecting in social media. In a Facebook group for detectorists around the world, posts presented photographic evidence of detecting near Jalal Abad (Khan, 2015; see also Bondi Treasure Hunter, 2016; Khan, 2016). Significantly, there is evidence of detecting that appears to be conducted completely outside the established and recognised, disorganised and organised, Afghan and Pakistani networks. Some potential participants are deterred because there are 'too many unexploded mines everywhere' (s.c.shooter, 2013). Nevertheless, U.S. Army personnel detect on their military bases (e.g. Shindand Airbase, see Tejaas, 2013a; they appear to have detected after military infrastructure work had removed a metre of soil, see Tejaas, 2013b). U.S. Navy personnel detect in acquaintances' 'enclosed yards', in order to avoid 'Taliban [and] landmines' (chudman, 2009). U.S. Air Force personnel recommend 'anywhere near Bagram [airbase]' as 'money' (in other words, a payload detecting location), where detectorists could find antiquities from the period of Alexander the Great, while they found Greco-Bactrian Hellenistic antiquities, such as 'a coin from 210 years before Christ' (Kolby72, 2012). Airport workers have their detectors 'mail[ed]' to them and appear to detect there (Gunshin, 2012).

It has been observed that, by destabilising any and all authority, the U.S.-led invasion has 'freed up', rather than closed down, 'the antique smuggling market' (Stewart, 2005, p. 170); freight inspection is inadequate, as private freight is inspected by 'U.S. soldiers who are only looking for explosives, not antiquities' (according to a Field Coordinator for the United Nations Conference on Trade and Development (UNCTAD), Reza Mohammadi, cited by Wendle, 2013); and foreign diplomats use their immunity from inspection and prosecution to facilitate boutique smuggling (McGirk, 1996). It is less well-documented that the U.S.-led forces may supply that market, way beyond souvenirs and trophies. While treasure-hunting by metal-detectorists among foreign militaries may pale in insignificance in comparison with the nationwide problem, it is an aspect of the illicit trade for which outside states bear a direct responsibility, which has been hiding in plain sight for years.

6.5 India

6.5.1 The structure and functioning of the illicit trade

As explained by the Archaeological Survey of India (ASI), under the laws of the Republic of India (RoI), excavation may only be conducted by authorised officials or licensed professionals (RoI, 2010, Article 21; Article 22; see also ASI, 2011). It is illegal to engage in unlicensed sale (RoI, 1972, p. 5) or unauthorised export of antiquities (RoI, 1972, Article 3; see also ASI, 2011).

Typically, thieves photograph targets – sometimes before theft, otherwise afterwards – and use those records to negotiate. According to Police ADG Prateep V Philip, 'usually' local dealers and/or foreign collectors review the photographs and agree on deals; then, the desired cultural objects are 'stolen to order' from sacred places and other sites (cited by Burke, 2015). Otherwise, the photos constitute a catalogue like one of an ordinary business.

There is 'no [significant] internal demand' for these objects (ibid.). In order to acquire documentation to falsely legitimise transfer, replicas are produced and either certified for export then switched, or delivered for export then switched in collaboration with corrupt customs officials (Pachauri, 2002, p. 273).

There appear to be tight bottlenecks in supply lines. According to the Idol Wing of Tamil Nadu Police, Vallaba Prakash and his son Aditya Prakash are suspected of having had 'a role in 80 [per cent] of idol theft cases in Tamil Nadu and also across India' (cited by Times News Network, 2017).

6.5.2 Metal-detecting/treasure-hunting

There is evidence of amateur(ish) detecting by local detectorists (e.g. sanjeebrosy, 2015, who detects on the lands of his property-letting family). However, according to an India-based numismatics hobbyist and aspiring metal-detecting hobbyist, 'hobby' detecting is 'still not very common for [a] poor developing nation like India' (Coinsforever, 2011a).

Estimated numbers of cultural property criminals do not appear to have been published, but there are some indications. For instance, it is suspected that there are around '200 treasure[-]hunt[ing] teams', who use 'sophisticated metal detectors' to loot archaeological sites, who are based in the district of Anantapur or based in the district of Karnataka and operating in Anantapur (Department of Archaeology and Museums, cited by Benjamin, 2016) – so, within a community of around 4,000,000 residents.

Suggesting that there is little detecting tourism, a USA-based detectorist had not seen 'any talk of India in the forums' (Tador, 2012) when that international forum had around 40,747 members (TreasureNet, 2012). Nevertheless, it is done by detectorists, for example, from the United Kingdom (according to vurda, 2013); France (according to LE.JAG, 2015); and Canada, the United States and Peru (who collaborated, cf. Kaushik, 2015). One USA-based, overland-travelling tourist planned to do 'alot [*sic* – a lot] of detecting' in India and 'north west' of it, seemingly Pakistan and other territories on the way to northern

Europe (bigstemz, 2015). The USA-based intermittent foreign resident 'spen[t] three months [each year] on the beaches' (Wostro, 2014), in other words, beach-combing with a metal-detector.

One aspiring hobby detectorist, who wanted to detect 'basically coins', even though 'the laws [were] not user friendly', observed that 'for each and every law there [were] loopholes' (Coinsforever, 2011b). Another India-based numismatist stated that laws against trespassing on property or committing criminal damage were 'not very effective or a deterrent', but the law for state ownership of archaeological remains *was* a somewhat effective deterrent (asm, 2011). If police learned that metal-detectorists had 'not willingly' reported and delivered metal-detected cultural property to the authorities, they 'would be a hassle'; and, even if metal-detectorists did report and deliver finds, 'the amount of time, money and energy' that would be involved would be a deterrent in and of itself (asm, 2011).

One seemingly USA-based intermittent foreign resident argued that India was a 'very complicated' territory, which required an 'understand[ing]' that the question was 'never' if something was 'legal or not' but, rather, 'if they let you' do it or not; he advised '[k]eeping a low profile [was] key' (Wostro, 2014). Asked whether he sold his finds in India or exported them to the United States and what the gold export laws were (by CapeTownBeachBum, 2016), he did not reply.

6.6 Nepal

6.6.1 Illicit trafficking of cultural objects

Under the Kingdom of Nepal, it is illegal to conduct unauthorised 'excavations at the site of ancient monuments' (KoN, 1970, Article 16), which encompass 'any' buildings or objects of 'historical, archeological or artistic importance' (KoN, 1970, Article 2), or otherwise to destroy, damage or misappropriate 'any ancient monument or archeological object' (KoN, 1970, Article 7). Furthermore, collecting, trading and/or export of cultural objects are prohibited, licensed or otherwise regulated activities (KoN, 1970, Article 13).

Due to the international demand for sacred objects ('exotic' art, according to an antiquities dealer in the United States, cited by Sassoon, 1991), cultural property crime has historically manifested in theft from standing buildings more than looting of archaeological sites, with or without a detector. The market emerged in the 1950s when 'local thugs and the mafia' stole sacred art (Kathmandu Post, 2014), then local elites and transnational foreign workers smuggled literal 'truck loads' (according to writer Thomas Bell, cited by Kunwar, 2015).

It is exceptionally difficult to document cultural goods in their original location, and thus to assess the scale of criminal activity and to recover stolen goods due to a common prohibition on photography of sacred objects (Sharma, 2015). Nonetheless, between 1964 (when art from Nepal was exhibited in the United States, cf. Pal, (1986, p. 7), cited by Brodie, (2006, p. 55)) and the 1990s, during which time Western professional smugglers established themselves as intermittent foreign residents and supplanted other smugglers such as diplomats

(Sassoon, 1991), perhaps 90 per cent of the country's 'rare idols' were stolen (according to art connoisseur Jürgen Schick, cited by Limbu, 2001). The remaining ones were less significant or less stealable; and the rate of theft had already decreased by the 1990s, because there was somewhat less demand and simply 'not much left to steal' (Ibid).

6.6.2 Metal-detecting/treasure-hunting

Since then, 'many' antiquities with 'accretions and dirt' have 'surfaced' on the market, where the evidence of their looting serves as evidence of their authenticity (Hawley, 2007, p. 230). Yet, on searching, there was extremely little evidence of concentrated online activity. The available evidence both demonstrates that there is online activity and appears to corroborate the impression that there is insignificant online social organisation of detecting.

Numerous coin collectors/traders, who seemingly could not find specialist online communities of knowledge and practice elsewhere, discussed offline and online market prices and sales strategies; advertised the available goods; and provided their full names, telephone numbers and/or e-mail addresses from their social media accounts under a YouTube video about ancient coins from Nepal (cf. discussion under Buda, 2015, who advised that cultural objects should be sold onto the 'international market via bidding sites' such as eBay). Again, a dearth of online activity does not *necessarily* indicate a dearth of offline activity, especially when only around 21.9 per cent of the population have access to the internet (MMG, 2017). Detectorists may have leapfrogged to private online trading, or they may simply engage in offline activity.

6.7 Pakistan

6.7.1 Conflict antiquities trafficking

Partly due to the geographical span of ancient societies and partly due to the political span of modern crises, cultural property crime in Afghanistan and Pakistan appears to be a highly transnational enterprise. In both countries, for instance, there is jihadi iconoclasm of cultural property (Allbritton, 2009; Malik, 2012; Rehman, 2012). During the chaos of the war in Afghanistan and the internationalisation of the response through Pakistan, diplomats exploited the opportunity to illicitly export antiquities from Pakistan (Delhi Times, 2011).

Indeed, recently, in North American and European security discourse, Afghanistan and Pakistan have been controversially 'conflat[ed]' into 'one geopolitical unit' – 'AfPak' or 'Af-Pak'[1] – that contains 'two separate but parallel

1 Due to objections from Pakistan, 'AfPak'/'Af-Pak' has been abandoned in official discourse (Rogin, 2010); due to objections from India, a subcontinental form, 'AfPakIn', was never adopted (Bhadrakumar, 2017).

conflicts – the insurgency in Afghanistan and militancy in Pakistan' (Khan, 2010, p. 5). Further afield, terrorist activity in the European Union is '[i]ncreasingly' supported with 'criminal financing... by core groups' and/or organised crime groups in 'AfPak', such as the transnational Haqqani Network (West Sands Advisory, 2012, p. 32; see also Makarenko and Mesquita, 2016, p. 53).

The similarly transnational Taliban is supported, and the Haqqani Network is controlled, by the Inter-Services Intelligence (ISI) agency of Pakistan (Dalrymple, 2013). And the Haqqani Network traffics cultural objects as well as other commodities. Antiquities are smuggled from Afghanistan and bartered for arms in Pakistan, then arms are smuggled from Pakistan and sold to the Taliban in Afghanistan (Campbell, 2013, pp. 127–128). Meanwhile, the Taliban racketeers that organisation and other traffickers of cultural objects (Peters, 2010, p. 36).

It should also be noted that, while international attention is focused on the connection between antiquities trading and political violence within Afghanistan, the connection exists within Pakistan as well. Pseudonymous warlord Zaman Khan raised 'millions of rupees' (thousands or tens of thousands of dollars) through the looting of 'statues, coins and ornaments' to finance 'guns, ammunition and guards' (Agence France-Presse, 2012b).

Gandharan culture spans eastern Afghanistan and north-western Pakistan. Persistently, according to the Director of Archaeology for the Province of Sindh, Qasim Ali Qasim, 'thieves and mafias' loot archaeological sites in north-western Pakistan 'with little control by the authorities', because it too has been deeply penetrated by Taliban (quoted and paraphrased by Agence France-Presse, 2012a).

6.7.2 *Organised cultural property crime*

Sometimes, antiquities from Afghanistan are fraudulently documented and illicitly transported by elements within the government and the military in Pakistan (McGirk, 1996). They are also collected by the most senior elements of the government and the military there. Such pervasive connections and flows raise the question of where corruption ends and state crime begins.

More often, antiquities are smuggled and dealt with by organised crime networks from Pakistan (Astill, 2003), which have significant influence over the activity of organisations in Afghanistan. They convinced the Taliban to remove and sell fragments of the Bamiyan Buddhas 'like pieces of the Berlin Wall' (according to then-Director of the Bibliotheca Afghanica and its Afghanistan Museum in Exile, Paul Bucherer-Dietschi, cited by McGirk, 2002). One gallery in Australia actively advertised 'rare historical artifacts', Afghan Gandharan Buddhist art that they had allegedly acquired when 'offered' in 'the days that followed' the destruction of the Bamiyan Buddhas (cited by Huffer, 2010). The sale-purchase was advertised as an act of 'preservation', a form of rescue-by-purchase. If the gallery had been selling such pieces, knowingly or unknowingly, it might have produced a revenue stream for organised crime and terrorist financing.

These networks also deliver 'orders for specific antiquities' (Astill, 2003), so organised cultural property crime and conflict antiquities trafficking from

Afghanistan through Pakistan encompass looting-to-order/theft-to-order. Bactrian and Kushan antiquities may be smuggled through Uzbekistan, then 'fenced to the "new Russian" mafia' in Russia (Lee, 2000). These channels include multi-commodity trafficking of antiquities, such as heroin-and-antiquities trafficking and antiquities-for-nuclear trafficking (McGirk, 1996).

In response to varying risks, the channels flow in both directions. Against the tide, 'millions of rupees" worth of antiquities were found in the baggage of a smuggler who was in the process of smuggling the objects from Pakistan to Afghanistan by land, on the overland route to European markets (Express Tribune, 2017). Some of these operations exploit other opportunities that have been created by the crisis. Whether an official vehicle was used by clandestine officials or by corrupt officials or whether an ordinary vehicle was disguised as an official vehicle, one intercepted operation tried to smuggle antiquities from Pakistan to Afghanistan 'in the garb of a NATO vehicle' (according to archaeology director Ali Qasim, quoted by Associated Press, 2012).

6.7.3 Metal-detecting/treasure-hunting

The Islamic Republic of Pakistan (IRP, 1992, Article 13A) owns all buried antiquities. It is illegal to treat a religious site in any way that is inconsistent or inappropriate with regard to its status (IRP, 1992, Article 17; Article 18); to conduct any unlicensed 'excavation or exploration for archaeological purposes' or to 'unearth or make any digging in any land or site for taking out antiquities' (IRP, 1992, Article 29); or otherwise to 'destroy, break, damage, alter, injure, deface or mutilate' antiquities (IRP, 1992, Article 19). It is also illegal to engage in antiquities fraud (IRP, 1992, Article 24), to engage in unlicensed dealing (IRP, 1992, Article 25), to engage in unlicensed export (IRP, 1992, Article 26), or otherwise to sell or remove antiquities 'to the detriment of Pakistan' (IRP, 1992, Article 27).

Yet underfunded services and overstretched security have left legal artefacts vulnerable to embezzlement or theft from cultural heritage institutions (Dunya News, 2016) and governmental institutions (Daily Capital, 2016). They even left seized antiquities vulnerable to embezzlement by police officers or theft from police stations (Express-Tribune, 2012). In such circumstances, it is unsurprising that looting and theft of cultural objects are widespread and intensive.

Antiquities looting has been so intensive that some archaeological sites have been 'destroyed' (Dawn, 2008); they 'do not exist at all' anymore (according to schoolteacher and voluntary cultural heritage worker Osman Ulasyar, cited by Khattak, 2016). In general, organised or disorganised, smugglers are 'influential people' who collaborate with officials, while local labourers use 'dynamites [*sic* – dynamite] and metal detectors to find coins and antiquities' (Dawn, 2008). For instance, in Taxila, a 'gang' of 'influential treasure hunters' used detectors to extract cultural objects, then used tractors to flatten the land, which thereby obscured indicators of looting (Rana, 2013). The outflow of antiquities has also created a market and mechanism for a forgery industry (cf. Associated Press, 2012).

6.8 Sri Lanka

6.8.1 Conflict antiquities trafficking

During the war between the Sri Lanka Armed Forces (SLAF) and the Liberation Tigers of Tamil Eelam (LTTE), control of territory by the LTTE prevented looting of at least some archaeological sites by treasure-hunters (according to the Head of the Special Unit for Prevention of Destruction and Theft of Antiquities of the Department of Archaeology, Udeni Wickramasinghe, cited by Fiedler, 2015; see also Kariyakarawana, 2013). At the same time, some sacred objects were looted from temples, 'when people could not go there' (according to Hindu prelate Padmanadan Sharma, cited by Wijedasa, 2013).

Such thefts may have been acts of organised criminals, who may have paid a cut to whichever authorities (or elements within those authorities) were in control of the places at the time. The stolen goods would constitute conflict antiquities, as they profited the racketeering armed groups. Or, the thefts may have been acts of conflict antiquities traffickers who were official or unofficial elements of state forces or non-state forces.

It is known that the LTTE subsidised their activities with the profits from illicit antiquities. For example, a 'valuable Indian stone frieze' was confiscated by police in the UK before it could be auctioned by 'Sri Lankan terrorists' (according to MP Richard Allan, cf. UKHC, 2003: Col. 1224).

Since the end of the war and the reduction in the risk of 'landmines and terrorists' (according to police spokesperson Ajith Rohana, cited by Kirinde, 2012), treasure-hunting has been increasing in scale, organisation and technological complexity in northern and eastern Sri Lanka (Kirinde, 2012; Wijedasa, 2013). It is now a revenue stream for at least 'several gangs' (Wijedasa, 2013). It must be a significant revenue stream, as operations sometimes invest tens of thousands of dollars, employ tens of looters and run for months (according to the Officer-in-Charge of the Antiquities Protection Division of the Archaeology Department in Colombo, Inspector Rohana Chaminda, cited by Rothfield, 2013).

6.8.2 Metal-detecting/treasure-hunting

Under the Parliament of the Democratic Socialist Republic of Sri Lanka (PDSRSL, 1956, Article 2), the state owns all 'undiscovered antiquities..., whether lying on or hidden beneath the surface of the ground or in any river or lake'. It is illegal to 'excavate for the purpose of discovering antiquities' without a licence (PSDRSL, 1956, Article 6), or otherwise to willfully destroy, injure, deface or tamper with antiquities (PDSRSL, 1956, Article 15B, as amended by PDSRSL, 1998, Article 4).

Treasure-hunting appears to involve intermittent entrepreneurs as well as part-time and full-time professionals. According to the Officer-in-Charge of the Special Task Force (STF) Camp at Mahabulankulama, Police Superintendent W. M. N. Wanigasekara, one full-time public servant changed career and became a full-time treasure-hunting consultant, who 'hir[ed] out a modified mine detector to treasure hunters' (cited by Wickremasekara, 2012).

Organised or disorganised, many treasure-hunters are 'armed' (Kariyakarawana, 2013). The 'organised gangs' comprise one or more financiers, one kattadiya (devil priest) to provide spiritual protection, plus one or more locals to provide labour. They have long used 'backhoes' (machine excavators or earthmovers), but are '[i]ncreasingly' using both 'modified and unmodified metal detectors' (in other words, adapted mine-detectors and specialist metal-detectors, cf. *Sunday Times*, 2013).

6.9 Discussion

6.9.1 Organised cultural property crime and conflict antiquities trafficking

Some of the illicit excavation, trafficking and dealing across the region is minor disorganised crime. Some of it is opportunistic. In Bangladesh, organised criminals followed Muslim nationalist violence against the Buddhist minority community and stole vulnerable cultural objects (Blitz, 2012). In Nepal, 'amateurs', as well as 'antique dealers, in connivance with local thugs', exploited an earthquake to steal cultural objects (Millennium Post, 2015; see also Wolfson, 2015); at least eight people were arrested for theft and attempted illicit sale (Soondas, 2015).

Nonetheless, as demonstrated in India and Sri Lanka, and particularly in Afghanistan and Pakistan, some persistent activity is the preserve of profit-driven organised criminals and politically-motivated armed groups. Hence, cultural property protection is often disincentivised and dangerous. For instance, in Afghanistan, not only do looters and smugglers make more money, but also law enforcement agents are 'murdered' in the line of duty (Astill, 2003). As evidenced in the investigation into one of the largest and farthest-reaching antiquities trafficking empires in the world, in India, antiquities trafficking is sometimes intertwined with drugs trafficking (*Press Trust of India*, 2017).

6.9.2 Corruption

While embezzlement and corruption are challenges everywhere, cultural property policing is hampered by embezzlement among cultural heritage professionals in Bangladesh (e.g. *Daily Star*, 2014), India (e.g. Ganjapure, 2017) and Pakistan (e.g. Tribal News Network, 2016). It is hampered by corruption among tourism workers, cultural heritage professionals, other public servants (who may provide permits for innocuous activities, such as quarrying, cf. Kirinde, 2012), law enforcement agents and/or security agents in India (e.g. Deccan Chronicle, 2017; Pachauri, 2002, p. 273), Nepal (e.g. Sassoon, 1991), Pakistan (e.g. Ashgar, 2017) and Sri Lanka (e.g. Herath, 2016; Kuruneru, 2014; Pothmulla, 2013; Randeniya, 2013; Wijedasa, 2013, where they include politicians, cf. *Sunday Times*, 2013; *Sunday Times*, 2014). At least in Pakistan, some organised crime groups are secreted throughout state structures, as museum workers, police officers and customs officials collaborate in criminal enterprises (Tribal News Network, 2016).

On top of economic challenges and political problems, social conditions undermine efforts to preserve cultural property. Frankly, there is a 'lack of interest among locals to protect' cultural property in Afghanistan (according to the deputy spokesperson for the Ministry of Interior Affairs, Najibullah Danesh, cited by TKG, 2016). Government officials 'show little concern' for cultural property in India (according to a senior research scholar in global studies, Vishakha Desai, cited by Mashberg and Bearak, 2015, p. AR1). The 'vast majority in Muslim Pakistan… have no interest' in pre-Islamic history (Khattak, 2016), while the handling of non-Islamic cultural objects suggests at least a 'lack of concern' among public servants (Tunio, 2017); cultural objects may even be exposed to decay by cultural heritage workers (Medrano, 2017). Again, at least in Pakistan, cultural property criminals believe that they are 'performing a religious duty', 'earning… *Sawab* (blessings of God)', as well as money, 'by digging out the 'remnants of infidels'' and thus committing (ethno)religious cleansing of the territory (Khattak, 2016).

6.9.3 Law and diplomacy

On top of everything else, source countries are vulnerable to political as well as economic exploitation. In an international forum discussion, a magistrate in Australia explained the 'hazzards [*sic* – hazards]' of metal-detecting tourism in Sri Lanka (metaldetective, 2011a).

He had consulted the High Commissioner of Sri Lanka in Canberra with regard to permission 'to take [his] machine into the country' (metaldetective, 2011a). The High Commissioner advised that it was legal to do so, as long as he paid a deposit that would be repaid when he took the machine out again. The magistrate also appears to have checked the regulations on metal-detecting in Australia (metaldetective, 2006a, 2006b). However, there is no indication that he consulted the High Commissioner or anyone else about the legality of using a metal detector on a known archaeological site or anywhere else in Sri Lanka.

Upon arrival, the magistrate had 'obtained permission from a [tour] guide', then proceeded to detect at an unnamed 'ancient site' near Colombo; evidently, it was a functioning temple, as there was at least one 'resident Monk' (metaldetective, 2011a). He was very quickly stopped by a 'very large man' who 'accused' him of 'being a Treasure Hunter' (metaldetective, 2011a). Later, he was questioned by the police and his car was searched; 'of course none [no treasure] was found', though that was presumably because he had been halted after 'about 5 minutes' (metaldetective, 2011a).

The magistrate did not sign a pre-written Sinhala-language statement but did not state whether or not he signed a subsequent English-language translation. By then, 'rather intolerant', the magistrate refused to relinquish his detector to the temple's monk and demanded contact with the Australian Consul in Colombo (metaldetective, 2011a).

When his 'friend and guide... advised' the police that the 'incident could be blown out of all proportions' if the magistrate contacted the consul, the police 'reluctantly allowed [them] to leave without further ado' (metaldetective, 2011a, via Regton, 2011). The magistrate himself appears to indicate the nature of the 'incident'. As he concluded, 'they all wear valuable jewlry [*sic* – jewelry]', so even metal-detecting on the beach would produce 'astounding' finds, '[i]f they ever ma[d]e it legal' (metaldetective, 2011b).

6.9.4 False evidence of looting and potential evidence of fraud

The public knowledge of source countries' vulnerability and exploitation can itself be exploited. OKM Metal Detectors (2018) has been in business since 1998 and its Facebook page indicates that it has at least 27,864 fans around the world (as of 19 January 2018). It manufactures purported detecting devices such as 'treasure-detectors', 'cavity-detectors' and 'long-range detectors'. Their efficacy has been questioned (for example, in discussion under ishtar hunter, 2011). The devices have been outright ridiculed as 'expensive sticks', 'junk', 'garbage', 'fake' or a 'scam' (for example, in discussion under Aziz, 2012; goverton, 2011; GrievousAngel, 2013; HeadsUp, 2013; Jeff30135, 2013; Karl, 2011; Skeeterbait, 2012; Vox veritas, 2011).

The brand advertises in markets where economic insecurity and rich legends of ancient treasures coincide, such as Iran, Tunisia, China and Greece (cf. OKM Metal Detectors, 2017). Although, judging by the prices, it does not target the poorest members of those societies; it targets members of the middle classes who are susceptible to suggestions of rapid enrichment and upward social mobility.

Advertising its 'very discrete [*sic* – discreet]', Android smartphone-controlled, Rover UC (undercover) detector, which is supposedly used to uncover 'buried objects', OKM Metal Detectors (2014) introduced perhaps its 'oldest customer': a 'very successful', 85-year-old 'treasure hunter' in Afghanistan, who had found 'a lot of valuable treasures'. Supposedly, such a device was also being used by a detectorist in Syria (see Syofi, 2014).

OKM Metal Detectors (2017) published another alleged find with a questionable testimonial from Afghanistan. Supposedly, it was a 'golden statue', which had 'been found with [a] metal detector Rover Deluxe.... 4–5 meters under the ground', for which its alleged finder had supposedly refused USD 800,000 from a local dealer, because it might have been 'worth more than that'. Yet it does not resemble any published examples of the excavated rhytons (drinking vessels) that had inspired its style.

It does resemble the practice where forgers of antiquities and dealers of forged antiquities advertise 'metal-detector finds', objects that have been 'found metal-detecting' or 'found with a metal-detector', in order to fabricate evidence of the authenticity of their objects. In the United Kingdom, for example, detectorist

David Hutchings was convicted of fraud, for registering fake coins on the UK Detector Finds Database (UKDFD), then selling them as genuine antiquities (Brown, 2009).

In Sri Lanka, there are 'several gangs' who sell forgeries by pretending to be 'expert treasure hunters' (according to the Special Unit for Prevention of Destruction and Theft of Antiquities in its Department of Archaeology, cited by Kariyakarawana, 2013). Since unlicensed excavation and unlicensed trading are illegal in Afghanistan and Sri Lanka, such activity is akin to advertising, 'this cultural object is guaranteed to be authentic, because it is looted; here is the metal-detector to prove it'.

6.9.5 Conclusion

Despite the sparsity of sources, the information that is available is instructive for academic and non-academic researchers, cultural heritage professionals and law enforcement agents. Analysis of online forums and social networks has identified evidence of: illicit trafficking of cultural objects, by a range of actors from local entrepreneurs to armed forces on deployment overseas; the nature of the market across South Asia, as experienced participants train novice participants; the social organisation of the market, as participants manage their own activity online; and strategies to evade regulation and prevent policing. Thus, such open-source research is a viable tool for advancing understanding and policing of transnational antiquities trafficking.

Adapting these methods and variations (e.g. Hardy, 2016b, 2017), this tool can be used by academic and non-academic researchers and analysts to expand and refine quantitative and qualitative data. Certainly, local-language-proficient studies will be able to significantly advance understanding of social organisation and online management of illicit activity. They may be able to identify sites that are being looted or that are being targeted for looting, as well as criminals' own testimony to the factors that disrupt or deter looting/theft, trafficking/smuggling and illicit sales. As demonstrated, police services may be able to identify active criminals and secure self-published incriminating evidence or leads to evidence, such as the listing of loot by soldiers from the United States in Afghanistan. Meanwhile, border forces and customs agencies may be able to target resources at bottlenecks in smuggling routes or techniques for bypassing inspections.

Altogether, this evidence may emphasise the difficulties of crime prevention in source countries and pressure the international community to intensify crime prevention in market countries. Market countries, anyway, are the places that create the demand that drives the supply. They draw in most of the profit in the illicit trade and channel out a fraction, which undermines social cohesion and the rule of law and finances organised crime and political violence in source countries. As highlighted by the financing of terrorism in Europe with profits from illicit trafficking in South Asia, which are ultimately largely derived from markets in Europe (and North America), it is a matter of stability and security for the market countries to support stability and security in the source countries.

Bibliography

Agence France-Presse (2012a) Smugglers lead police to ancient loot. *news.com.au*, 8 July. Available at: www.news.com.au/world/breaking-news/smugglers-lead-police-to-ancient-loot/news-story/f03e49e66983d46de65299bb5cefa2e5 (accessed 7 July 2018).

Agence France-Presse (2012b) Millionaires unveil Pakistan's artefact smuggling secrets. *Dawn*, 9 August. Available at: www.dawn.com/news/740942/millionaires-unveil-pakistans-artefact-smuggling-secrets [Archived at: http://web.archive.org/web/20160224132233/http://www.dawn.com/news/740942/millionaires-unveil-pakistans-artefact-smuggling-secrets (accessed 7 July 2018).

Alejandro (2013) When the embassy doesn't know… *Friendly Metal Detecting Forum*, 31 December. Available at: https://metaldetectingforum.com/showthread.php?t=175783 (accessed 24 January 2018).

Allbritton, C. (2009) Pakistan's turmoil endangers its archaeological treasures. *Time*, 25 December. Available at: http://content.time.com/time/world/article/0,8599,1950034,00.html (accessed 7 July 2018).

Ashgar, M. (2017) Two customs officials booked in antiques smuggling case. *Dawn*, 17 August. Available at: www.dawn.com/news/1352045/two-customs-officials-booked-in-antiques-smuggling-case (accessed 24 January 2018).

ASI (Archaeological Survey of India) (2011) Legislations. *Archaeological Survey of India*, 21 July. Available at: http://web.archive.org/web/20110721192659/http://www.asi.nic.in/asi_legislations.asp (accessed 24 January 2018).

asm (2011) Re: Metal detecting hobby in India. *World of Coins*, 21 September. Available at: www.worldofcoins.eu/forum/index.php/topic,11669.msg78879.html#msg78879 (accessed 24 January 2018).

Associated Press (2012) Pakistan struggles to control smuggling of Buddhist antiquities for black market trade. *CBS News*, 4 October. Available at: www.cbsnews.com/news/pakistan-struggles-to-control-smuggling-of-buddhist-antiquities-for-black-market-trade/ (accessed 7 July 2018).

Astill, J. (2003) Plunder goes on across Afghanistan as looters grow ever bolder. *Guardian*, 13 December. Available at: www.theguardian.com/world/2003/dec/13/highereducation.artsandhumanities (accessed 24 January 2018).

Aziz (2012) Scam alert! *Australian Electronic Gold Prospecting Forum*, 28 March. Available at: http://australianelectronicgoldprospectingforum.com/general-chat-and-discussion-forum/scam-alert!/?action=printpage (accessed 24 January 2018).

Benjamin, R.P. (2016) Treasure hunters ravage temples. *Hans India*, 4 March. Available at: www.thehansindia.com/posts/index/Andhra-Pradesh/2016-03-04/Treasure-hunters-ravage-temples/211234 (accessed 24 January 2018).

Bhadrakumar, M.K. (2017) An open-ended Afghan war can serve 'America First'. *Asia Times*, 15 June. Available at: http://web.archive.org/web/20170615073918/https://www.atimes.com/open-ended-afghan-war-can-serve-america-first/ (accessed 7 July 2018).

Bigstemz (2015) Trip to India and what detectors to take. *Friendly Metal Detecting Forum*, 1 February. Available at: https://metaldetectingforum.com/showpost.php?p=2270249&postcount=1 (accessed 24 January 2018).

Blitz (2012) Stolen Buddhist artifacts reaching international racket. *Facebook*, 21 October. Available at: www.facebook.com/BuddhistDefenceLeague/photos/a.3

38260486266521.78842.326560140769889/353642594728310/?type=1&theater (accessed 24 January 2018).

Bondi Treasure Hunter (2016) This guy goes metal detecting in Afghanistan. *Facebook*, 23 June. Available at: www.facebook.com/bonditreasurehunter/photos/a.512918108890255.1073741829.486831268165606/568395196675879/?type=3&theater (accessed 24 January 2018).

Bopearachchi, O. (2006) Preserving Afghanistan's cultural heritage: What is to be done? In: Agnew, N. and Bridgland, J. (eds.) *Of the Past, for the Future: Integrating Archaeology and Conservation*. Los Angeles: Getty Conservation Institute, pp. 266–274.

Brodie, N. (2006) An archaeologist's view of the trade in unprovenanced antiquities. In: Hoffman, B.T. (ed.) *Art and Cultural Heritage: Law, Policy, and Practice*. Cambridge: Cambridge University Press, 52–63.

Brown, D. (2009) Metal detector user David Hutchings jailed for selling fake coins. *Times*, 11 May. Available at: www.thetimes.co.uk/article/metal-detector-user-david-hutchings-jailed-for-selling-fake-coins-7rjx8vsb5gh (accessed 24 January 2018).

Buda, G. (2015) Early coins (circular), Nepal. *YouTube*, 11 April. Available at: www.youtube.com/watch?v=ARhgC5i7uNE (accessed 24 January 2018).

Burke, J. (2015) India struggles to halt multimillion dollar trade in stolen artworks. *Guardian*, 3 August. Available at: www.theguardian.com/world/2015/aug/03/india-struggles-to-halt-multimillion-dollar-trade-stolen-artworks-temples (accessed 24 January 2018).

Campbell, P.B. (2013) The illicit antiquities trade as a transnational criminal network: Characterising and anticipating the trafficking of cultural heritage. *International Journal of Cultural Property* 20(2): 113–153.

CapeTownBeachBum (2016) Detecting in India? The gold must fall like leaves in autumn. *TreasureNet*, 20 March. Available at: www.treasurenet.com/forums/beach-shallow-water/305469-detecting-india-gold-must-fall-like-leaves-autumn-2.html#post4908754 (accessed 24 January 2018).

Channa, A. (2015) Customs Air Freight Unit foils bid to smuggle antiques worth $10 million out of country. *Customs Today*, 23 December. Available at: www.customstoday.com.pk/customs-air-freight-unit-recovers-precious-antiquities-worth-10m/ (accessed 24 January 2018).

Chudman (2009) First Afghanistan Hunt. Friendly Metal. *Detecting Forum*, 21 November. Available at: https://metaldetectingforum.com/showpost.php?s=4a614dd502449c4e7bb20e58b95b2b1d&p=408192&postcount=1 (accessed 24 January 2018).

Coinsforever (2011a) Re: Metal detecting hobby in India. *World of Coins*, 21 September. Available at: www.worldofcoins.eu/forum/index.php/topic,11669.msg78817.html#msg78817 (accessed 24 January 2018).

Coinsforever (2011b) Re: Metal detecting hobby in India. *World of Coins*, 23 September. Available at: www.worldofcoins.eu/forum/index.php/topic,11669.msg78995.html#msg78995 (accessed 24 January 2018).

Curtis, J. (2011) Archaeology and cultural heritage in war zones. In: British Academy (ed.) *History for the Taking? Perspectives on Material Heritage*. London: British Academy, 55–76.

Daily Capital (2016) Valuable antiquities were stolen from PA premises. *Capital TV*, 4 March. Available at: http://dailycapital.pk/valuable-antiquities-were-stolen-from-pa-premises/ (accessed 7 July 2018).

Daily Star (2014) Barendra museum heist: Punish culprits, recover artefacts. *Daily Star*, 17 December. Available at: www.thedailystar.net/barendra-museum-heist-55672 (accessed 24 January 2018).

Dalrymple, W. (2013) A deadly triangle: Afghanistan, Pakistan and India. *Brookings Institution*, 25 June. Available at: http://csweb.brookings.edu/content/research/essays/2013/deadly-triangle-afghanistan-pakistan-india-c.html (accessed 7 July 2018).

Davis, J.L. and Capron, A. (2015) Rendons au Népal ses statues volées [let us return Nepal's stolen statues]. *France* 24, 11 May. Available at: http://observers.france24.com/fr/content/20150424-trafic-statues-volees-nepal-katmandou-seisme-musee-france-carte-artiste-peinture (accessed 24 January 2018).

Dawn (2008) Mardan: Illegal digging at archaeological sites continues. *Dawn*, 27 April. Available at: www.dawn.com/news/300050 (accessed 24 January 2018).

Deccan Chronicle (2017) Tamil Nadu: Absconding DSP held for idol robbery. *Deccan Chronicle*, 15 September. Available at: https://web.archive.org/web/20170915105902/http://www.deccanchronicle.com/nation/crime/150917/tamil-nadu-absconding-dsp-held-for-idol-robbery.html (accessed 24 January 2018).

Delhi Times (2011) Christie's auction house selling stolen merchandise. *The Delhi Times*, 19 September. Available at: http://web.archive.org/web/20160212022820/http://www.cultureindevelopment.nl/News/Discussing_Looting/1319/Christie's_Auction_House_selling_stolen_merchandise (accessed 7 July 2018).

Docekal, C. (2014) I am metal detecting and picking up shells right now <3. *Facebook*, 8 November. Available at: www.facebook.com/connie.docekal/posts/613825505413159 (accessed 24 January 2018).

Dunya News (2016) Real artifacts stolen, replaced with fake ones at Peshawar museum. *Dunya News*, 26 March. Available at: http://dunyanews.tv/en/Crime/329390-Real-artifacts-stolen-replaced-with-fake-ones-at- (accessed 7 July 2018).

Dupree, N.H. (1998) Museum under siege. *Archaeology*, 20 April. Available at: http://archive.archaeology.org/online/features/afghan/ (accessed 24 January 2018).

Express-Tribune (2012) Gandhara relics: Stolen or not, police and archaeologists can't agree on one number. *Express-Tribune*, 22 July. Available at: http://tribune.com.pk/story/411469/gandhara-relics-stolen-or-not-police-and-archaeologists-cant-agree-on-one-number/ (accessed 7 July 2018).

Express Tribune (2017) Bid to smuggle Mughal-era antiquities foiled. *Express-Tribune*, 7 October. Available at: https://tribune.com.pk/story/1524795/bid-smuggle-mughal-era-antiquities-foiled/ (accessed 24 January 2018).

Fanelli, J. (2015) Brooklyn art dealer accused of selling stolen ancient artifacts for $500K. *DNAinfo*, 2 April. Available at: www.dnainfo.com/new-york/20150402/greenpoint/brooklyn-art-dealer-accused-of-selling-stolen-ancient-artifacts-for-500k (accessed 24 January 2018).

Ferguson, A. (2009) Treasure-hunting in Afghanistan. *Time*, 26 February. Available at: http://content.time.com/time/photogallery/0,29307,1882179,00.html (accessed 24 January 2018).

Fiedler, D. (2015) An island's damaged heritage. *Deutsche Press*, 9 March. Available at: www.nationmultimedia.com/life/An-islands-damaged-heritage-30255488.html (accessed 24 January 2018).

Ganjapure, V. (2017) Missing ancient coins: Ex-HOD still missing. *Times of India*, 25 April. Available at: https://timesofindia.indiatimes.com/city/nagpur/missing-ancient-coins-ex-hod-still-missing/articleshow/58350403.cms (accessed 24 January 2018).

goverton (2011) Rover UC metal detector (walking stick) ?! Anyone use this? *TreasureNet*, 17 November. Available at: www.treasurenet.com/forums/metal-detecting/268686-rover-uc-metal-detector-walking-stick-anyone-use.html (accessed 20 January 2018).

GrievousAngel (2013) OKM Black Hawk: Wort the big $$$? *TreasureNet*, 5 September. Available at: www.treasurenet.com/forums/brands/374297-okm-black-hawk-wort-big.html (accessed 24 January 2018).

Gunshin (2012) First Afghanistan hunt. *Friendly Metal Detecting Forum*, 3 September. Available at: https://metaldetectingforum.com/showpost.php?s=4a614dd502449c4e7bb20e58b95b2b1d&p=1355526&postcount=9 (accessed 20 January 2018).

Hardy, S.A. (Under review) Antiquities rescue or ransom? The cost of buying back stolen cultural property. In: Republic of Turkey Ministry of Culture and Tourism (ed.) Proceedings of the 5th International Conference of Experts on the Return of Cultural Property, Nevşehir, Turkey, 18–22 October 2015. Ankara: Republic of Turkey Ministry of Culture and Tourism. Available at: https://conflictantiquities.files.wordpress.com/2011/08/hardy-2016-icercp-article-draft-160331.pdf (accessed 24 January 2018).

Hardy, S.A. (2016a) *Illicit Trafficking, Provenance Research and Due Diligence: The State of the Art*. Paris: UNESCO. Available at: http://web.archive.org/web/20190418153528/http://www.unesco.org/new/fileadmin/MULTIMEDIA/HQ/CLT/pdf/Hardy_2016_UNESCO_antiquities_trafficking_review_materia.pdf (accessed 20 January 2018).

Hardy, S.A. (2016b) 'Black archaeology' in Eastern Europe: Metal detecting, illicit trafficking of cultural objects and 'legal nihilism' in Belarus, Poland, Russia and Ukraine. *Public Archaeology* 15(4): 214–237.

Hardy, S.A. (2017) Quantitative analysis of open-source data on metal detecting for cultural property: Estimation of the scale and intensity of metal detecting and the quantity of metal-detected cultural goods. *Cogent Social Sciences* 3. Available at: http://dx.doi.org/10.1080/23311886.2017.1298397 (accessed 24 January 2018).

Hawley, J.K. (2007) The international illicit trade in cultural heritage: Can museum professionals help stop it? In: Argyropoulos, V., Hein, A. and Abdel Harith, M. (eds.) *Strategies for Saving our Cultural Heritage*, 228–233. Athens: TEI of Athens.

HeadsUp (2013) OKM machines. *Prospecting Australia*, 17 April. Available at: www.prospectingaustralia.com.au/forum/viewtopic.php?id=936 (accessed 24 January 2018).

Herath, B. (2016) Treasure hunting Johnny's SO arrested. *Ceylon Today*, 15 November. Available at: www.ceylontoday.lk/print20161101CT20161231.php?id=9342 (accessed 24 January 2018).

Huffer, D. (2010) Gandhara Galleries: 'Statue-ary rape'. *It Surfaced Down Under!*, 25 April. Available at: http://itsurfaceddownunder.blogspot.co.uk/2010/04/gandhara-galleries-statue-ary-rape.html (accessed 24 January 2018).

IRP (Islamic Republic of Pakistan) (1992) *Antiquities Act*. Islamabad: Islamic Republic of Pakistan – Department of Archaeology and Museums. Available at: http://web.archive.org/web/20190418154958/https://en.unesco.org/sites/default/files/pakistan_act7_1975_eng_orof.pdf (accessed 24 January 2018).

ISA (Islamic State of Afghanistan) (2004) *Law on the Protection of Historical and Cultural Properties [21 May 2004]*. Kabul: Ministry of Justice of the Islamic State of Afghanistan. Available at: http://web.archive.org/web/20190418155219/https://en.unesco.org/sites/default/files/afghanistan_law_preservation_heritage_2004_engtno.pdf (accessed 24 January 2018).

Ishtar hunter (2011) My test by okm exp4000–visulizer3D. *Geotech*, 9 August. Available at: www.geotech1.com/forums/showthread.php?18009-My-test-by-okm-exp4000-visulizer3D&s=193c0f129b625c890ece360b68a58366 (accessed 24 January 2018).

Jeff30135 (2013) OKM Exp 5000 Pro. Wow! *Friendly Metal Detecting Forum*, 15 March. Available at: https://metaldetectingforum.com/showthread.php?t=146600 (accessed 24 January 2018)30135.

Kariyakarawana, K.K. (2013) Treasure hunting goes on unabated in remote areas. *Sunday Observer*, 14 April. Available at: http://web.archive.org/web/20130414042636/http://www.sundayobserver.lk/2013/04/14/fea09.asp (accessed 24 January 2018).

Karl (2011) Metal detectors from OKM. *Thunting*, 11 May. Available at: www.thunting.com/smf/metal_detecting_in_general/metal_detectors_from_okm-t23656.0.html (accessed 24 January 2018).

Kathmandu Post (2014) Stolen idols. *Kathmandu Post*, 3 April. Available at: http://kathmandupost.ekantipur.com/printedition/news/2014-04-03/stolen-idols-261239.html (accessed 24 January 2018).

Kaushik, N. (2015) Tourist haunt. *Bangkok Post*, 19 October. Available at: www.pressreader.com/thailand/bangkok-post/20151019/282681866102372 (accessed 24 January 2018).

Khaama Press (2016) Iran-made treasure hunting equipment seized in Bamyan Province. *Khaama Press*, 13 July. Available at: www.khaama.com/iran-made-treasure-hunting-equipment-seized-in-bamyan-province-01475 (accessed 24 January 2018).

Khan, A.R. (2010) *Conceptualizing AfPak: The Prospects and Perils*. London: Chatham House.

Khan, H. (2015) At Afghanistan. *Facebook*, 24 November. Available at: www.facebook.com/groups/1624680771142551/permalink/1674092652868029/ (accessed 24 January 2018).

Khan, H. (2016) At Afghanistan 2012. *Facebook*, 11 June. Available at: www.facebook.com/groups/1624680771142551/permalink/1758694294407864/ (accessed 24 January 2018).

Khattak, D. (2016) Pakistan's vanishing history. *Diplomat*, 2 July. Available at: https://thediplomat.com/2016/07/pakistans-vanishing-history/ (accessed 24 January 2018).

Khattak, I. (2015) Large number of artifacts smuggled to US, EU: Pervaiz. *Nation*, 7 August. Available at: https://nation.com.pk/07-Aug-2015/large-number-of-artifacts-smuggled-to-us-eu-pervaiz (accessed 24 January 2018).

Kirinde, C. (2012) Hunting the treasure hunters. *Sunday Times*, 20 May. Available at: www.sundaytimes.lk/120520/News/nws_20.html (accessed 24 January 2018).

Kolby72 (2012) First Afghanistan hunt. *Friendly Metal Detecting Forum*, 3 September. Available at: https://metaldetectingforum.com/showpost.php?s=4a614dd502449c4e7bb20e58b95b2b1d&p=1356147&postcount=16 (accessed 24 January 2018).

KoN (Kingdom of Nepal) (1970) *Ancient Monuments Protection Act [28 October 1970]*. Kathmandu: Kingdom of Nepal. Available at: http://web.archive.org/web/20190418155449/https://en.unesco.org/sites/default/files/nepal_act_consolidated_text_28_10_1970_eng_tno.pdf (accessed 24 January 2018).

Kunwar, N. (2015) The lost sculptures of Kathmandu. *Huffington Post*, 14 April. Available at: www.huffingtonpost.com/niranjan-kunwar/the-lost-sculptures-of-kathmandu_b_7059524.html (accessed 24 January 2018).

Kuruneru, P. (2014) Priceless gem recovered. *Island*, 3 August. Available at: www.island.lk/index.php?page_cat=article-details&page=article-details&code_title=107914 (accessed 24 January 2018).

LE.JAG (2015) Detecting in India? The gold must fall like leaves in autumn. *TreasureNet*, 10 January. Available at: www.treasurenet.com/forums/beach-shallow-water/305469-detecting-india-gold-must-fall-like-leaves-autumn-2.html#post4340429 (accessed 24 January 2018).

Lee, D. (2000) History and art are being wiped out in Afghanistan. *Art Newspaper*, 7 June. Available at: http://web.archive.org/web/20000607160522/http://www.allemandi.com/TAN/news/article.asp?idart=1033 (accessed 24 January 2018).

Limbu, R. (2001) In the land of gods, thieves have a field day. *Nepali Times*, 28 September–4 October. Available at: http://nepalitimes.com/news.php?id=7311 (accessed 24 January 2018).

Live at 7 News (2016) Nidhan horu koṭuveyi [treasure hunters arrested]. *YouTube*, 22 July. Available at: www.youtube.com/watch?v=DhsejDljD5Q (accessed 24 January 2018).

Makarenko, T. and Mesquita, M. (2016) Categorising the crime-terror nexus in the European Union. In: Carrapico, H., Irrera, D. and Tupman, B. (eds.) *Criminals and Terrorists in Partnership: Unholy Alliance*. Abingdon: Routledge, 47–62.

Malik, S. (2012) Illegal digs threaten Pakistan's past. *Independent Online*, 21 July. Available at: www.iol.co.za/scitech/science/discovery/illegal-digs-threaten-pakistan-s-buddhist-past-1.1346250 (accessed 7 July 2018).

Mashberg, T. and Bearak, M. (2015) The ultimate temple raider? Inside an antiquities-smuggling operation. *New York Times*, 26 July, AR1. Available at: http://www.nytimes.com/2015/07/26/arts/design/the-ultimate-temple-raider-inside-an-antiquities-smuggling-operation.html (accessed 24 January 2018).

McGirk, T. (1996) A year of looting dangerously. *Independent on Sunday*, 24 March. Available at: www.independent.co.uk/arts-entertainment/a-year-of-looting-dangerously-1343741.html (accessed 24 January 2018).

McGirk, T. (2002) Third Buddha found? *Time*, 20 May. Available at: https://content.time.com/time/magazine/article/0,9171,238674,00.html (accessed 24 January 2018).

Medrano, K. (2017) Pakistan: Ancient Buddha statues saved from smugglers. Museum then dumps them in the trash. *Newsweek*, 17 November. Available at: www.newsweek.com/pakistan-ancient-buddha-statues-saved-smugglers-museum-then-dump-them-trash-714874 (accessed 7 July 2018).

"metaldetective (2011a) Metal detecting in a foreign country. Thunting, 30 September. Available at: http://www.thunting.com/smf/metal_detecting_in_general/metal_detecting_in_a_foreign_country-t27728.0.html;msg196653#msg196653 (accessed 24 January 2018)."

"metaldetective (2011b) Metal detecting in a foreign country. Thunting, 10 October. Available at: https://www.thunting.com/smf/metal_detecting_in_general/metal_detecting_in_a_foreign_country-t27728.0.html;msg197488#msg197488 (accessed 24 January 2018)."

Millennium Post (2015) Antique dealers eye priceless artefacts at Nepal sites. *Millennium Post*, 28 April. Available at: www.millenniumpost.in/NewsContent.aspx?NID=112683 (accessed 24 January 2018).

MMG (Miniwatts Marketing Group) (2017) Internet, Facebook and population stats for Europe. *Internet World Stats*, 30 June. Available at: www.internetworldstats.com/stats3.htm#asia (accessed 24 January 2018).

OKM Metal Detectors (2017) Valuable golden statue detected in Afghanistan. *OKM Metal Detectors*, 3 July. Available at: www.okmmetaldetectors.com/en/treasure-finds/golden-statue-afghanistan/ (accessed 24 January 2018).

OKM Metal Detectors (2014) OKMs oldest customer? *Facebook*, 15 October. Available at: https://www.facebook.com/okmmetaldetectors/posts/700143463414579 (accessed 24 January 2018).

OKM Metal Detectors (2017) Metal detector finds, treasure finds and discoveries. *OKM Metal Detectors*, 11 October. Available at: www.okmmetaldetectors.com/en/treasure-finds/ (accessed 24 January 2018).

OKM Metal Detectors (2018) OKM Metal Detectors. *Facebook*, 19 January. Available at: www.facebook.com/okmmetaldetectors/about/ (accessed 24 January 2018).

Pachauri, S.K. (2002) Plunder of cultural and art treasures – The Indian experience (2002). In: Brodie, N. and Tubb, K.W. (eds.) *Illicit Antiquities: The Theft of Culture and the Extinction of Archaeology*. London: Routledge, 268–278.

Pal, P. (1986) *American Collectors of Asian Art*. Bombay: Marg.

PDSRSL (Parliament of the Democratic Socialist Republic of Sri Lanka) (1956) *Antiquities Ordinance*. Colombo: Parliament of the Democratic Socialist Republic of Sri Lanka. Available at: http://web.archive.org/web/20190418152614/https://en.unesco.org/sites/default/files/ceylon_legislative_enactments_1956_engl_orof.pdf (accessed 24 January 2018).

PDSRSL (Parliament of the Democratic Socialist Republic of Sri Lanka) (1998) Antiquities (Amendment) Act [No. 24, 21 May 1998]. Colombo: Parliament of the Democratic Socialist Republic of Sri Lanka. Available at: www.archaeology.gov.lk/web/images/pdf/A-Antiquity_(Amendment)_Act_No_24_of_1998.pdf (accessed 24 January 2018).

Peters, G. (2010) *Crime and Insurgency in the Tribal Areas of Afghanistan and Pakistan*. New York: West Point Combating Terrorism Center.

Pothmulla, L. (2013) US-bound artefacts discovered. *Daily Mirror*, 4 June. Available at: www.dailymirror.lk/news/30370-us-bound-artefacts-discovered.html (accessed 24 January 2018).

Press Trust of India (2017) HC dismisses antique dealer Kapoor's bail plea. *Press Trust of India*, 21 July. Available at: https://web.archive.org/web/20170721205906/http://www.ptinews.com/news/8909215_HC-dismisses-antique dealer-Kapoor-s-bail-plea.html (accessed 24 January 2018).

Rana, M.R. (2013) Taxila: Treasure hunters steal ancient items illegally. *Pakistan Observer*, 4 January. Available at: http://web.archive.org/web/20130107000021/http://pakobserver.net/detailnews.asp?id=190028 (accessed 24 January 2018).

Randeniya, R. (2013) Unending treasure hunting. *Island*, 3 September. Available at: www.island.lk/index.php?page_cat=article-details&page=article-details&code_title=87253 (accessed 24 January 2018).

Regton (2011) METAL DETECTING in Sri-lanka. Regton, 30 September. Available at: https://www.facebook.com/Regton.Metal.Detectors/posts/239193226127783 (accessed 28 January 2018)."

Rehman, Z.U. (2012) Karachi police foil Gandhara artefact-smuggling plot. *Central Asia Online*, 9 July. Available at: http://centralasiaonline.com/en_GB/articles/caii/features/pakistan/main/2012/07/09/feature-01 (accessed 7 July 2018).

Richardson, B.G. (2012) Trafficking in antiquities during a time of war – Analysis. *Eurasia Review*, 8 June. Available at: www.eurasiareview.com/08062012-trafficking-in-antiquities-during-a-time-of-war-analysis/ (accessed 24 January 2018).

Rogin, J. (2010) Team Obama scuttles the term 'AfPak'. *Foreign Policy*, 20 January. Available at: https://web.archive.org/web/20100125145128/http://thecable.foreignpolicy.com/posts/2010/01/20/team_obama_scuttles_the_term_afpak (accessed 7 July 2018).

RoI (Republic of India) (1972) *Antiquities and Art Treasures Act*. New Delhi: Republic of India. Available at: http://web.archive.org/web/20190418152344/https://en.unesco.org/sites/default/files/in_actantiquitiesartreasures1972_engorof.pdf (accessed 24 January 2018).

RoI (Republic of India) (2010) *Ancient Monuments and Archaeological Sites and Remains Act 1958 [as of 29 March 2010]*. New Delhi: Republic of India. Available at: http://web.archive.org/web/20190418152155/https://en.unesco.org/sites/default/files/inde_act24_1958_enorof.pdf (accessed 24 January 2018).

RoM (Republic of Maldives) (1979) *Law of Historical and Cultural Properties [No. 27/79, 22 July 1979]*. Malé: Republic of Maldives. Available at: http://web.archive.org/web/20190418152509/https://en.unesco.org/sites/default/files/maldives_law_22_07_1979_englorof.pdf (accessed 24 January 2018).

Rothfield, L. (2013) Economics of looting: The costs of production. *Punching Bag*, 11 February. Available at: http://larryrothfield.blogspot.co.uk/2013/02/economics-of-looting-costs-of-production.html (accessed 24 January 2018).

Ruiz, C. (2010) 9/11 hijacker attempted to sell Afghan loot: Mohammed Atta offered artefacts to German archaeologist. *Art Newspaper*, 27 January. Available at: www.theartnewspaper.com/articles/9/11-hijacker-attempted-to-sell-Afghan-loot/20188 (accessed 24 January 2018).

sanjeebrosy (2015) Detecting in India? The gold must fall like leaves in autumn. *TreasureNet*, 4 September. Available at: www.treasurenet.com/forums/beach-shallow-water/305469-detecting-india-gold-must-fall-like-leaves-autumn-2.html#post4667686 (accessed 24 January 2018).

Sassoon, D. (1991) The antiquities of Nepal: It is time to start listening to communities whose possessions have become objects of international consumption. *Cultural*

Survival Quarterly 15(3). Available at: www.culturalsurvival.org/publications/cultural-survival-quarterly/antiquities-nepal-it-time-start-listening-communities (accessed 24 January 2018).

s.c.shooter (2013) Metal detecting in Afghanistan. *TreasureNet*, 7 November. Available at: http://www.treasurenet.com/forums/metal-detecting/383789-metal-detecting-afghanistan.html#post3681059 (accessed 24 January 2018).

Serii Kopatel v Poiskakh Klada (2016) Maldives – A paradise for treasure hunters! *YouTube*, 10 January. Available at: www.youtube.com/watch?v=siSSlFhu1m8 (accessed 24 January 2018).

Sharma, S.M. (2015) Protecting the ruins. *Nepali Times*, 24–30 July. Available at: http://nepalitimes.com/article/Nepali-Times-Buzz/religious-objects-of-Kathmandu-vulnerable-to-threat-after-the-earthquake,2437 (accessed 24 January 2018).

Skeeterbait (2012) Anyone ever hear of this MD? Rover? *Friendly Metal Detecting Forum*, 9 February. Available at: https://metaldetectingforum.com/showthread.php?t=102890 (accessed 24 January 2018).

Soondas, A. (2015) Can Nepal save riches beneath its ruins? *Times of India*, 4 May. Available at: http://timesofindia.indiatimes.com/world/south-asia/Can-Nepal-save-riches-beneath-its-ruins/articleshow/47143358.cms (accessed 24 January 2018).

SPACH (Society for the Preservation of Afghanistan's Cultural Heritage) (2004) About SPACH. *Society for the Preservation of Afghanistan's Cultural Heritage*, no date. Available at: http://spach.af/ehistoryplan.htm (accessed 24 January 2018).

Stein, G.J. (2015) The war-ravaged cultural heritage of Afghanistan: An overview of projects of assessment, mitigation, and preservation. *Near Eastern Archaeology* 78(3): 187–195.

Stewart, R. (2005) *The Places in Between*. London: Picador.

Sunday Times (2013) Poson reflections: Save our heritage". Sunday Times, 23 June. Available at: http://www.sundaytimes.lk/130623/editorial/poson-reflections-save-our-heritage-49884.html (accessed 24 January 2018).

Sunday Times (2014) Magistrate's court wants report on archaeology site following arrests. *Sunday Times*, 10 August. Available at: www.sundaytimes.lk/140810/news/magistrates-court-wants-report-on-archaeology-site-following-arrests-110407.html (accessed 24 January 2018).

Syofi, N. (2014) أيضاً صديق لي عنده واحده مثلها [Also a friend of mine has one like it]. *Facebook*, 15 October. Available at: www.facebook.com/okmmetaldetectors/photos/a.190744904354440.40201.109904952438436/700128163416109/?type=3&comment_id=700334703395455 (accessed 24 January 2018).

Tador (2012) Detecting in India? The gold must fall like leaves in autumn. *TreasureNet*, 29 July. Available at: www.treasurenet.com/forums/beach-shallow-water/305469-detecting-india-gold-must-fall-like-leaves-autumn.html#post2873628 (accessed 24 January 2018).

Tejaas (2013a) Metal detecting in Afghanistan. *TreasureNet*, 29 October. Available at: www.treasurenet.com/forums/metal-detecting/383789-metal-detecting-afghanistan.html#post3666108 (accessed 24 January 2018).

Tejaas (2013b) Metal detecting in Afghanistan. *TreasureNet*, 3 November. Available at: www.treasurenet.com/forums/metal-detecting/383789-metal-detecting-afghanistan.html#post3681068 (accessed 24 January 2018).

Times News Network (2017) Idol theft case: Masterminds arrested. *Times of India*, 7 November. Available at: https://timesofindia.indiatimes.com/city/trichy/idol-theft-case-masterminds-arrested/articleshow/61537754.cms (accessed 24 January 2018).

TKG (2016) Haven for smugglers. *The Killid Group*, 19 October. Available at: http://tkg.af/english/2016/10/19/haven-for-smugglers/ (accessed 24 January 2018).

TreasureNet (2012) What's going on? *TreasureNet*, 2 August. Available at: https://web.archive.org/web/20120802004058/http://www.treasurenet.com/forums/forum.php (accessed 24 January 2018).

Tribal News Network (2016) Probe committee confirms antiquities stolen from Peshawar Museum. *TNN*, 18 May. Available at: www.radiotnn.com/probe-committee-confirms-antiquities-stolen-from-peshawar-museum/ (accessed 24 January 2018).

Tunio, H. (2017) 1,500 year old statues left in the trash at National Museum. *Express Tribune*, 17 November. Available at: https://tribune.com.pk/story/1560429/1-1500-year-old-statues-left-trash-national-museum/ (accessed 24 January 2018).

UKHC (UK House of Commons) (2003) Dealing in Cultural Objects (Offences) Bill [4 March 2003]'. *Hansard* 402: 1219–1235. Available at: www.publications.parliament.uk/pa/cm200203/cmhansrd/vo030404/debtext/30404-15.htm (accessed 24 January 2018) 402. Hansard, 1219–1235 (2003).

USICE (United States Immigration and Customs Enforcement) (2013) ICE returns stolen antiquities to Islamic Republic of Afghanistan. *U.S. Immigration and Customs Enforcement (ICE)*, 9 September. Available at: www.ice.gov/news/releases/1309/130909washingtondc.htm (accessed 24 January 2018).

Vox veritas (2011) OKM Bionic X4. Your opinion. *TreasureNet*, 18 October. Available at: www.treasurenet.com/forums/metal-detecting/263730-okm-bionic-x4-your-opinion.html.

vurda (2013) Re: Metal detector. *TripAdvisor*, 30 November. Available at: www.tripadvisor.in/ShowTopic-g297604-i6045-k7019145-Metal_detector-Goa.html (accessed 24 January 2018).

welsh john (2014) Detecting in the Maldives. *Detecting Wales*, 28 January. Available at: www.detectingwales.com/index.php?topic=20002.0 (accessed 24 January 2018).

Wendle, J. (2013) Who's stealing Afghanistan's cultural treasures? *National Geographic*, 1 August. Available at: http://news.nationalgeographic.co.uk/news/whos-stealing-afghanistan-cultural-treasures/ (accessed 24 January 2018).

West Sands Advisory (2012) *Europe's Crime-Terror Nexus: Links between Terrorist and Organised Crime Groups in the European Union [Study for the Committee on Civil Liberties, Justice and Home Affairs of the European Parliament]*. Brussels: Policy Department C, Citizens' Rights and Constitutional Affairs, European Parliament. Available at: www.europarl.europa.eu/RegData/etudes/etudes/join/2012/462503/IPOL-LIBE_ET(2012)462503_EN.pdf (accessed 7 July 2018).

Wickremasekara, D. (2012) Two cases a day: Treasure-hunters on the rampage. *Sunday Times*, 8 April. Available at: www.sundaytimes.lk/120408/News/nws_43.html (accessed 24 January 2018).

Wijedasa, N. (2013) Archaeological sites islandwide plundered for priceless artefacts. *Sunday Times*, 10 February. Available at: www.sundaytimes.lk/130210/news/

archaeological-sites-islandwide-plundered-for-priceless-artefacts-32652.html (accessed 24 January 2018).

Wolfson, E. (2015) Theft in Kathmandu: Can Nepal's cultural legacy be saved? *Newsweek*, 29 April. Available at: www.newsweek.com/theft-kathmandu-can-nepals-cultural-legacy-be-saved-326684 (accessed 24 January 2018).

Wostro (2014) Detecting in India? The gold must fall like leaves in autumn. *TreasureNet*, 29 December. Available at: www.treasurenet.com/forums/beach-shallow-water/305469-detecting-india-gold-must-fall-like-leaves-autumn.html#post4321277 (accessed 24 January 2018).

7 Using Routine Activity Theory to explain illegal fishing in the Indo-Pacific

Jade Lindley and Erika Techera

7.1 Introduction

The vast Indo-Pacific region borders several States, supports many important trade routes and is home to countless species of marine life. This combination exposes the region to maritime crime. Illegal fishing is one of many crimes that exist at sea. Oftentimes, illegal fishing is interlocked with several other organised maritime crimes (United Nations Office on Drugs and Crime, 2011, p. 3). Clandestine links onshore aid the transfer of fish to market (United Nations Office on Drugs and Crime, 2011, p. 3). Data captured by governments and international organisations attempt to measure the scale and cost of illegal fishing, however, beyond estimates, these figures lack accuracy due to the wide regional reach, number of species involved and the ability to mix legitimately with illegitimately caught fish at market. Estimates do, however, suggest the global black market for seafood is worth more than US$20 billion (Agnew et al., 2009). The global reliance on the Indo-Pacific for a multitude of reasons cements the preservation of fish stocks as a priority.

Due to the doctrine of the freedom of the high seas, cooperative arrangements must apply to regulation and policing of areas beyond national jurisdiction as they are not owned by any one State (United Nations, 1982, Art 87(1)). Illegal fishing causes billions of dollars of harm to victimised States, through lost revenue in licensing, taxes and duties, monies lost to corruption of border control, and economic growth through legitimate investments (United Nations Office on Drugs and Crime, 2011, p. 97). States also lose revenue and income they would otherwise have gained through legitimate fisheries, and economic growth through foreign investment and employment (United Nations Office on Drugs and Crime, 2011, p. 97). Crime threatens the fishing industry, livelihoods reliant on subsistence and the marine conservation of the region. Recently, there has been an increase in awareness-raising of declining stocks and the impact of illegal fishing among the general population (Jacquet and Pauly, 2007, p. 8). However, there has been limited effort to measure the effectiveness of the awareness-raising campaigns (Jacquet and Pauly, 2007, p. 10).

Criminals embroiled in illegal fishing are highly motivated and well-connected (Gulbrandsen, 2009, p. 654; Telesetsky, 2014, p. 939). This combination allows them to not only fish outside regions where they are licensed to do so, but also to clear port and seamlessly on-sell fish to legal markets. Syndicates using this successful business model contribute to the statistic that approximately 20 per cent of fish consumed globally is caught illegally (Urbina, 2016). Greater insight into how these criminals operate, and ways in which their activities can be limited, is the focus of this chapter. This is done by critically exploring the nature and extent of illegal fishing in the Indo-Pacific and measures to control it are explained through Routine Activity Theory. While the existing illegal fishing regulatory regime is extensive, it lacks effectiveness. This chapter considers how motivated offenders, the vulnerability of the targets and the (in)adequacy of guardianship contributes to ongoing offending. This analysis will draw out the underlying causes and enablers. By understanding the issue through this analytical assessment of the problem, it is possible to help law enforcers, regulators, policymakers and industry to determine a more appropriate response. This chapter further explores the concept of super controllers and their role in providing large-scale, long-term control of illegal fishing. Super controllers exert direct or indirect influence or create incentives to prevent crime (Sampson and Eck, 2008, p. 8; Townsley et al., 2016, p. 537). The role of the consumer is discussed in this context. Consumers may be unaware of the nature and extent of illegal fishing, but their purchasing power is an effective means of addressing the demand for overfished species and reducing supply. Consumers, and indeed other members of the public, can place political pressure on governments to increase regulatory control over the fishing industry to make sustainability policies effective and to ensure marine and fish conservation is a paramount consideration.

7.2 Nature and extent of illegal fishing in the Indo-Pacific

The bounds of the Indo-Pacific region extend from 'South Africa up to the Red Sea, east through Indonesia and Australia to Hawaii and the South Pacific Islands, all the way to Easter Island' (Helfman et al., 1997, p. 331). Significantly, it contains about one-third of the species of shallow marine fish, about 3,000 species, compared to no more than 1,200 in any other region (Helfman et al., 1997, p. 331). Seafaring, fishing and maritime piracy are old practices linked to all regions and cultures historically and in modern times (Puchala, 2005). Unscrupulous criminals seek out opportunity to profit through fishing illegally by targeting vulnerable and unprotected regions. Illegal, unregulated and unreported (IUU) fishing has grown in significance in recent years. IUU fishing is made up of three separate concepts, defined in the United Nations Food and Agricultural Organization (FAO) *International Plan of Action to Prevent, Deter and Eliminate Illegal, Unreported and Unregulated Fishing* (IPOA-IUU), adopted in Rome in 2001 (United Nations Food and Agricultural Organization, 2001). IUU fishing is a broad catchall concept for a variety of (mostly) illicit fishing activities. It violates international, regional and local fishing laws and regulations in order to yield the greatest catch. Fish are wild and belong to no specific nation, however, every littoral State has the right to fish in their territory or license others to do so (UNCLOS, 1982, Article 116). IUU fishing may involve stretching the parameters of the licence or agreement or blatantly disregard the rules in place. IUU fishing is a multifaceted problem, crossing environmental, legal, economic, criminological and political disciplines; therefore, addressing it through a multidisciplinary approach is logical and appropriate. This chapter addresses only the illegal aspect of the collective IUU fishing definition.

Each year, approximately 15–20 per cent of global fisheries are caught illegally (United Nations Food and Agricultural Organization, 2016, p. iii; Urbina, 2016). Vulnerable fish stocks are at serious risk of endangerment and potential depletion. Further worsening the issue, evidence has emerged of the link between organised crime and illegal fisheries, including the use of forced labour. The scale and organisation of these enterprises demand horizontal (regional) and vertical (international community) responses to address it, combining measures against illegal fishing and transnational organised crime (Lindley and Techera, 2017; Telesetsky, 2014, p. 939). Without a holistic approach, the likelihood of responses having real impact is limited.

Illegal fishing is enabled by a number of factors, in particular, corruption and lax regulatory enforcement at several points along the supply chain. Most commonly, vessels are registered in States with little or no regulatory controls and/or weak governance: flags of convenience. The use of transhipment (mixing illegal with legal catches at sea), ports of convenience and tax havens all contribute to illegal fishing (Martini, 2013, p. 3). Each of these methods intends to disregard or in some way evade controls in place to protect marine life, promote fair market share and provide the relevant State with its due revenues.

Unlike many other crimes committed by individual criminals, or even organised gangs of criminals, illegal fishing is frequently systemic, occurring at an industry-wide level by highly organised syndicates. It requires multilayered organisation across jurisdictions at ports, markets, vessel owners and flag States. It is unlikely that all levels of vessel ownership, flagging and crew are unaware of the intention to carry out illegal fishing, though it is possible. Official illegal fishing vessel and organisational blacklists published by Regional Fisheries Management Organisations (RFMOs), among others, purport to identify problem vessels and companies, but given the propensity of rebranded phantom vessels to emerge, it is unclear whether the blacklists have any real effect. The quality of the blacklists varies between RFMOs, and in fact, the level of detail reported is unlikely to lead to any recognition of a banned vessel (see, for example, the Indian Ocean Tuna Commission, 2017). The Indo-Pacific is not alone in facing illegal fishing, however, the combination of vast oceans, weak governance operating in littoral States, limited regional enforcement and the existence of abundant (though declining) high-value fish stocks such as tuna, makes the region a target for illicit activity.

7.3 Routine Activity Theory to explain illegal fishing

Lawrence Cohen and Marcus Felson developed Routine Activity Theory to explain assumptions of crime (Cohen and Felson, 1979). This theory states that crime occurs due to the convergence of three elements: the presence of motivated offenders; access to suitable targets and the absence of capable guardians (Cohen and Felson, 1979). Routine Activity Theory can be applied to various crime settings, providing justification for its inclusion and longevity within mainstream crime prevention applications (for example, Somali piracy, Lindley, 2016; online youth victimisation, Marcum et al., 2010; street robbery Groff, 2007; cybercrime, Yar, 2005; property and personal crime, Rotton and Cohn, 2003). Routine Activity Theory commonly explains offences committed by individuals, but as this chapter shows, can also be used to explain the motivations of illegal fishing occurring at the gang, syndicate or company level. The following sections explore the elements of Routine Activity Theory in the illegal fishing context.

7.3.1 Motivated offenders

To explain illegal fishing using Routine Activity Theory, reliance is placed on the existence of motivated offenders. A 2002 Australian Government report identified three types of illegal fishers: the habitual or repeat offenders; the opportunists and the ignorant (Victorian Parliament Environment and Natural Resources Committee, 2002, p. 244). While the majority of illegal fishers are organised criminals, some 'ignorant' or non-organised 'opportunist' illegal fishers disregard the law to yield a greater catch by taking advantage of absent regulation of the commercial fishing industry and poor law enforcement. Organised criminals engage in opportunities to profit in low risk, high return ventures and therefore are likely to be more damaging to human and food security than ignorant or opportunist fishers (United Nations Office on Drugs and Crime, 2011). Illegal fishing provides opportunity for organised offending through various paths. Organised criminal hierarchies use lower-level criminals to conduct the offences rather than the criminal leaders. Oftentimes, but dependent on the size and level of organisation of the group, illegal fishing may be one of many illicit activities run by a syndicate (United Nations Office on Drugs and Crime, 2011).

Illegal fishing relies on corrupt officials at borders to facilitate the entry of black or grey market fish into the legitimate market (Sundström, 2013; Tsamenyi and Hanich, 2008, p. 9). These same officials may also enable border crossings of drugs, weapons, undocumented people (who may be destined for working aboard illegal fishing vessels) and other contraband. Effective port regulation is essential to prevent illegal catches entering the marketplace and being onsold to consumers. Illegal fishers evade effective port regulation by concealing their illegitimate catches before entering port through transhipment, mixing illegitimate with legitimate catches, making it virtually impossible to tell one product from the other (Martini, 2013). Those responsible for providing foreign vessels access to territorial fishing grounds, distributing fishing licences and vessel registrations have been found to be vulnerable to corruption, particularly in developing States (United Nations Office on Drugs and Crime, 2011, p. 4). Limited, ineffective and corrupt border control directly and indirectly facilitates the illegal fishing problem. While it is understood that these criminals are highly organised, the criminal organisational structure that facilitates their nimble responses to proactive policing is not well understood (see, for example, Benson and Decker, 2010; Telesetsky, 2014; Walton and Dinnen, 2016) and are key research questions for future research.

Dishonesty is an essential part of the illegal fishing business. Flagrant disregard for rules occurs at the highest level of industry whereby fleet owners under-report vessel tonnage, fleet size and areas of operation (Pauly, 2009, p. 215; Telesetsky, 2014, p. 939). These vessel details are used to not only calculate applicable fees (i.e. smaller boats pay less) but also determine allowable catch sizes, regardless of any intention to comply with those limits, therefore undermining the international regulatory regimes in place to ensure equitable access among all vying for their market share (International Maritime Organization, 1982). Distorting actual catch sizes to reduce fees payable financially affects the licensing State and unfairly depletes the marine environment. Some fishing companies may conduct large-scale illegal fishing operations. In these instances, they may avoid criminal interception and State responsibility by failing to fly a flag or flag-hopping between States (Balton, 2004, pp. 3–5; United Nations Office on Drugs and Crime, 2011, pp. 104–105). An un-flagged vessel is therefore not the responsibility of any one State and avoids being reprimanded for any wrongdoing (Rosen, 2016). Criminals engaged in illegal fishing seek to meet the demand of consumers while the benefit outweighs the environmental cost. If the consumer demand remains, the criminals' motivation is unlikely to waver.

7.3.2 *Suitable targets*

In engaging in illegal fishing, criminals either target specific fish stocks or particular fishing jurisdictions. In situations when fish stocks are the targets, they are not necessarily preyed upon in all regions. The following sections briefly explore both fish species and States' maritime areas as potential targets for illegal fishing.

7.3.2.1 Fish as targets

Increased demand and limited supply of certain fish may lead some fishers into illegal fishing practices, particularly to gain greater potential for profits. In some instances, a well-intentioned fisher may operate beyond his or her licence. As fish are unaware of jurisdictional borders, they may journey across a boundary and therefore be captured illegally, for example, in a region where a vessel has no authority to fish. The *freedom of the seas* doctrine implies that the high seas are accessible to all States and sovereignty cannot be claimed (United Nations, 1982, Article 87(1)). This results in poor policing. It is most likely that these fishers do not individually cause global detriment to fishing stocks due to their small-scale illegal fishing. As noted in the previous section, these illegal fishers are most likely to be ignorant or opportunists seeking to take advantage of poor regulatory control. While this may be true for artisanal and subsistence fishers, some fishers seek out certain fish stocks due to their high value. This is the case for shark fin, abalone, seahorse and Patagonian toothfish (Anderson and McCusker, 2005, p. 1; Grilly et al., 2015). International standards to prevent illegal fish entering international markets seek to enforce control over fishers involved in the complex supply chains (Grilly et al., 2015). Supply of high-value fish is demand driven; therefore, involving the consumer may affect markets and prevent illegal fishing of certain species. Fishers seeking the greatest potential financial yield offend with disregard for environmental and legal obstacles. Abundant fish stocks can be decimated through unsustainable fishing practices, in turn increasing prices and therefore earnings by criminal syndicates. Highly financially motivated illegal fishers may intentionally overfish a specific species to drive up prices and reduce supply, increasing their profits. While consideration of short selling stock is beyond the scope of this work, it may be worthwhile to consider the global impact on supply and demand.

7.3.2.2 Regions as targets

As noted previously, fish are wild and do not belong to any one State. Their migratory patterns may enable some States to fish certain species in their territorial waters to a greater extent than others. Legal licences allow fishing, however, actions become illegal when fishing beyond the agreed quota occurs (overfishing) or fishing species outside the licence conditions are caught. The effectiveness of the international community's framework for control is only as effective as the State's willingness to enforce it.

Reviewing the literature, it appears that the criminals' motivation to target a particular region is more to do with lax law enforcement and port controls rather than more extreme political motivations that would be associated with terrorism (see, for example, Lindley, 2016; Telesetsky, 2014; United Nations Office on Drugs and Crime, 2011; Walton and Dinnen, 2016). Apart from the lax regulatory controls, some regions may be targeted more than others due to access to the region, vastness of territorial waters, favourable fishing conditions and abundance of fish stocks. As an example, Somalia experienced detrimental illegal foreign fishing in the 1990s. Somalia was deemed a suitable target, having more than 3,000 kilometres of coastline, coupled with weak governance, systemic corruption and lax (in some areas non-existent) law enforcement. Furthermore, warlords issued fake fishing licences to foreign fishers, meaning that any foreign fishing in Somali waters amounted to illegal fishing. Overfishing and highly destructive fishing practices depleted stocks, leaving local fishers unable to support their industry. In response, local fishers retaliated by threatening offending vessels with extreme violence and demanding payments (taxes) to fish within Somali territorial waters (Lindley, 2016). This effective 'business model' quickly escalated into piracy involving local organised criminals, dissimilar to piracy experiences in any region previously (Lindley, 2016). Threatened by poverty and lost earning potential, this example highlights the plight local fishers face when fishing stocks are depleted.

Risks associated with various States based on the level of actual or perceived control of the exclusive economic zone (EEZ) may influence the likelihood of offending. Vulnerable countries with limited law enforcement and catch oversight within their EEZs are more likely to be targeted due to their perceived laxness. The international community developed RFMOs to take responsibility for the control and management of sustainable fishing practices within a particular region. There are approximately 17 RFMOs, five of which are dedicated to sustainable tuna fishing practices alone. Members can join according to vested interests in the region, such as ownership over territories located in the relevant region (Organisation for Economic Co-operation and Development, 2014, para. 29). While the role of RFMOs in protecting against illegal fishing is clear, their ability to operationalise oversight may be fraught with complications.

7.3.3 Capable guardianship

Both fish species and regions are exposed as suitable targets of illegal fishing in the Indo-Pacific. Capable guardians to control illegal fishing are critical to protect and prevent further environmental harm in the Indo-Pacific. Guardians of illegal fishing can be viewed in two ways: legal instruments and enforcers. This section briefly reviews both in the context of illegal fishing to better understand the extent of capable guardianship.

7.3.3.1 Legal instruments

Under the UN Convention on the Law of the Sea (UNCLOS), States have legal and enforcement jurisdiction within their territorial waters. As illegal fishing is a transnational crime, this section explores only overarching international law. Local laws should be drafted in accordance with international rules by which States are bound to meet obligations and avoid fragmentation. International law provides the legal landscape to guide and implement control over fisheries activities. The legal frameworks for controlling fishing, maritime security, criminal and labour issues are disparate with rules and regulations contained in a number of international and regional instruments, as discussed below. This results in a patchwork of responses driven by different organisations and their various mandates.

UNCLOS is the overarching legal 'constitution for the oceans', setting out maritime zones and the rights that States have within them. It establishes obligations to protect and preserve the marine environment (UN, 1982). UNCLOS broadly guides States to establish collaborative and/or regional approaches, either directly or through international organisations for straddling stocks and highly migratory species (United Nations, 1982, Articles 63 and 64). Further, the 1995 Fish Stocks Agreement supplements UNCLOS on highly migratory species on the high seas (United Nations, 1995). RFMOs represent member States with fishing interests based either on geographic location or on the fishing activities of their nationals. Their binding regulations cover some of the most valuable fishing regions in the world. In response to illegal fishing, several RFMOs collect and share basic information on illegal fishing vessels and provide rules for inspections and enforcement (Food and Agriculture Organization of the United Nations, 2001; Trygg Mat Tracking, n.d.). The lack of uniformity between RFMO conservation management measures impedes responses to fishery crimes, in addition to the States' failure to impose penalties on wrongdoers.

The FAO has an important role in eliminating hunger and food insecurity. Part of its mandate is to ensure sustainable management and use of marine living resources, instrumental in addressing illegal fishing. The FAO established the Code of Conduct for Responsible Fisheries, which sets out general measures for sustainable fisheries development (Food and Agriculture Organization of the United Nations, 1995). The FAO International Plan of Action on IUU Fishing (IPOA-IUU) is another relevant soft law instrument (Food and Agriculture Organization of the United Nations, 1995). The IPOA-IUU supports conservation of stocks and sustainable development of fisheries by providing States with a framework to implement domestic responses (Food and Agriculture Organization of the United Nations, 1995). With regard to issues analysed in this research, the IPOA-IUU requires flag States to ensure vessels are authorised to fish in waters beyond their jurisdiction, via a license or otherwise, but does not specifically address living and working conditions on board vessels. The FAO Agreement on Port State Measures to Prevent, Deter and Eliminate Illegal, Unreported and Unregulated Fishing is the first legally binding international treaty that specifically focuses on IUU fishing (Hagan, 2014; Food and Agriculture Organization of the United Nations, 2016a).

While RFMO regulations largely focus on coastal and flag States, the Port State Measures Agreement centres on the point at which fish are landed. Importantly, authorities have power to deny landings and refuse permission to dock if they suspect illegal fishing (Food and Agriculture Organization of the United Nations, 2009, Article 9, paragraph 4). The Agreement establishes standards to ensure compliance with conservation and fisheries regulations, harmonise port State measures, enhance regional and international cooperation and block the flow of illegally-caught fish into national and international markets (Food and Agriculture Organization of the United Nations, 2009, Article 9, paragraph 4). As this instrument entered into force in June 2016 (Food and Agriculture Organization of the United Nations, 2016a, 2016b), its full effect has yet to be felt. Importantly for the Indo-Pacific, Thailand, Indonesia and several Pacific Island States are parties to the Agreement (Food and Agriculture Organization of the United Nations, 2016b). Significantly, the IPOA-IUU does not address fisheries crime and neither do most of the measures adopted by RFMOs.

Extensive legal frameworks in place evolved over a number of years attempting to create safe, secure and sustainable waters (Lindley and Techera, 2017). Despite the wealth of fisheries regulation, vertical and horizontal fragmentation among legal regimes create obstacles for good oceans governance. Evidenced by the continuation of illegal fishing and the estimated losses affecting coastal nations, overwhelmingly, the success of illegal fishing outweighs the effectiveness of regulatory frameworks in place.

7.3.3.2 Enforcement

Fishing is a legitimate industry that coexists with illegal fishing. Unlike other illegal commodities, such as drugs, fish are a legal commodity and therefore it can be a challenge for regulators to police and enforce what may or may not be legitimate catches. As such, the importance of present and competent regulators to uphold adequate rules is critical. All littoral States are entitled to 12 nautical miles of territorial waters (United Nations, 1982, Article 3). Every country, whether coastal or landlocked, has the right to flag ocean-going vessels (United Nations, 1982, Article 90). With the shared environment also comes varying and oftentimes conflicting legal regimes. In practical terms, policing and monitoring within and outside territorial waters can become a logistical nightmare. These challenges are magnified when States' maritime areas are adjoining, as is commonly the case among several States throughout the Indo-Pacific.

Due to the vastness of the Indo-Pacific region, even if some amount of monitoring and control is in place, it is unlikely to be completely effective. It is the duty of the flag State to enforce jurisdiction over a flagged vessel, whether in its territorial waters or on the high seas (United Nations, 1982, Article 94). Returning the responsibility of control to the flag State may lead to some improvement, though the issue of vessels registering in States with lax regulations may challenge this requirement. Commonly, coast guards provide protection within a State's territorial waters, often supported by naval forces. For States with weak governance, scarce resources are more appropriately applied to other essential services such as education and healthcare. As such, foreign fishing vessels may be provided the opportunity to offend without fear of interception. To resolve the resultant loopholes in border control, cooperative agreements seek to close the gap on offending opportunities, such as ship rider agreements (Hurndell, 2014). In order for such agreements to be available and work effectively, political will to engage in an agreement among all States involved is essential. In addition, to enable an agreement it must be feasible, logistically and geographically, through all seasons. Oftentimes, a lack of cohesion between neighbouring territories amplifies pre-existing policing issues in the maritime space. The importance of effective RFMOs should overcome these neighbourly conflicts; however, enforcement of these rules is critical.

For many States, policing the EEZ is already a challenge, so the high seas present an even greater hurdle as all nations are equally responsible for managing their own nationals and vessels within these vast regions. RFMOs are charged with the responsibility to oversee fishing activities of that region for their member States. The role varies between regions but can extend to identifying and policing the movement of known illegal fishing vessels. Member States must perform collaborative policing activities within the RFMO, as RFMOs do not generally perform surveillance. Lax monitoring and enforcement by RFMOs, governments and industry enable illegal fishing. Collaboratively monitoring and enforcing regulation in regions reduces fragmentation and delivers a mutually beneficial outcome. Bi- and multilateral agreements for monitoring and enforcement depend on political will and agreed outcomes. Australia and Indonesia jointly collaborate to control illegal fishing within the narrow region between the two States (Australian Fisheries Management Authority, 2016). The collaboration involves both Australian and Indonesian patrol vessels and personnel (Australian Fisheries Management Authority, 2016). By pooling resources, the net effect improves for both States. This arrangement achieves a positive outcome as the political will aligns. Some States fail to agree on the perceived detrimental impact of illegal fishing exposure or may be unable to contribute resources equally. Failure to align motivations and intended outcomes will surely result in legal fragmentation.

Ship rider agreements are collaborative arrangements though require heavy reliance on one State to carry out the patrol effort. Ship rider agreements are solutions-focused regional interventions that make use of existing resources in order to benefit all involved stakeholders. These agreements allow an enforcement officer of one State to ride on the vessel of another foreign State, extending the surveillance capability of the local state. The United States (US) has ship rider agreements with several Pacific Islands, due to its interest in protecting against crimes penetrating its western border. Through ship rider agreements with the Cook Islands, Kiribati, the Federated States of Micronesia (FSM), the Marshall Islands, Nauru, Palau, Samoa, Tonga and Tuvalu, the US Coast Guard bridges the capacity and capability gap by providing patrols (United States Department of State, 2011). Ship rider operations typically occur when US Coast Guard vessels patrol US waters, amounting to approximately 70 days of Pacific patrolling annually (Hurndell, 2014; United States Department of State, 2011). Enhanced US Coast Guard ship rider agreements negotiated with Palau and FSM enables the US to enforce local laws without local authorities being aboard the vessel (Hurndell, 2014). Expanding enhanced bi- and multilateral ship rider agreements with other Pacific Islands would introduce a layer of regulatory control otherwise absent to protect against illegal fishing and other maritime crimes. Political will is possibly the biggest issue challenging effective policing. Most States are a party to the essential international instruments and have legal frameworks in place. The ability to implement in an effective manner consistently appears to be the largest obstacle.

Sanctions are a common method of general and specific criminal deterrence. If severe, swift and certain, the sanction should achieve specific deterrence (DiIulio, 2010). Theorists believe that rational actors will desist from offending if the sanctions outweigh the potential gain from the criminal act; but this in turn depends upon surveillance and enforcement efforts, and the sanctions being applied (DiIulio, 2010). Conceptually, sanctions imposed should discourage the specific fisher, company or flag State from reoffending. Punishment of specific offenders also achieves a general deterrence effect amongst those not yet participating in those activities or discourages those also engaging in that criminal activity (DiIulio, 2010).

The European Union (EU) has a tough stance on illegal fishing. In 2010, an EU regulation entered into force to make accountable and even blacklist States that fail to enforce rules against illegal fishing (European Union, n.d.). As one of the largest importers of seafood, the EU puts pressure on States to comply. The EU issues sanctions banning non-complying States from exporting to its members, though reversible if the blacklisted States improve their practices. The EU has ceased trade with Belize, Guinea, Cambodia and Sri Lanka. Thailand is on notice to put in place greater measures to combat illegal fishing (International Centre on Trade and Sustainable Development, 2015). The EU's visible sanctions serve as a warning to other wrongdoing States and have a general deterrent effect on all States that implicitly or explicitly support illegal fishing.

While the lack of effective monitoring is an issue in and of itself, if authorities capably intercept and prosecute offenders, the sanctions must have future deterrent effects. Globally, there is criticism of the low financial impact of fines for illegal fishing and their consequent failure to have specific or general deterrent effects on illegal fishers at a personal or company level. To be effective, criminal sanctions must significantly outweigh the potential benefit; otherwise, offenders will continue to offend. In many cases, however, fines are adapted to the company/fishers ability to pay (Martini, 2013, p. 3). Oftentimes, the fishers, who themselves often work in very poor conditions and receive very low salaries, are the ones arrested and forced to pay the fines. In such situations, these sanctions have limited, if any effect, on the highest level of the criminal organisation. Several issues impede the effectiveness of fisheries sanctions, most of which relate back to the size of the Indo-Pacific region and the inability to effectively police wrongdoers.

As noted in this section, effective policing of illegal fishing presents several challenges and while guardianship exists, it lacks effectiveness. Extensive international law and regulations are aimed at fisheries and RFMOs to prevent illegal fishing by protecting suitable targets, both regions and species. Lacking capable guardianship and having suitable targets invites motivated offenders. Illegal fishers are unlikely to waver unless it becomes less profitable or too physically challenging, that is, effort exceeds potential yield. While law enforcement efforts can be enhanced to decrease the motivation among offenders, reduce suitable targets and increase capable guardianship, they require large-scale, long-term and coordinated efforts. Interim solutions can bridge the gap through non-traditional regulators, as explored in the following section.

7.4 Consumers as super controllers

Critically exploring illegal fishing in the Indo-Pacific against the elements of Routine Activity Theory shows that coordinated regional responses require strengthening to increase capable guardianship. Illegal fishers are motivated to meet the demand, therefore, informing consumers about seafood sourcing may influence purchasing, which in turn forces governments to better regulate to ensure sustainable fisheries are supplied to market. This may be an influential method of decreasing suitable targets and reducing motivation among offenders. Routine Activity Theory does not provide a full explanation of why the controllers may be absent or ineffective (Sampson et al., 2010, p. 37). Eck's extension of the Routine Activity Theory triangle includes handlers of the offenders, guardians of the target and managers of the place (Eck, 2003, p. 89). Super controllers overlay the handlers, guardians and managers and exert indirect influence on a problem (Sampson and Eck, 2008, p. 8). Super controllers are institutions, organisations and people that can provide incentives to controllers to act in ways that prevent crime (Sampson and Eck, 2008, p. 9). The premise of the super controller concept is that crime is multilayered and therefore there are many ways to reduce crime by exerting influence over offenders (Sampson and Eck, 2008, p. 33). Exploring consumers as super controllers of illegal fishing can provide an innovative and otherwise absent layer of governance that seeks to prevent the convergence of the three elements of the Routine Activity Theory triangle, resulting in illegal fishing. Consumers' purchasing practices affect all three elements by extension; without the demand, there need not be any supply. The super controller concept confirms that there are multiple ways to reduce crime (Sampson and Eck, 2008, p. 33).

Consumers should fully engage in decisions about food security. Most consumers would be unaware of the complexities governing and the irregularities surrounding their fish dinner. Purchasing power is an effective way to send a message to industry and government, conveying greater consumer expectations for regulatory control (Lindley, 2019, p. 416). In its 2016 annual report, the Marine Stewardship Council (MSC) reported 286 certified fisheries in 36 countries (Marine Stewardship Council, 2016). Only 10 per cent of certified fisheries harvest wild caught fish (Marine Stewardship Council, 2016). While this is positive, it is not representative of the fishing fleets operating on oceans. As such, most ocean fisheries are uncertified and therefore could also be illegal, in part or in whole. These facts reaffirm the need for clear and unfragmented regulatory controls supported and upheld by States that have the political will to preserve the fish stocks through sustainable practices. These controls must apply to fish harvesting, on-selling and delivering the fish to the consumer.

Some regions and States have very strong and clear regulations on fresh and cooked seafood labelling requirements. The EU requires vendors to label all seafood, fresh and cooked, with mandatory requirements including the accurate species name, production method, catch location and method of fishing used (European Union, 2014, p. 3). In the context of the Indo-Pacific, Australia is an island nation with one of the largest EEZs and approximately 80 per cent of its population living coastally, yet, it lacks progressive regulation on seafood labelling, i.e. analogous to that in the EU (Cechet et al., 2011). Despite a federal requirement to identify the source of seafood available for purchase in supermarkets and fishmongers, it is unreasonable to expect the consumers to question whether criminal activities were involved at any point in the process, for example, in terms of the location of catch and gear and equipment used. Furthermore, there is no requirement in Australia for restaurants and other food services to disclose the source (or accurate variety) of seafood on the menu once cooked.

Seafood imported from developing States may have been caught in polluted waters, containing banned antibiotics and mercury, details which the consumer need not be informed of due to limited labelling requirements (Hasham, 2015). Evidence submitted to a Federal Senate inquiry on seafood showed more than 75 per cent of seafood consumed by Australians is imported, despite 70 per cent of Australians preferring to purchase local seafood (Commonwealth of Australia Senate, Rural and Regional Affairs and Transport References Committee, 2014, paras. 1.7 and 1.8). However, 'Australian seafood is constrained by affordability, with two-thirds of Australian consumers already unable to afford fresh local seafood regularly' (Restaurant and Catering Australia, 2015, p. 4). Australian seafood consumption is trending upwards (Commonwealth of Australia and Fisheries Research and Development Corporation for the Strategy Working Group, 2010, p. 18); increased demand and limited labelling requirements provides illegal fishers opportunity. As such, government should actively ensure seafood sold at any retailer is clean, fair and legal. In 2015, the Federal Parliament voted down the Food Standards Amendment (Fish Labelling) Bill in Parliament (Parliament of Australia, 2015). The Bill sought to require food services to label cooked and pre-prepared seafood served in their businesses (Parliament of Australia, 2015). Through purchasing power, consumers have a role in influencing government to improve regulatory requirements placed on the fisheries industry to benefit consumers, reduce opportunity for illegal activities and help create a sustainable marine environment. Further research is needed to extensively explore the role of the MSC and other bodies on purchasing power through labelling, looping back to the effect on the supply of illegal fish.

7.5 Conclusion

The purpose of this chapter was to analyse illegal fishing by viewing it through a theoretical lens allowing a clearer understanding of the gaps exposing the Indo-Pacific to continued illegal fishing. Reframing the problem of illegal fishing allows looking at its causes to find more appropriate controls. Using Routine Activity Theory to better understand illegal fishing exposes what motivates offenders, who the suitable targets are and discusses the capability of guardians.

Existing responses to illegal fishing impose restrictions on acceptable practices through legal frameworks. Fragmented and lacking global policing to adequately enforce and sanction wrongdoers, the frameworks fail to achieve set goals. Focusing instead on what motivates offenders and how they are enabled by others, such as border and port control officials, facilitates targeted enforcement. Similarly, understanding the targets, both species and regions, clarifies why criminals choose them.

Through Routine Activity Theory, this research uncovered that while adequate regulation exists, greater effort is needed beyond the existing regimes to bring about change. In this context, there is a role for the consumer as the super controller. Informing consumers about what creates a suitable target can be integral in applying government pressure for changes in regulation and through purchasing power, affecting the demand. Articulating the lack of capable guardians of illegal fishing and identifying improved methods for control can lead to a stronger and allied approach. From this research, it can be seen that while the legal regimes in place are in fact sound, the failure to integrate a broader range of issues – such as measures to demotivate offenders, the role of the consumer in reducing suitable targets and methods to bolster control using existing frameworks – causes reduced effectiveness.

All URLs correct as at 4 October 2018.

References

Agnew, D.J., Pearce, J., Pramod, G., Peatman, T., Watson, R., Beddington, J.R., Pitcher, T.J. (2009) 'Estimating the Worldwide Extent of Illegal Fishing' *PLOS ONE* 4(2) p. e4570. www.plosone.org/article/info:doi/10.1371/journal.pone.0004570.

Australian Fisheries Management Authority (2016) 'Joint Australia/Indonesia Illegal Fishing Patrol a Success', Media Release 23 August 2016. www.afma.gov.au/joint-australiaindonesia-illegal-fishing-patrol-success/?utm_source=feedburner&utm_medium=feed&utm_campaign=Feed%3A+AustralianFisheriesManagementAuthority+%28Australian+Fisheries+Management+Authority%29.

Balton, D. (2004) 'IUU Fishing and State Control over Nationals' AGR/FI/IUU/RD(2004)2, submitted as a background paper for the IUU Fishing Workshop, 19–20 April 2004, www.oecd.org/greengrowth/fisheries/31426742.PDF.

Benson, J.S., Decker, S.H. (2010) 'The Organizational Structure of International Drug Smuggling' *Journal of Criminal Justice* 38(2) pp. 130–138.

Cechet, B., Taylor, P., Griffin, C., Hazelwood, M. (2011) 'Australia's Coastline: Adapting to Climate Change', *AusGeo News* March 2011 Issue No. 101. Canberra: Geoscience Australia. www.ga.gov.au/ausgeonews/ausgeonews201103/climate.jsp.

Cohen, L.E., Felson, M. (1979) 'Social Change and Crime Rate Trends: A Routine Activity Approach' *American Sociological Review* 44(4) pp. 588–605.

Commonwealth of Australia, Fisheries Research and Development Corporation for the Strategy Working Group (2010) *'Working Together: The National Fishing and Aquaculture RD&E Strategy 2010. A Component of the National Primary Industries Research, Development and Extension Framework'* Canberra. www.frdc.com.au/-/media/Fish-FRDC/Corporate-documents/RDE-plan/National-RDE-Strategy-for-Fishing-and-Aquaculture-2010.ashx?la=en.

Commonwealth of Australia Senate, Rural and Regional Affairs and Transport References Committee (2014), *'Current Requirements for Labelling of Seafood and Seafood Products'*. Canberra: Senate Standing Committees on Rural and Regional Affairs and Transport..

DiIulio, J.J. Jr. (2010) *'Deterrence Theory'*, pp. 233–236. https://marisluste.files.wordpress.com/2010/11/deterrence-theory.pdf.

Eck, J. (2003) 'Police Problems: The Complexity of Problem Theory, Research and Evaluation' *Crime Prevention Studies* 15, www.popcenter.org/library/crimeprevention/volume_15/04eck_problem_theory.pdf.

European Union (n.d.) *'Fisheries – IUU Fishing: The EU Rules to Combat Illegal, Unreported and Unregulated Fishing'*, http://ec.europa.eu/fisheries/cfp/illegal_fishing/index_en.htm.

European Union (2014) *'A Pocket Guide to the EU's New Fish and Aquaculture Consumer Labels'*, Luxembourg: Publications Office of the European Union. https://ec.europa.eu/fisheries/sites/fisheries/files/docs/body/eu-new-fish-and-aquaculture-consumer-labels-pocket-guide_en.pdf.

Food and Agriculture Organization of the United Nations (1995) *'Code of Conduct for Responsible Fisheries'*, www.fao.org/3/a-v9878e.htm.

Food and Agriculture Organization of the United Nations (2001) *'International Plan of Action to Prevent, Deter and Eliminate Illegal, Unreported and Unregulated Fishing'*, Rome. www.fao.org/docrep/003/y1224e/y1224e00.htm.

Food and Agriculture Organization of the United Nations (2009) *'Agreement on Port State Measures to Prevent, Deter and Eliminate Illegal, Unreported and Unregulated Fishing, 2009'*, www.fao.org/3/a-i5469t.pdf.

Food and Agriculture Organization of the United Nations (2016a) *'Port State Measures Agreement'*, www.fao.org/fishery/psm/agreement/en.

Food and Agriculture Organization of the United Nations (2016b) *'Agreement on Port State Measures to Prevent, Deter and Eliminate Illegal, Unreported and Unregulated Fishing – Signatories'*, www.fao.org/fileadmin/user_upload/legal/docs/037s-e.pdf.

Grilly, E., Reid, K., Lenel, S., Jabour, J. (2015) 'The Price of Fish: A Global Trade Analysis of Patagonian (*Dissostichus eleginoides*) and Antarctic Toothfish (*Dissostichus mawsoni*)' *Marine Policy* 60 pp. 186–196.

Groff, E.R. (2007) 'Simulation for Theory Testing and Experimentation: An Example Using Routine Activity Theory and Street Robbery' *Journal of Quantitative Criminology* 23(2) pp. 75–103. doi:10.1007/s10940-006-9021-z.

Gulbrandsen, L.H. (2009) 'The Emergence and Effectiveness of the Marine Stewardship Council' *Marine Policy* 33(4) pp. 654–660.

Hagan, S.A. (2014) 'Too Big to Tackle? The Persistent Problem of Pirate Fishing and the New Focus on Port State Measures' *Suffolk Transnational Law Review* 37(1) p. 109.

Hasham, N. (2015) 'Australian Consumers Kept in the Dark about Seafood Origins' *The Sydney Morning Herald*, 29 August 2015, www.smh.com.au/federal-politics/political-news/consumers-kept-in-the-dark-on-seafood-origins-after-senate-vote-20150827-gj9nbj.html.

Helfman, G.S., Collette, B.B., Facey, D.E., Bowen, B.W. (1997) '*The Diversity of Fishes*', Chichester: Wiley-Blackwell Publishing.

Hurndell, J. (2014) 'The Value of Ship Rider Agreements in the Pacific', *Center for Strategic and International Studies*, 10 December 2014, http://cogitasia.com/the-value-of-ship-rider-agreements-in-the-pacific/.

Indian Ocean Tuna Commission (2017) *'Compliance: List of IUU Vessels'*, www.iotc.org/vessels#iuu.

International Centre for Trade and Sustainable Development (2015) *'EU Warns Thailand on Illegal Fishing'*, 8 May 2015, www.ictsd.org/bridges-news/biores/news/eu-warns-thailand-on-illegal-fishing.

International Maritime Organization (1982) *'International Convention on Tonnage Measurement of Ships'*, 18 July 1982. www.imo.org/en/About/Conventions/ListOfConventions/Pages/International-Convention-on-Tonnage-Measurement-of-Ships.aspx.

Jacquet, J.L., Pauly, D. (2007) 'The Rise of Seafood Awareness Campaigns in an Era of Collapsing Fisheries' *Marine Policy* 31(3) pp. 308–313.

Lindley, J. (2016) '*Somali Piracy: A Criminological Perspective*'. London: Routledge Publishers.

Lindley, J. (2019) 'Sustainably Sourced Seafood: A Criminological Approach to Reduce Demand for Illegal Seafood Supply'. In: Leal Filho, W. and Consorte McCrea, A. (eds.) *Sustainability and the Humanities*, pp. 407–420. Hamburg: Springer.

Lindley, J., Techera, E.J. (2017) 'Overcoming Complexity in Illegal, Unregulated and Unreported Fishing to Achieve Effective Regulatory Pluralism' *Marine Policy* 81 pp. 71–79.

Marcum, C.D., Higgins, G.E., Ricketts, M.L. (2010) 'Potential Factors of Online Victimization of Youth: An Examination of Adolescent Online Behaviors Utilizing Routine Activity Theory' *Deviant Behavior* 31(5) pp. 381–410. doi:10.1080/01639620903004903.

Marine Stewardship Council (2016) *'From Sustainable Fishers to Seafood Lovers: Annual Report 2015–16'*, www.msc.org/docs/default-source/default-document-library/about-the-msc/msc-annual-report-2015-16-english.pdf.

Martini, M. (2013) *'Illegal, Unreported and Unregulated Fishing and Corruption', U4 Expert Answer*.

Organisation for Economic Co-operation and Development (2014) *'Fishing For Development – Background Paper For Session 5: The Role of Regional Fisheries Management Organisations (RFMOs)'*, TAD/FI(2014)11, 20 March 2014, Paris: OECD. www.oecd.org/tad/events/fishing-for-development-2014-session-5-RFMOs.pdf.

Parliament of Australia (2015) *'Food Standards Amendment (Fish Labelling) Bill 2015'*. 1 August 2015. www.aph.gov.au/Parliamentary_Business/Bills_Legislation/Bills_Search_Results/Result?bId=s1004.

Pauly, D. (2009) 'Beyond Duplicity and Ignorance in Global Fisheries' *Scientia Marina* 73(2) pp. 215–224. doi:10.3989/scimar.2009.73n2215.

Puchala, D.J. (2005) 'Of Pirates and Terrorists: What Experience and History Teach' *Contemporary Security Policy* 26(1) pp. 1–24.

Restaurant and Catering Australia (2015) 'Extending Mandatory Country of Origin Labelling to Seafood: A Perspective from the Foodservices Sector', http://rca.asn.au/rca/wp-content/uploads/2016/05/RPT_FINAL_SeafoodLabelling_2015_lowres.pdf.

Rosen, M.E. (2016) 'Challenges to Public Order and the Law of the Sea'. In: Inge Bekkevold J. and Till G. (eds.) *International Order at Sea: How It Is Challenged. How It Is Maintained*, pp. 15–38. London: Palgrave Macmillan.

Rotton, J., Cohn, E.G. (2003) 'Global Warming and U.S. Crime Rates: An Application of Routine Activity Theory' *Environment and Behavior* 35(6) pp. 802–825. doi:10.1177/0013916503255565.

Sampson, R., Eck, J.E. (2008) 'Super Controllers: Can I Be Your Superman?' 19th Annual Problem-Oriented Policing Conference, Bellevue, Washington, 22–24 September 2008. www.popcenter.org/conference/conferencepapers/2008/supercontrollers.pdf.

Sampson, R., Eck, J.E., Dunham, J. (2010) 'Super Controllers and Crime Prevention: A Routine Activity Explanation of Crime Prevention Success and Failure' *Security Journal* 23(1) pp. 37–51.

Sundström, A. (2013) 'Corruption in the Commons: Why Bribery Hampers Enforcement of Environmental Regulations in South African Fisheries' *International Journal of the Commons* 7(2) pp. 454–472.

Townsley, M., Leclerc, B., Tatham, P.H. (2016) 'How Super Controllers Prevent Crimes: Learning from Modern Maritime Piracy' *British Journal of Criminology* 56(3) pp. 537–557. doi:10.1093/bjc/azv071.

Trygg Mat Tracking (n.d.), 'Combined IUU Vessel List', http://iuu-vessels.org/iuu.

Tsamenyi, B.M., Hanich, Q.A. (2008) *'Addressing Corruption in Pacific Islands Fisheries: A Report/Prepared for IUCN PROFISH Law Enforcement, Corruption and Fisheries Project'*, http://ro.uow.edu.au/cgi/viewcontent.cgi?article=1229&context=lhapapers.

United Nations (1982) *'Convention on the Law of the Sea (UNCLOS)'*. New York: UN.

United Nations (1995) *'United Nations Agreement for the Implementation of the Provisions of the United Nations Convention on the Law of the Sea of 10 December 1982 Relating to the Conservation and Management of Straddling Fish Stocks and Highly Migratory Fish Stocks (Fish Stocks Agreement)'*, New York: UN www.un.org/depts/los/convention_agreements/convention_overview:fish_stocks.htm.

United Nations Office on Drugs and Crime (2011) '*Transnational Organized Crime in the Fishing Industry: Focus on Trafficking in Persons, Migrant Smuggling and Illicit Drugs Trafficking*', Vienna: UNODC.

United States Department of State (2011) *'US Engagement in the Pacific'*, 17 September 2011, www.state.gov/p/eap/rls/2017/267084.htm.

Urbina, I. (2016) 'Palau vs. the Poachers', *New York Times Magazine*, 17 February 2016, www.nytimes.com/2016/02/21/magazine/palau-vs-the-poachers.html?_r=0.

Victorian Parliament Environment and Natural Resources Committee (2002) '*Inquiry into Fisheries Management: Second Report*', Melbourne: Parliament of Victoria. www.parliament.vic.gov.au/images/stories/Reports/VPARL1999-2002No166.pdf.

Walton, G., Dinnen, S. (2016) 'The Dark Side of Economic Globalisation: Politics, Organised Crime and Corruption in the Pacific', *Development Policy Centre Discussion Paper 48*, October 2016, Crawford School of Public Policy, The Australian National University, pp. 1–31, papers.ssrn.com/sol3/papers.cfm?abstract_id=2848016.

Yar, M. (2005) 'The Novelty of 'Cybercrime': An Assessment in Light of Routine Activity Theory' *European Journal of Criminology* 2(4) pp. 407–427, http://journals.sagepub.com/doi/pdf/10.1177/147737080556056.

Part IV

Criminal networks and politics

8 Meet the in-betweeners

Exploring the quality and strength of ties in the 'Mafia Capitale' network in Rome

Anna Sergi

The Italian Antimafia Operation 'Mondo di Mezzo' (the World in Between) has presented the so-called 'Mafia Capitale' as a mafia-type group born and bred in Rome, with links to all major Italian criminal organisations in the capital city, but eventually autonomous and reaching into public administration and politics. A trial has established that the corruption employed by associates of Mafia Capitale, together with the entrepreneurial nature of the group, is enough to qualify the group as a mafia-type criminal association according to article 416-bis of the Italian Penal Code.

By analysing court documents, including interceptions, pre-trial documentation and courts' preliminary hearings, this chapter will look at the network of Mafia Capitale, in particular focusing on the quality of ties among the World Above (politicians), the World Below (criminals) and the in-betweeners (facilitators). A qualitative analysis will help in understanding the *modus operandi* of Mafia Capitale, their systematic use of corruption to secure access to privileged channels and the way ties have been formed and maintained in the illicit network. This study will shed light on the characteristics of a modern mafia group; this could open up new debates around organised crime groups' strategies of infiltration in the public sector, including outside of Italy.

8.1 Introduction and methods

On 2 December 2014, the District Antimafia Prosecutors in Rome revealed the findings of Operation 'Mondo di Mezzo' by arresting 38 people, among them Massimo Carminati, well known for his terrorist activities in far-right militia groups in the capital during the 1970s and 1980s. Forty-four people were arrested in June 2015 as a result of the same operation. The group led by Carminati and his associates has been named 'Mafia Capitale'. The appeal trial ended in July 2018, confirming that the group can be qualified as a mafia group under Italian law. Aside from its legal definition, Mafia Capitale has attracted a lot of attention from the media and analysts for its setting – the capital city of Rome – and because it was extremely successful and for a long time went unpunished. Politics, public administration and the business world mixed with underworld figures belonging to both far-right terrorist groups and other organised crime or mafia groups in the territory. Charges include mafia-type association, corruption, extortion, loan-sharking, money laundering and collusive tendering.

Relying on judicial information gathered in the past three years, this chapter will look at Mafia Capitale from a network perspective by assessing the nature of ties among the principal players as presented by the Antimafia through interceptions, wiretaps and witness statements. Over 2,000 pages in court documents enable a qualitative analysis of the network and represent a very rich source of data, especially as they include all participants of the network (Campana, 2011). While social network analysis (SNA), as a research method relies heavily on quantitative approaches (Carrington, 2011), a qualitative approach to SNA helps explore the content and meaning of ties, which is essential for understanding network patterns and dynamics. As noted by Edwards (2010, p. 2), 'qualitative approaches enable analysts to consider issues relating to the construction, reproduction, variability and dynamics of complex social ties'.

This chapter goes beyond the traditional literature on social network analysis, organised crime and criminal networks. This study is intended as a preliminary exploration of Mafia Capitale and an exercise of interpretative social network analysis. This study will explore the types of relationships among the main players of the Mafia Capitale network by performing a content and discourse analysis of intercepted communications as transcribed in the main judicial documents presented by the Antimafia prosecutors in Rome. As the study is based on the construction of the network as presented by the prosecutors, it might be considered biased. However, these documents present intercepted materials and in-depth investigation analysis that are surely reliable and useful for the case study. A further limit might be that a network analysis performed qualitatively might eventually be only a preliminary step into the study of this case. As noted by Walthers and Christopoulos (2015, p. 501) in their descriptive social network analysis of terrorist groups based on media sources, 'missing actors or missing links are likely to alter the centrality measures produced here, which calls for caution'. Nevertheless, as has been argued, the use of qualitative methods can be the first step for informed data collection in SNA (Coviello, 2005; Jack, 2005; Edwards, 2010).

This chapter is based on an exploration of the Mafia Capitale network as presented by the authorities in the two years following the arrests. The first section briefly describes the current state of the trial and its outcome. The second section will lay out the literature on network analysis relevant to a qualitative analysis of this group and then the following sections will provide an analysis of the case study. By applying Granovetter's (1973) theory on the strength of weak ties, this work will explore and discuss: 1) the content and quality of ties and interactions among individuals charged in the Mafia Capitale trial who were crucial for the functioning of the network in order to assess how strong ties and weak ties have shaped the network; 2) the context in which these ties have operated for Mafia Capitale's success and reputation in the capital city; and 3) the implications of these ties for a deeper understanding of the network.

8.2 Background: Mafia Capitale and its status in the law

On 5 November 2015, the trial for the Mafia Capitale case started in Rome with an ending date for preliminary hearings in July 2016. In the course of this first trial, 59 people faced trial, among whom were the leaders of the criminal group, Massimo Carminati and Salvatore Buzzi. Also charged were local politicians and entrepreneurs, including the former mayor of Rome – the *in-betweeners* who supported Mafia Capitale. The trial ended in convictions of almost all those charged, but in the first instance, the group was not recognised as a mafia-type group. However, on appeal, Mafia Capitale was recognised as a mafia-type group. The law, in article 416-bis of the Italian Penal Code, requires a certain number of 'ingredients' to 'make' a mafia group: the power of intimidation of the criminal association and the resulting conditions of submission and silence (*omertà*) to commit criminal offences, to manage or control, directly or indirectly, economic activities and concessions. The main challenge for the prosecutors in the Mafia Capitale case, therefore, was to detach the legal definition of 'mafia-type' organised crime from its commonly accepted one – evoking images of clans operating illegal businesses and able to corrupt and infiltrate all sectors of economy and society – by proving the ingredients of article 416-bis for the criminal organisation led by Massimo Carminati (Dalla Chiesa, 2015).

According to the prosecutors, Mafia Capitale is all about the so-called 'Mondo di Mezzo', the 'World in Between'. The in-betweeners are public officials, counsellors, local politicians, mediators and brokers who are close enough to figures in power (the 'World Above', the upperworld) and are likely to accept promises of a better career and/or other benefit/income through exchange of favours with figures in the 'World Below', the underworld. Mafia Capitale was not only involved in various criminal activities but, through influence over public tenders and contracts and persistent corruption of all sectors of public administration, also obtained and maintained its economic and social connections.

In Operation 'Mondo di Mezzo',[1] we read that Mafia Capitale is:

> An organisation that uses, overtly, the power of intimidation originating from the associative bonds in areas of the Capital city. (…) It is a power of intimidation that does not have a privileged physical, institutional or social territory, but that is instantly felt by anyone who experiences it.

The Antimafia prosecutors add:

> Because of its power of intimidation originating from the associative bonds and its ability to cross physical, institutional, economic, and criminal

1 Translated from Italian – Operazione Mondo di Mezzo, Ordinanza di applicazione delle misure cautelari, 28 novembre 2014, No. 30546/10 R.G. Tribunale di Roma, p. 36.

> territories, Mafia Capitale has the capacity to maintain equilibriums and create illicit synergies between very different worlds.[2]

The Court of Cassation – Italian Supreme Court – validated the view of the prosecutors in Operation 'Mondo di Mezzo' in March 2015. The Court said the power to intimidate – typical of the 'mafia method' as it enables the preservation of territorial influence and social prestige of mafia groups – can be acquired and maintained through corruption and not only through violence, as usually maintained in jurisprudence (Sergi, 2016). The Court of Cassation affirmed:

> Notwithstanding the association's ability to resort to violence, the power of intimidation can be acquired with the creation of an organisational structure. Because of its proximity to political actors, through repeated usurpations and systemic activities of corruption, this organisational structure can influence the allocation of contracts and licensing, and can control entire portions of public works and public companies, so to effectively nullify competition and frustrate any new initiative that does not obey the rules of the association.[3]

According to the Court of Cassation, therefore, the power of intimidation of Mafia Capitale does not originate from threats or violence only, but also from corruption and from the reputation of the leaders of the organisation, in both worlds, above and below.

> The same systemic corruption, on one side, has contributed to the criminal 'reputation' of the organisation. Especially among those entrepreneurs unwilling to comply with the 'rules' of the illegal market, the organisation could rely upon an aura of invincibility originating from a wide and stable supporting network made of suborned public officials. On the other side, the systemic use of corruption has been functional to foster relationships of *omertà*, consolidated through blackmail if necessary to ensure secrecy.[4]

The Mafia Capitale case is notable both for its urban setting and for Mafia Capitale's reach into the public administration of the Capital city of Rome. Its difference from traditional Italian mafias can be found, according to both the Antimafia Prosecutors and the Supreme Court, in its endemic use of corruption as the chosen method of intimidation. The use of corruption by associates and leaders of the criminal group certainly throws a new distinctive light

2 Translated from Italian – Operazione Mondo di Mezzo, Ordinanza di applicazione delle misure cautelari, 28 novembre 2014, No. 30546/10 R.G. Tribunale di Roma, p. 37.

3 Corte di Cassazione, sez. VI pen., 10th March 2015 [motivations deposited on 9th June 2015], no. 24535, Pres. Agro, Rel. De Amicis, p. 48.

4 Corte di Cassazione, sez. VI pen., 10th March 2015 [motivations deposited on 9th June 2015], no. 24535, Pres. Agro, Rel. De Amicis, p. 35.

on the importance of facilitators – the in-betweeners of the Operation 'Mondo di Mezzo'.

8.3 Relationships, ties and criminal networks

In reading the transcripts of interceptions of Operation 'Mondo di Mezzo', it appears appropriate to look at Mafia Capitale from the point of view of network analysis and the strength of ties among leaders and affiliates. In organised crime studies, network analysis has been used both for theoretical conceptualisations and as a methodology tool (Carrington, 2011). Joseph Albini (1971), in his attempt to challenge the mainstream approach to the Italian-American mafia (Albanese, 2014), maintained that organised crime groups and activities are a system of loosely structured and profit-oriented relationships. Together with Albini, other early work (Ianni and Reuss-Ianni, 1972) on the Italian-American mafia families referred to the concept of network to explain how the organisation in criminal groups works bottom-up and cannot be assumed *a priori* (Von Lampe, 2009). Eric Wolf (1966) maintained that the system of patrons and clients operating in Sicily, which contributed to the development of mafia groups, works in the same way for both legal and illegal interactions; the patron provides protection while the client offers respect, information or political support. As argued by Albini and McIllwain (2012, p. 27), this 'system of patron-client relationships forms a matrix of interactions that weaves itself through both legitimate and illegitimate sectors of Sicilian society itself'. In works that focus on the relationships among mafia members, affiliates and externals, weaknesses and strengths of the groups are often related to the groups' structures. Studies have focused on the cohesiveness of the groups, on the reach of their ties, on communication flows and certainly on the existence of hierarchies or internal agreements and specialisation of labour in the organisation of criminal activities (Morselli, 2005; Varese, 2006; Morselli, 2009; Campana, 2011).

When analysing the strength of ties in criminal networks, certain scholars have relied upon organisational, business, anthropological and sociological studies (Nohria, 1992). While there is consensus on the benefits of networks in developing business relationships, for example, there are still gaps in understanding the content of network interactions (Jack, 2005). Scholars have studied the nature and effects of interactions and the type of exchanges among individuals. Interactions and links among individuals can originate as 'friends of friends' (Boissevain, 1974), group obligations (Bourdieu, 1986) and strong and weak ties (Granovetter, 1973). As argued by Kleemans and de Poot (2008, p. 75), organised crime networks work within a social opportunity structure with 'social ties providing access to profitable criminal opportunities'. Interactions, links and ties among individuals in a network create different types of relationships which are more or less beneficial for the network's success.

As reminded by Campana (2016, p. 2), while a substantive approach to networks focuses on structures, an instrumental approach focuses 'on the presence of two constitutive sets of elements: actors (nodes) and relationships (ties)'.

Even though the relationships between these two approaches is far from settled, the study of ties and their strength is dominant in the study of networks (Jack, 2005). As famously argued by Mark Granovetter (1973, p. 1361) in his Strength of Weak Ties theory, the strength of a tie is 'a combination of the amount of time, the emotional intensity, the intimacy and the reciprocal services which characterises the tie'. Very interestingly, the difference between strong and weak ties, according to Granovetter's theory, is in their origin; strong ties are associated with homogeneous groups, while weak ties are heterogeneous. This means that the value and strength of weak ties are related to the connections to *other* social systems and groups not immediately available through strong ties (Granovetter, 1985). Weak ties allow reaching out to a broader society, while strong ties, even though they are trustworthy, rich and accurate, are often believed to offer redundant information within the same circle (Burt, 1992). Focus on and analysis of the relationships among the various entities of a network is particularly useful when we look at the *intentions* of the actors and their *relational* ties within *social* systems (Robins, 2015). Social network analysis, in this sense, looks at social relations and the way ties are formed and maintained within social systems, including criminal ones. Notwithstanding the outstanding issues and problems associated with network analysis (Campana, 2016), the study of criminal networks (qualitative or quantitative) by focusing on ties and relationships is useful because it is empirical and not *a priori*.

Significantly, when we look at network analysis, the issue of *trust* becomes quite crucial in understanding how criminal organisations employ their social capital, how ties are cemented and why certain relationships are more successful than others. Obviously, as scholars have pointed out on various occasions, because of the nature of certain crimes, trust is what substitutes for the lack of recourse to legal means to enforce agreements, as agreements operate outside the law (Carrington, 2011). Trust is essential for the functioning of the network. In fact, whether trust is pre-existing to the formation of the criminal network or develops in the course of the criminal collaboration (Von Lampe and Johansen, 2004; Kleemans and de Poot, 2008; Morselli, 2009), it is trust that shapes the reputation of the group and cements its ties when interacting with other groups, with suppliers, with customers and various others. Criminal networks – and mafias especially – succeed because of trust among members and because of reputation based on that trust among non-members (Sergi and Lavorgna, 2016).

8.4 Mafia Capitale: upperworld, underworld and in-betweeners

The criminal network known as Mafia Capitale pivots around a central figure – its 'boss' Massimo Carminati. It is beyond the scope of this chapter to present and evaluate the criminal career of Carminati, who, well known to Italian authorities, has a past with right-wing terrorism and organised crime groups in the capital city of Rome (Mazzeo, 2015). It is the opinion of the authorities, both Antimafia authorities and an Inquisitive Commission – which scrutinised offices and departments of the municipality of Rome to evaluate mafia penetration after the Antimafia carried out the arrests in 2014 – that Mafia Capitale has become a powerful network because of the specific strategy and the personality of Carminati. The idea of connecting worlds normally detached from one another is well expressed by Carminati himself during an intercepted conversation with some associates, revealing the existence and the ultimate aim of the criminal network.

> [I]t is the theory of the world in-between mate...there are...how to say...the living above and the dead below and we are in the middle (...) a world in between where everybody meets and you ask...how the hell is this possible that tomorrow I can be at dinner with Berlusconi (...) you understand...all meet, every social class. It's not a question of social class, it's about merit, right? (...) in between also the person in the upperworld has interest for someone in the underworld to do something for them that no one else would do'.[5]

As noted by the District Antimafia Prosecutors, it has always been in Carminati's nature 'to interact with different realities and to be at the same time emancipated from them and their limits, operating always in autonomous and transversal ways'.[6]

8.4.1 The underworld

Notwithstanding its links with politicians or entrepreneurs in the city of Rome, the Mafia Capitale network is born in, and cannot leave, the underworld. As confirmed by Massimo Carminati, the underworld makes the whole organisation operational, attractive and reputable among those in the upperworld. The ties in the underworld of the Mafia Capitale network are of three categories: 1) Carminati's friends and associates mainly from the years of the Banda della Magliana and the far-right armed militia, running extortion and debt collection on behalf of the network; 2) street criminals, such as robbers, who are helpful for securing control over different areas of the city; and 3) other criminal groups, including other mafia groups operating in the capital city, who are at the same time partners and competitors for the network.

Certainly, the underworld of Mafia Capitale is cast in the mould of Carminati himself. Riccardo Brugia, one of his associates, is linked to Carminati by a strong bond; the two come from the same past in the far-right militia in the city of Rome

5 Operazione Mondo di Mezzo – R.G.N.R. 30546/10 Tribunale di Roma – Ordinanza di Custodia Cautelare 13/12/2012 – Vds. pag. VI – Premessa all'informativa del ROS Reparto Anticrimine, p. 37.

6 Operazione Mondo di Mezzo – R.G.N.R. 30546/10 Tribunale di Roma – Ordinanza di Custodia Cautelare, p. 38.

during the 1970s and 1980s and have been friends since their teenage years. Their relationship has been cemented over different types of criminal activities; Brugia is the right-hand man of the boss. He shows an *affectio societatis* to the criminal network to whom he is essential and, at the same time, he accepts the primary role of Carminati as leader. As noted by one of the witnesses of the prosecution: 'they have been friends for many years and, as far as I know, what Riccardo does he always seeks Massimo's consent because, basically, Massimo is still a bit more important than he is, pretty sure of that'.[7] Brugia appears to be involved in various criminal activities, including the custody of weapons, extortion, debts collection and intimidation; he is also constantly informed about on-going relationships with the upperworld. As a representative of the underworld of the criminal network of Mafia Capitale, Brugia is also the one that handles the connections with street gangs and with other criminals in different areas of the city.

These ties are still strong as both Carminati and Brugia have historically been involved in street crimes such as robberies and vehicle thefts, for example, so these are ties formed in homogenous worlds. However, the quality of these ties is different, as they are opportunistic and linked to mutual support when needed. For example, as noted by one of the individuals arrested during the investigation, the relationship between his own clan and the network headed by Carminati was based on 'certain things to do in the Capital…for example, killing someone (…) having territorial support, receiving help in the acquisition of weapons as well as getting information if someone did not pay'.[8] This relationship is particularly interesting both when it comes to local mafia clans in the city of Rome and to clans of other mafias, such as the 'ndrangheta clans or the camorra clans well established in the capital city as well as in other parts of Italy and abroad. For example, it is very visible from both interceptions and testimonies how the relationship between Mafia Capitale and the 'ndrangheta clan Mancuso is based on mutual recognition of each group's criminal reputation, with constant exchanges both in Calabria and in Rome, through trusted intermediaries.

In terms of local mafia groups, in the city of Rome, it was essential for Mafia Capitale to establish links, for example, with the Senese clan from Naples and operating in the capital since the 1970s, through direct connections between Carminati and the Senese brothers. Also, links were established with the Casamonica clan, a clan in the south-east of Rome, the Esposito brothers, a mixed clan with links to the camorra and Albanian connections, as well as other criminal groups around the city. The relationships with these groups are more than just occasional; they are continuous and based on mutual support, mainly linked to drug provisions and protection on the clans' territories as well as business ventures. Each relationship with the various mafia-style groups in Rome is cemented through individual

7 Witness Roberto Grilli, 20 April 2012, Operazione Mondo di Mezzo – R.G.N.R. 30546/10 Tribunale di Roma – Ordinanza di Custodia Cautelare, p. 285.

8 Operazione Mondo di Mezzo – R.G.N.R. 30546/10 Tribunale di Roma – Ordinanza di Custodia Cautelare, p. 255.

connections. These are connections that either Massimo Carminati or Riccardo Brugia personally cultivated. Ernesto Diotallevi, for example, once belonging to the infamous criminal group known as the 'Banda della Magliana' with Massimo Carminati, ensured access to local gangs as well as clans close to Cosa Nostra. Similarly, Luciano Casamonica supported the network (and Salvatore Buzzi, the other *dominus*, in particular) as a mediator with a group of gypsies in an area where Mafia Capitale wanted to invest. Giovanni De Carlo, close to Carminati, Diotallevi and the Senese clan, acted as another handyman for Carminati thanks to their connection dating back to the years in the far-right militia.

Other individuals, such as Matteo Calvio and Fabio Gaudenzi, are other important nodes in the network. Talking about Calvio, one witness declares: 'He was one of the soldiers, you know, an offshoot of Riccardo [Brugia]'.[9] Calvio's role is confirmed by Calvio himself in an intercepted conversation with one of the entrepreneurs close to the network: 'I cannot say that I am a bandit (...) I certainly cannot say that I am in charge of collecting debts, what the fuck can I say?'.[10] Massimo Carminati, however, does not consider him one of the important pieces of the puzzle; not only does Calvio come from a different, middle-class world, but he is considered 'an ignorant, one of those with a stupid ignorance',[11] so that he could only be trusted with minor activities as an executioner. Different story for Fabio Gaudenzi, who comes from the same far-right militia and knows both Carminati and Brugia since the 1970s–1980s. Carminati entrusts Gaudenzi with various tasks. In an intercepted conversation, a witness notes how 'in Rome there is a hierarchy...you know...it's not like the one there [Carminati] tells Fabio [Gaudenzi] to call him and Fabio doesn't call...eh...Fabio must call'.[12]

8.4.2 The upperworld

It is recognised that the strength of Mafia Capitale is in the ability to accumulate and employ/exploit *social* capital in the underworld as well as enter into agreements with *institutional* capital – individuals in different roles in society, i.e. entrepreneurs, politicians, professionals, public officials (Dalla Chiesa, 2015; De Bonis, 2015). As Mazzeo (2015, p. 47) has already noticed, next to the 'black charisma' of Massimo Carminati, Mafia Capitale is centred around the *'red dominus'* Salvatore Buzzi. Buzzi met Carminati in prison while serving a sentence for murder. However, his background is neither in the far-right militia nor in the underworld. Buzzi is the alter ego of Carminati in the upperworld; a world he has access to because of his closeness to, and good reputation within, the political

9 Oitness Roberto GRILLI, 09.05.2012, Operazione Mondo di Mezzo – R.G.N.R. 30546/10 Tribunale di Roma – Ordinanza di Custodia Cautelare, p. 379.

10 Matteo Calvio and Cristiano Guarnera, intercepted conversation at 16:31 of 21.03.2013, Operazione Mondo di Mezzo – R.G.N.R. 30546/10 Tribunale di Roma – Ordinanza di Custodia Cautelare, p. 380.

11 Massimo Carminati, conversation no. 867 of 15.01.2013 – RIT 3850/12.

12 Filippo Maria Macchi, conversation no. 110 at 9:25 of 14.06.2014.

left wing of the region. Buzzi and Carminati are partners and Buzzi deals with the economic aspects of the partnership. Buzzi is the one monitoring the illegal economy of the group as well as the activities and the people able to direct it; he is also in charge of keeping, renewing and fostering the relationships with politicians and most of all administrators and public officials. In an intercepted conversation[13] while in a car with Giovanni Campennì (also charged with mafia association) – an entrepreneur close to the Mancuso clan of the 'ndrangheta – Buzzi says:

> You have to be good at it, as our *cooperative* lives through politics; the work I do a lot of people do, so why me? I sponsor newspapers, advertisement, and events. I pay for secretaries, for dinners, for banners. On Monday I have a dinner worth 20,000 euros you know…this is the period you pay the most because there are the local elections, then for five years you only pay depending on what they do for you. This is the moment I pay more…with the council elections…we spend a lot of money for the city council.

The role of Salvatore Buzzi, similarly to that of Carminati, is one of linking different worlds. He is the one making sure that people close to the network are appointed to the highest ranks of the public administration also because he has his own interests in companies tendering for public works in the municipality of Rome and in the Lazio region. Within the strategies Buzzi and Carminati agree upon, three categories of people in the upperworld are essential to the Mafia Capitale network: entrepreneurs, public administrators and politicians.

When it comes to entrepreneurs, some have been active supporters of the network, like Cristiano Guarniera in the property sector, Agostino Gaglianone in the construction sector or Giuseppe Ietto in the restaurant and catering business. Others have been victims, like Luigi Seccaroni in the automobile sector, a victim of Brugia's extortion, or Marco Iannilli, in whose name Carminati had bought a property for purposes of money laundering. As reminded by the prosecutors:

> The difference between corrupted entrepreneurs and victim entrepreneurs is in the mutual benefit, i.e. in the mutually useful relationship that the criminal network can establish with the company. The corrupted entrepreneur, in contrast to the victim, has awareness of the profit that a relationship with the mafia network brings.[14]

13 Salvatore Buzzi and Giovanni Campenni talking in Buzzi's car, RIT 3240-13 prog. no. 54 h. 17.00.00 of 20.04.2013 – Operazione Mondo di Mezzo – R.G.N.R. 30546/10 Tribunale di Roma – Ordinanza di Custodia Cautelare, p. 157.

14 Operazione Mondo di Mezzo – R.G.N.R. 30546/10 Tribunale di Roma - Ordinanza di Custodia Cautelare, p. 463.

Cristiano Guarniera gets involved in the business of Mafia Capitale through Riccardo Brugia, asking for protection while demanding to be put in contact with Buzzi and Carminati. Brugia assigns Matteo Calvio as his 'protector' and proposes a business arrangement for 90 flats in Monteverde. Brugia passes on the proposal to Carminati, who involves Gaglianone to support the construction of the flats with a declared objective: 'I want him to gain with his own investments, and us to gain with his money too without spending anything!'.[15] Guarnera benefits from this partnership as Carminati manages to reduce his costs by asking Gaglianone for preferential treatments, as well as supporting with the bureaucratic process to get access to the land. As Guarnera puts it: 'he [Carminati] has been able to do something which I have been trying to do for two years...in three days he got it done!'.[16] After this event, Guarnera becomes organic to the group, meeting regularly with Brugia, Carminati and Buzzi and working on common projects related to property investments. As he himself recognises: 'in Rome no one can touch me, not even Jesus Christ...here, in Rome, I have become untouchable...or I can have you talk to the person in charge [Carminati]'.[17]

Together with the establishment of financial relationships like the one with Guarnera, Mafia Capitale builds its reputation on the penetration in the public administration and in politics. As already said, public administration and politics are the main domains of Salvatore Buzzi. The list of relationships, supporters and activities is too long to be presented in this chapter. However, as reminded by the Inquisitorial Commission, the expansion of the network happens mainly after the election of the previous Mayor of Rome, Gianni Alemanno, in 2008. Access to Alemanno and his entourage, especially through his Chief of Staff Antonio Lucarelli, was fundamental for Carminati and Buzzi to place various individuals in prominent positions, thereby controlling and distorting the governance of the capital city (Prefetto di Roma, 2015). These individuals would afterwards become very useful when in 2013 the mayor changes and new alliances are needed. This is, for example, the case of Fabrizio Franco Testa, who is one of the closest men to Buzzi and Carminati and who coordinates all the corruptive activities of Mafia Capitale by handling the appointment of chosen individuals in key sectors of the public administration. Testa also ensures that public contracts (such as the outsourcing of waste management) get assigned to companies and entrepreneurs close to the network. A very complex network of relationships between the companies owned by Salvatore Buzzi and other entrepreneurs who are close to the

15 Massimo Carminati, intercepted conversation in a car, no. 718 at h. 11:00 of 09.01.2013 – Operazione Mondo di Mezzo – R.G.N.R. 30546/10 Tribunale di Roma – Ordinanza di Custodia Cautelare, p. 473.

16 Cristiano Guarnera, intercepted conversation no. 1238 of 22.03.2013 – Operazione Mondo di Mezzo – R.G.N.R. 30546/10 Tribunale di Roma – Ordinanza di Custodia Cautelare, p. 473.

17 Cristiano Guarnera, intercepted conversation no. 1238 of 22.03.2013 – Operazione Mondo di Mezzo – R.G.N.R. 30546/10 Tribunale di Roma – Ordinanza di Custodia Cautelare, p. 476.

group, paired with perpetual manipulation of public tenders, allows influence and control over the public administration mechanisms of the capital city. Even when there are sectors that require a more political 'push', such as, for example, the management of centres for refugees, Mafia Capitale members can lay their hands on the money. For example, Luca Odevaine, a high-ranking public official in the previous administration, is the one who supports the assignment of funds and refugees to the companies linked to Buzzi and his associates. As noted by Buzzi when learning that Odevaine (who gains up to 5,000 euros per month from Mafia Capitale[18]) might have been nominated in the entourage of the mayor: 'everything is falling into place…now we need a bunch of right counsellors and… we'll have fun!' [19]

These contacts are fundamental for the network. As noticed by Massimo Carminati, talking with Riccardo Brugia:

> [W]ell…now he [an associate, Gaglianone, entrepreneur] needs the approval, now it's not in his hands anymore, now my friend with Fabrizio Testa, at the town hall, now they deal with it, they get the contracts, then they approve them…by the beginning of January he [Gaglianone] can start.[20]

Carminati's 'friend' is Luca Gramazio, a politician, head of the PDL (centre-right party) in the town hall, who together with Testa allegedly controls the competition over public works, for example, interfering with the board of directors of the Azienda Municipalizzata Ambiente (AMA S.p.A.) through direct discussions of possible candidates with the Mayor Alemanno and other politicians in the capital.

There are many more examples of the collusion of entrepreneurs with politicians and public officials via the key members of the Mafia Capitale network, as presented by the prosecutors and at trial during 2016. The crucial factor, however, is that there is always a way – a willing public official, a politician or an entrepreneur – through which the network can access its areas of interests and create new opportunities. As reminded, once again, by Carminati talking to Buzzi, on the occasion of the change of the Mayor of Rome from Gianni Alemanno to Ignazio Marino in 2013, it is necessary to find a way in.[21] Buzzi is lamenting that he finds it difficult to keep the relationships he has in the town hall as they are now a minority and that he is worried that some of the nomina-

18 Intercepted conversation Salvatore Buzzi No. Q5 (RIT 3240/13) of 20.04.2013 - Operazione Mondo di Mezzo – R.G.N.R. 30546/10 Tribunale di Roma - Ordinanza di Custodia Cautelare, p. 808

19 Operazione Mondo di Mezzo – R.G.N.R. 30546/10 Tribunale di Roma – Ordinanza di Custodia Cautelare, p. 135.

20 Operazione Mondo di Mezzo – R.G.N.R. 30546/10 Tribunale di Roma – Ordinanza di Custodia Cautelare, p. 55.

21 Massimo Carminati and Salvatore Buzzi, intercepted phone conversation no. 10 h 09:56:49 of 14.06.2013 RIT 4955/13 – Operazione Mondo di Mezzo – R.G.N.R. 30546/10 Tribunale di Roma – Ordinanza di Custodia Cautelare, p. 134.

tions might go wrong. Carminati reminds him: 'you need to sell the product, my friend. We need to be like whores now (...) put on your miniskirt and go hang with them'. According to the Commission that scrutinised the status of public administration in Rome, the network managed to reinforce their interests through the new administration, after all, when Giovanni Fiscon, with the support of Buzzi, remained manager of AMA S.p.A. (Prefetto di Roma, 2015; Commissione Parlamentare Antimafia, 2016).

8.5 The relationships between the underworld and the upperworld

The fundamental aim of the Mafia Capitale network is to achieve a functioning set of relationships between the underworld and the upperworld through discrete and methodical activities of the in-betweeners. While it is certainly the case that Massimo Carminati belongs to the underworld, his intention of stepping out of it and being 'in between' is the core strategy of the network. As he puts it while talking to Riccardo Brugia about some 'friendly' entrepreneurs:

> We need to go straight to the point...they have to be our executioners, they have to work for us...we can't do things like we used to...arriving afterwards and collecting debts (...) We are not interested in that anymore...collecting debts means also war with those who don't want to pay...people steal and we have to collect money? (...) We are not people who can do this anymore, for some spare change![22]

And he continues:

> It has to be an equal partnership...you have to tell him...you can try and give me a million euros to take care of all of this, I am not interested (...) it's normal that from our friendship comes the possibility to do business together, that's it. (...) Thing is, in the street, you have to tell him - to whatshisname – we rule...someone like you will never rule in the street...in the street you will always need us.

With this clarity of mind in relation to roles and potential of the different worlds, the network of Mafia Capitale is successful in establishing stable relationships between upperworld and underworld. The key to these relationships is certainly the mutual benefit, the shared assessment of risks and opportunities on both sides. The success of Mafia Capitale is essentially based on the systemic use of corruption reinforced by the reputation of the consortium in the underworld

22 Massimo Carminati and Riccardo Brugia, conversation of 13.12.2012 – Operazione Mondo di Mezzo – R.G.N.R. 30546/10 Tribunale di Roma – Ordinanza di Custodia Cautelare, pp. 58–59.

as well as in the upperworld.[23] This success primarily comes from the relationship between Carminati and Buzzi. As perfectly summarised by the Antimafia Commission (Commissione Parlamentare Antimafia, 2016, p. 97):

> The link between the two worlds – criminal and entrepreneurial – was in the transversal alliance between Massimo Carminati, from the extreme right wing and Salvatore Buzzi, head of an important group of companies with over 1300 stakeholders. (…) The companies, the acquaintances, and the 'clean face' of Buzzi together with the criminal prestige of Carminati and his historical links with the far-right in Rome whose members in the years had accessed public offices, allowed effects no one else could achieve but them.

On one side, the opposite political views of the two individuals (Carminati comes from the extreme right and Buzzi from the left) do not seem to represent an obstacle 'in their common purpose of seeking illicit profits through the systemic planning of the most diverse forms of influence on public administration's activities in the capital city in specific sectors of interest'.[24] On the other side, their continuous bond and their stable relationships with others in the network both ensure protection in case of set-backs due to political changes or policing activities. For example, when Riccardo Mancini, a corrupt administrator, is arrested, Carminati and Buzzi ensure that the man, considered weak and untrustworthy,[25] does not talk about what he knows. Buzzi says to Campennì – his associate entrepreneur close to the 'ndrangheta clan of the Mancuso – 'before they took him we went there and told him "you either shut up and calm down or if you talk then there is no place to hide", we went one week before it happened…to remind him…how is life'.[26] Just to have Campennì confirm that they managed to make sure that he had support in prison: 'sure…but inside [in prison] I made him find a bit of friendships, warmth…'. The network is therefore in charge, on one side securing cooperation and on the other side taking care of its associates. By alternating between intimidation and care, the network secures its longevity.

As noted more than once by the Antimafia prosecutors and by the Court of Cassation, the ability of Carminati and Buzzi, through their main associates, to place trusted individuals in positions of power in public administration and private companies supporting public administration gives the network its precious institutional capital. Very telling is the cooperation of Luca Gramazio – elected in the regional council for the Lazio region and member of the regional commission for budgetary policies and financial planning – who could affect the allocation of

23 Corte di Cassazione., sez. VI pen., 10.03.2015 [dep. 9.06.2015], no. 24535.

24 Corte di Cassazione, sez. VI pen., 10.03.2015 [dep. 9.06.2015], no. 24535, p. 20.

25 Operazione Mondo di Mezzo – R.G.N.R. 30546/10 Tribunale di Roma – Ordinanza di Custodia Cautelare, p. 90.

26 Conversations no. 53, 54, 55 starting at h.16:00 of 20.04.2013 – Operazione Mondo di Mezzo – R.G.N.R. 30546/10 Tribunale di Roma – Ordinanza di Custodia Cautelare, p. 91.

funds to local councils for the management of local policies. Gramazio supports the election of Tommaso Luzzi as preferred candidate as mayor in the municipality of Sacrofano near Rome, in concert with the interests over that territory shared by Buzzi and Carminati. Carminati discusses with the entrepreneur Gaglianone how Luzzi has to accept the requests made once elected as 'he can't do anything else, I say, as the money comes from the Region; if he doesn't do what we tell him, Luca [Gramazio] will stall everything (...) for everything he has to do!'.[27]

By being at the same time firm and flexible, the network manages to preserve and acquire institutional capital to safeguard its interests. As concluded by the Antimafia Commission, the most worrying result of the partnership between Carminati and Buzzi and of the quick development of their criminal network is indeed the emergence of the 'world in between' (Commissione Parlamentare Antimafia, 2016, p. 97):

> Buzzi, who had the legitimacy necessary to interact with public officials and politicians, was the official channel through which the upperworld – made of white collars, entrepreneurs and institutions – and the underworld with Carminati – made of robbers, drugs and arms traffickers – could meet in the middle.

8.6 The quality, the context and the strength of ties in Mafia Capitale

Figure 8.1 shows the results of a qualitative assessment of the ties linking the main players of Mafia Capitale, as presented in these sections. Strong ties are formed when there are either ideological links together with longevity of the connection or when one of the two above is missing but there is an intense contact anyway. Weak ties are established where there is neither shared ideology nor is there longevity of the relationship even if there is an intense contact. In the Mafia Capitale network, there is a clear distinction between the ties in the upperworld (much more varied and with a predominance of weak ties) and those in the underworld (certainly stronger). These differences are crucial to understanding the influence and growth of the Mafia Capitale network. Figure 8.2 shows the network of Mafia Capitale by using Gephi network analysis network.

8.6.1 Content and quality of ties: the strength of weak ties

The basis for the analysis of the quality of ties is Granovetter's (1983, 1978, 1973) consideration that *homophily* – the tendency in social groups for similar people to be connected together – allows for matching of, and close relationships among, similar individuals. As reminded by Matsueda (2006, p. 18), 'strong ties

27 Conversation no. 21600 h. 13:07 of 18.04.2014 - Operazione Mondo di Mezzo – R.G.N.R. 30546/10 Tribunale di Roma – Ordinanza di Custodia Cautelare, p. 146.

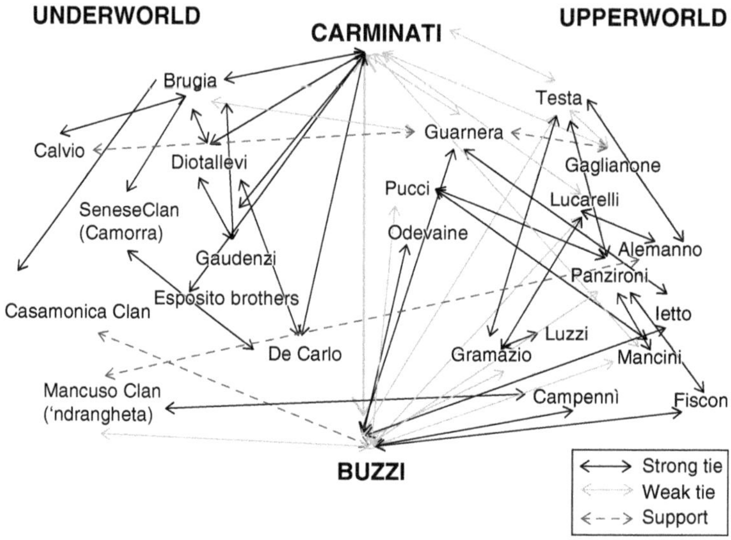

Figure 8.1 The basic ties of the Mafia Capitale network.

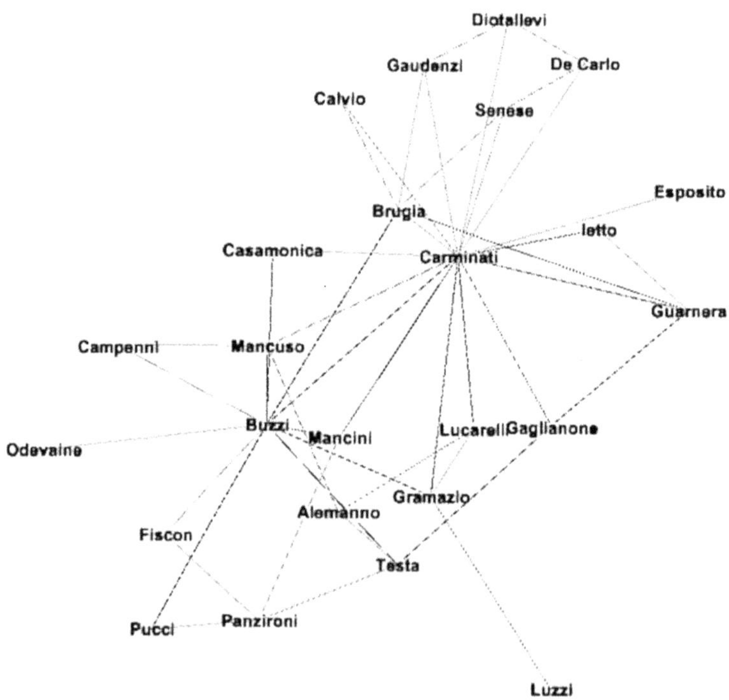

Figure 8.2 The network of Mafia Capitale in Gephi based on author's notes[18] Intercepted conversation Salvatore Buzzi No. Q5 (RIT 3240/13) of 20.04.2013 - Operazione Mondo di Mezzo – R.G.N.R. 30546/10 Tribunale di Roma - Ordinanza di Custodia Cautelare, p. 808

within a homogenous group not only encourage conformity but also lead to the circulation and recirculation of similar ideas', while 'groups that are not entirely closed, but have weak ties to other groups, will benefit from information flows between groups'. An assessment of the content of ties in the Mafia Capitale network based on the homogeneity as well as the intensity and longevity of ties reveals, as in Figures 8.1 and 8.2, how the group's success is largely based on the strength of weak ties. First and foremost, as said earlier in this chapter, the main tie, the one between Massimo Carminati and Salvatore Buzzi, can be considered substantially a weak tie. In fact, even though in the course of the years of activity of Mafia Capitale, the intensity of the relationship between the two grows (hence the boldness of the arrow in figure 8.1), the two men are not only coming from two heterogeneous worlds, they had not known each other for long and their diversity mirrors in their roles in the criminal network. Differently from the relationship between Carminati and Brugia, which dates back to a common past in the far-right militia and the underworld – a strong tie – the tie existing between Carminati and Buzzi is neither ideological nor personal: it is instrumental. As noted by Newton (1997), the product of weak ties is 'thin' trust, intended as a less personal, more instrumental, social relation. Thin trust between Carminati and Buzzi allows for the integration between the upperworld and the underworld. Thin trust is not a second rate form of trust (compared to what is instead known as 'thick' trust typical of smaller, homogenous, gated communities); rather, it allows the bridging of different types of social capital (Putnam, 2000). The success of Mafia Capitale starts with the ability to access and maintain 'institutional capital'; it is based on a system of relationships with politicians and mildly influential public officials and bureaucrats who support, and benefit from, the strategy of Buzzi and Carminati. The world of the in-betweeners is possible because of the quality of ties that Carminati has in the underworld and partially in the upperworld as much as those that Buzzi has in the upperworld. In fact, on one side, strong ties allow for a tighter control over the activities of the underworld, thus enhancing the criminal reputation of the criminal groups and increasing the possibilities to intimidate and corrupt. These ties, especially for Carminati, are mostly based on years of common and shared ideological grounds and contacts with 'friends of friends'. As suggested by Campana and Varese (2013), we can argue that people who have shared information about violent acts are more likely to form strong ties and cooperate. At the same time, Carminati's own weak ties represent the possibility to foster and influence other groups in the upperworld, thus realising his own strategy of the world in between. Buzzi's ties are predominantly weak ties, based on opportunistic, even though intense at times, contact with people who might be useful for the network's purposes again by bridging different but close enough worlds. Some of Buzzi's ties, however, for example the one with Campennì, fellow entrepreneur, allow for a strong bond not necessarily because of the shared ideological background, as it is the case for Carminati, but rather because of the strength of common future interests and criminal opportunities to come; this strong tie comes from systemic contact and impunity. Common future interests not only strengthen the ties between Buzzi and other members he introduces to, or approaches for, the network, but might also have facilitated the development of weak ties with the underworld. For example, in the case of Campennì, the strong tie with Buzzi allows Buzzi himself and other members of the upperworld to get in contact with a powerful mafia-type clan of the Calabrian 'ndrangheta, the Mancuso clan.

8.6.2 Context of ties: reputation and external recognition

The heterogeneity of the worlds connected in this network via a successful mix of strong and weak ties of the major players allows for a very peculiar phenomenon. Mafia Capitale, in fact, can count on the reputation of its leader, Carminati, in part because he does not belong to the upperworld that the network exploits. In other words, the differences between the individuals in the underworld and those in the upperworld make Carminati the boss of the underworld and a feared character in the upperworld. It is arguably in the heterogeneity of the two sides that we find an explanation of why this happens. The lack of shared ideologies, the opportunism of relationships and the thin trust that characterise weak ties in the upperworld make the strong ties of the underworld and Carminati's criminal past stable and alarming at the same time. As noticed by Buzzi talking to Campennì,[28] (after a meeting with Lucarelli who had previously talked to Carminati and by him was persuaded to talk to Mayor Alemanno):

> We called Massimo and I said 'I am having difficulties with those three hundred thousand euros (…)' and he told me 'ok go to the Campidoglio [meaning the official residence of the Mayor of Rome], at three o'clock and Lucarelli will come down to talk to you', so I said 'Massimo, but I am not allowed to go up…he is not coming down either!?' and he replied 'go there at three, don't worry'. You know what, at five to three he [Lucarelli] comes down, for real, and he says 'I have talked to Massimo, it's all good for tomorrow'…and it was all good! They are scared of him…they really are, they can't do much else.

Episodes like this are not isolated, as the criminal reputation of Mafia Capitale is largely based on the criminal charisma of and resulting obedience to Massimo Carminati (Mazzeo, 2015). The reputation of Mafia Capitale is part of the argument for its legal recognition as a mafia-type group, as argued by the Court of Cassation as well as the Antimafia prosecutors. Indeed, the criminal reputation of Carminati and his network has various effects: it instils fear of the group; it increases the prestige of the organisation; it allows intimidating those outside the group; and it ensures omertà in the group. The recognition of the criminal

28 Conversation between Salvatore Buzzi and Giovanni Campennì, 20.4.2013, ROS Final Report anticrimine, page 1191 – Operazione Mondo di Mezzo – R.G.N.R. 30546/10 Tribunale di Roma – Ordinanza di Custodia Cautelare, pp. 93–94.

prestige of Mafia Capitale by those external to the network is dependent on the perception of the quality of the bonds among members and their ability to reach non-members/others. This recognition comes from both the upperworld and the underworld. In fact, as has been pointed out repeatedly, the fact that established mafia-type criminal groups, like the Mancuso clan of the 'ndrangheta, for example, choose to do business with the Mafia Capitale network is essentially an *endorsement* of the network's capability and reach (Prefetto di Roma, 2015). The context in which the Mafia Capitale network operates is not free from other competing powers, both in the upperworld and in the underworld. The reputation of the group is in the perception of the strength of both strong and weak ties among the main players and others close to the main players.

8.6.3 *Effects of ties: the mafia method and behaviour*

This criminal group has been recognised as a mafia group for the purposes of Italian law. Indeed, the ability to create and foster a tight network of mildly or highly influential and useful contacts in both the underworld and the upperworld, through the effective exploitation of both strong and weak ties, distinguishes mafia groups from other organised crime groups (Dalla Chiesa, 2015; Sergi, 2017a). The systematic and strategic use of corruption, the influence over the public and private sectors and politics and the exploitation of privileged channels represent the modus operandi of Mafia Capitale. This can indeed be considered as manifestation of the 'mafia method', which aims at intimidating through the strength and reach of corruption pacts as well as through violence if needed to increase the prestige and influence of the network and its supporters. Indeed, through exchange of benefits and favours at every level and in different worlds, Mafia Capitale could count on an increasingly large network of contacts, ever expanding through the strength of weak ties that could be used to access other contacts. This snowballing approach is very typical of mafia groups and their behaviours, whereby *proximity* to politics and public administration is symptomatic of the growing reputation of the group as well as being one of the means of securing power and money (Sergi, 2017b; Sergi and Lavorgna, 2016). The escalation of Mafia Capitale's power, as previously discussed, can only be explained by looking at the quality of the ties the network has fostered, which become stronger during the 2008–2013 administration. As said, the successful links between politics, public administration and entrepreneurial mafia members have been repeatedly confirmed as differentiating mafia groups from other criminal groups (Sergi, 2017a). These links in some cases are characterised by strong ties, like in the case of certain 'ndrangheta clans in the south of Italy (Sergi, 2015b), but in many more cases, with some examples from Cosa Nostra, 'ndrangheta and camorra clans in various parts of Italy (Sciarrone, 2011) and also abroad (Sciarrone and Storti, 2014; Sergi, 2015a) are secured through weak ties. The strength of weak ties, as previously noted, lies in the possibility to link heterogeneous worlds and personalities, which, in the case of criminal groups, creates new opportunities and criminal ventures. Mafia Capitale has been able to take advantage of this through contacts in the upperworld. This explains the quick growth of the reputation of the group, but it would have not been possible, as seen, without the strong ties and the trust in the underworld as well. Like any other mafia group, Mafia Capitale enjoys both stable and dynamic forms of trust, based on common business interests and mafia-style methods to react and interact with those outside the group.

8.7 Conclusion

This chapter has qualitatively analysed the relationships among founders, affiliates and supporters of the criminal network known as Mafia Capitale in the city of Rome. The qualitative analysis, based on an understanding of ties as strong and weak ties as postulated by Granovetter (1973), has looked at the judicial documents supporting the Antimafia operation 'Mondo di Mezzo' (world in-between) to evaluate the nature of the ties linking individuals in the network. While conscious of the limits of such, an analysis from the point of view of social network analysis research methods and, more generally, from the point of view of research into criminal networks, this chapter has come to interesting findings.

First of all, weak ties are confirmed to be as important, if not more important, as strong ties when it comes to enlarging the network and opening up new possibilities and ventures. The main relationship of the group, the one between Carminati and Buzzi, starts as a weak tie when we look at their ideological background and where they come from; this tie gives the strong ties that Carminati fosters in the underworld a chance to emerge. Many of the ties established in the upperworld by both Buzzi and Carminati are weak ties, based on opportunistic exchanges and on the corruptive capability of the network.

Second, the corruptive capability of the network when approaching different people in different positions in the upperworld is strengthened and supported by the reputation and the prestige of the group. Reputation and prestige depend upon the strength of strong ties in the underworld. These ties project an image of a network that can both intimidate and resort to violence should corruption not be enough. The network can prosper and establish new ties because of its reputation in resorting to the mafia method (intimidation and omertà).

Third and finally, a group which is based on reputation and potential to intimidate, whether through the ability to corrupt or through the use of violence, is, in the latest interpretations of Italian law, a mafia-type group. The recognition of Mafia Capitale as a mafia-type group can be seen as a step towards abandoning stereotypes and misunderstandings surrounding the common concept of mafia both in Italy and elsewhere. Indeed, it would confirm that mafias are not just the traditional criminal organisations from the South of Italy, but instead manifest also through: 1) the existence of a criminal system with a reputation maintained through intimidation via corruption pacts and/or violence; 2) the trafficking of illicit favours and benefits, which reinforces the reputation of the group and increases fear of repercussions for externals; and 3) the reliance on in-betweeners, people able to connect underworld and upperworld, from armed militia to entrepreneurs, from criminals to politicians. This revised conceptualisation of a mafia group would separate, without denying, the idea of mafias from the traditional mafia groups linked to the Southern territories of Italy and would advance the analysis of the characteristics of the mafia phenomenon as a dynamic and fluid criminal behaviour detached from particular cultures and ethnic groups. The trial of Mafia Capitale is therefore a great opportunity to revisit the concept of mafias and in so doing support the dialogue between Italy and the rest of the world in the fight against organised crime.

References

Albanese, J. (2014) The Italian-American Mafia. In: Paoli, L. (ed.) *The Handbook of Organized Crime.* Oxford and New York: Oxford University Press. pp. 79–109

Albini, J.L. (1971) *The American Mafia: Genesis of a Legend.* New York: Appleton-Century-Crofts.

Albini, J.L. and McIllwain, J.S. (2012) *Deconstructing Organized Crime: An Historical and Theoretical Study.* North Carolina: McFarland & Co. Inc. Publishers.

Boissevain, J. (1974) *Friends of Friends, Networks, Manipulators and Coalitions.* Oxford: Basil Blackwell.

Bourdieu, P. (1986) The forms of capital. In: Richardson, J.G. (ed.) *Handbook of Theory and Research for the Sociology of Education.* New York: Greenwood. pp. 313–326.

Burt, R.S. (1992) The social structure of competition. In: Nohria, N. and Eccles, R.G. (eds.) *Networks and Organizations: Structure, Form and Action.* Harvard, MA: Harvard Business School Press. pp. 66–97.

Campana, P. (2011) Eavesdropping on the mob: The functional diversification of Mafia activities across territories. *European Journal of Criminology* 8(3), pp. 213–228.

Campana, P. (2016) Explaining criminal networks: Strategies and potential pitfalls. *Methodological Innovations* 9, pp. 1–9.

Campana, P. and Varese, F. (2013) Cooperation in criminal organizations: Kinship and violence as credible commitments. *Rationality and Society* 25(3), pp. 263–289.

Carrington, P.J. (2011) Crime and social network analysis. In: Scott, J. and Carrington, P.J. (eds.) *The SAGE Handbook of Social Network Analysis.* London: SAGE Publications Ltd. pp. 10–40.

Commissione Parlamentare Antimafia. (2016) Relazione sulla situazione dei comuni, sciolti per fenomeni di infiltrazione e condizionamento di tipo mafioso o sottoposti ad accesso ai sensi dell'art. 143 del decreto legislativo 18 agosto 2000, n. 267, di San Sostene (CZ), Joppolo (VV), Badolato (CZ), Sant'Oreste (RM), Platì (RC), Ricadi (VV), Diano Marina (IM), Villa di Briano (CE), Morlupo (RM), Scalea (CS), Finale Emilia (MO), Battipaglia (SA) e Roma Capitale, in vista delle elezioni comunali del 5 giugno 2016.

Coviello, N.E. (2005) Integrating qualitative and quantitative techniques in network analysis. *Qualitative Market Research* 8(1), pp. 39–60.

Dalla Chiesa, N. (2015) A proposito di Mafia Capitale. Alcuni Problemi Teorici. *Rivista di Studi e Ricerche sulla Criminalità Organizzata* 1(2), pp. 1–15. DOI: 10.13130/cross-16634.

De Bonis, A. (2015) *The World In-Between: Mafia Capitale Blurs the Lines of Organized Crime.*

Edwards, G. (2010) *Mixed-Method Approaches to Social Network Analysis*. ESRC National Centre for Research Methods Review Paper. University of Manchester: National Centre for Research Methods.
Granovetter, M.S. (1973) The strength of weak ties. *American Journal of Sociology* 78(6), pp. 1360–1380.
Granovetter, M.S. (1978) Threshold models of collective behavior. *American Journal of Sociology* 83(6), pp. 1420–1443.
Granovetter, M.S. (1983) The strength of weak ties: A network theory revisited. *Sociological Theory* 1, pp. 201–233.
Granovetter, M.S. (1985) Economic action and social structure: The problem of embeddedness. *American Journal of Sociology* 91(3), pp. 481–510.
Ianni, F.A.J. and Reuss-Ianni, E. (1972) *A Family Business : Kinship and Social Control in Organized Crime*. London: Routledge and K. Paul.
Jack, S.L. (2005) The role, use and activation of strong and weak network ties: A qualitative analysis. *Journal of Management Studies* 42(6), pp. 1233–1259.
Kleemans, E.R. and de Poot, C.J. (2008) Criminal careers in organized crime and social opportunity structure. *European Journal of Criminology* 5(1), pp. 69–98.
Matsueda, R.L. (2006) Differential social organization, collective action, and crime. *Crime, Law and Social Change* 46(1–2), pp. 3–33.
Mazzeo, M. (2015) Mafia Capitale. Anatomia dei protagonisti. *Rivista di Studi e Ricerche sulla Criminalita' Organizzata* 1(2), pp. 32–56.
Morselli, C. (2005) *Contacts, Opportunities, and Criminal Enterprise*. Toronto, London: University of Toronto Press.
Morselli, C. (2009) *Inside Criminal Networks*. New York: Springer.
Newton, K. (1997) Social capital and democracy. *American Behavioral Scientist* 40(5), pp. 575–586.
Nohria, N. (1992) Is a network perspective a useful way of studying organisations? In: Nohria, N. and Eccles, R.G. (eds.) *Networks and Organisations: Structure, Form and Action*. Harvard, MA: Harvard Business School Press. pp. 45–57.
Prefetto di Roma. (2015) Commissione di Accesso presso Roma Capitale, ex art. 143, comma 2, TUOEL. *Decreto Prefetto di Roma 15 dicembre 2014 no. 292944/2014*.
Putnam, R. (2000) *Bowling Alone: The Collapse and Revival of American Community*. New York: Simon & Schuster.
Robins, G. (2015) *Doing Social Network Research*. Thousand Oaks, CA: SAGE.
Sciarrone, R. (2011) Mafie, relazioni e affari nell'area grigia. In: Sciarrone, R. (ed.) *Alleanze nell'ombra. Mafie ed economie locali in Sicilia e nel Mezzogiorno*. Roma: Donzelli.
Sciarrone, R. and Storti, L. (2014) The territorial expansion of mafia-type organized crime. The case of the Italian mafia in Germany. *Crime, Law and Social Change* 61(1), pp. 37–60.
Sergi, A. (2015a) The evolution of the Australian 'ndrangheta. An historical perspective. *Australian and New Zealand Journal of Criminology* 48(2), pp. 155–174.
Sergi, A. (2015b) Mafia and politics as concurrent governance actors. Revisiting political power and crime in Southern Italy. In: Van Duyne, P.C., Maljević, A., Antonopoulos, G.A., Harvey, J. and von Lampe, K. (eds.) *The Relativity of Wrongdoing: Corruption, Organised Crime, Fraud and Money Laundering in Perspective*. Oisterwijk: Wolf Legal Publishers. pp. 1–25.
Sergi, A. (2016) A proposito di Mafia Capitale. Spunti per portare il dibattito fuori dall'Italia. *Rivista di Studi e Ricerche sulla Criminalita' Organizzata* 2(1), pp. 96–116.

Sergi, A. (2017a) *From Mafia to Organised Crime. A Comparative Analysis of Policing Models.* London, New York: Palgrave Macmillan.

Sergi, A. (2017b) Countering the Australian 'ndrangheta. The criminalisation of mafia behaviour in Australia between national and comparative criminal law. *Australian and New Zealand Journal of Criminology* 50(3), 321–340.

Sergi, A. and Lavorgna, A. (2016) *Ndrangheta. The Glocal Dimensions of the Most Powerful Italian Mafia.* London, New York: Palgrave Macmillan.

Varese, F. (2006) The structure of a criminal network examined: The Russian Mafia in Rome. Oxford Legal Studies Research Paper (21).

Von Lampe, K. (2009) The study of organised crime: An assessment of the state of affairs. In: Ingvaldsen, K. and Lundgren Sorli, V. (eds.) *Organised Crime: Norms, Markets, Regulation and Research.* Oslo: Unipub. pp. 45–57.

Von Lampe, K. and Ole Johansen, P.O. (2004) Organized crime and trust: On the conceptualization and empirical relevance of trust in the context of criminal networks. *Global Crime* 6(2), pp. 159–184.

Walther, O.J. and Christopoulos, D. (2015) Islamic terrorism and the Malian rebellion. *Terrorism and Political Violence* 27(3), pp. 497–519.

Wolf, E. (1966) Kinship, friendship and patron-client relations in complex societies. In: Banton, M. (ed.) *The Social Antrhopology of Complex Societies.* London: Routledge. pp. 1–25.

9 Power and trust networks in the organisation of crime in Ukraine

Anna Markovska and Petrus C. van Duyne

9.1 Introduction

This chapter discusses the nature of organised criminality and its dynamics in Ukraine. An important element of our discussion is corruption and the many ways corrupt connections can influence power. Organised crime and particularly the corruption of senior state officials in Ukraine is regularly reported locally and internationally. However, Ukraine is by no means unique. Historically, the Soviet Union saw many cases of corruption. For example, the 'Cotton Affair scandal', which took place in the late 1980s (Keller, 1988, Handelman, 2002), exposed corruption within various Soviet Republics where 'cotton magnates' had misappropriated billions of rubles over many years by inflating cotton harvest statistics. Such corruption included 'protection rackets, bribery, and the sale of government offices' (Keller, 1988). Specifically, a network of corrupt officials regulating the production of cotton in Uzbekistan engaged in selling cotton on the black market and thereby laundered billions of roubles. According to some sources, up to 2,600 officials were arrested when the affair was uncovered and about 50,000 cotton producers faced sanctions. In April 1988, a senior military tribunal sentenced the son-in-law of Leonid I. Brezhnev, the former Soviet leader, 'to 12 years in a labour camp for taking bribes, concluding a corruption trial that was widely read as an indictment of an era' (Keller, 1988), an example of powerful individuals organising a professional context in order to engage in serious financial crime. The Uzbek cotton affair was successful because of the high level of secrecy that enabled the organisation of a corrupt network within the legal system.

The cooperation of the individuals involved in the affair was based on fear of authority and their willingness to engage in illegal profit-sharing, features that may be considered symptomatic of traditional 'underworld' organised criminality. During the early Soviet period, this traditional organised criminal underworld was represented by so-called 'thieves-in-law', in reality professional criminals. However, this class of criminals operated in the then very different landscape of the Soviet Gulag, where different classes within the criminal world moved through short life cycles of criminal fraternity. Varese (2002) notes that when these traditional 'thieves-in-law' refused cooperation with the prison authorities, criminal bandits, 'the suki' ('bitches'), emerged and were happy to work with the authorities and against 'the thieves'. By the early 1950s, this struggle between 'the suki' and 'the thieves' was won by 'the suki'. Subsequently, 'the myth of the vory [thieves], as dashing heroes of the criminal world' who preferred death to betrayal of 'their "ideals" was born' (Varese, 2002, p. 531).

By the 1980s, the organising upper-level criminals gained significant power. In a general climate of corruption, they were able to take advantage of the scarcity of those consumer goods to which they had access and could then sell to the elite. After 1991, such organisers successfully adapted to the chaos engendered by the collapse of the Soviet Union. The illegalities of the Cotton Affair were in effect normalised.

In Ukraine, such practices have led to the emergence of an oligarchy (Kupatadze, 2012) composed of powerful industrial groups who, in the chaos of the first ten years of independence, transformed from being communist state officials to private owners of former state enterprises (Ibid.). The result is a continuing dominating legacy of Soviet Union corruption that has permeated all sectors of Ukraine, which has inherited this state of affairs.

This is evidenced by various international indices of public functioning, such as the World Economic Forum's Global Competitiveness Index 2017–2018, which analyses the performance of 137 countries according to selected indicators of competitiveness. Ukraine was ranked 81st of 137 countries, between Brazil and Bhutan. The ranking of organised crime interference in business in Ukraine is recorded at a high level. The presence of organised crime was measured according to the following criterion, 'To what extent does organised crime (mafia – oriented racketeering, extortion) impose costs on business?' [1 – to a greater extent, 7 – not at all]. On this scale, Ukraine arrived at an index of 3.9. Among all 137 countries on this scale, Ukraine was 113th, between Uganda (112th place) and Trinidad and Tobago (114th place).

So, what is the extent of organised crime in the Ukrainian context? According to a 2008 opinion poll, 60% of Ukrainians described organised criminals as a 'mafia created by oligarchs, representatives of the government, and law enforcement officers' (Kupatadze, 2012, p. 98). In order to understand this description in the Ukrainian context, it is necessary to integrate the concepts of white collar crime and state crime with traditional views on organised criminality in the underworld. Within this amalgamation, we need to then identify specific factors leading to the organisation of criminal conduct. For the purpose of this study, we identify two important principles: *trust* and *power*. We hold that these are basic principles in any entrepreneurial relationship and all the more so in criminal enterprises, where trust is largely absent and power essential.

In this chapter, we consider the interaction between the underworld and 'upper-world' in the light of trust and power networks in Ukraine. We intend to focus on the gambling sector in Ukraine and more specifically on the 'dark' or illegal side. This choice is not only motivated by the importance of the sector, either in its legal form before 2009 or in its illegal manifestation thereafter, but also because the sector has generated a substantial amount of qualitative data and academic insight (Markovska and Zabyelina, 2016).

Since 1991, the Ukrainian gambling industry has followed two parallel courses: legal and illegal. When gambling was legal many clubs nevertheless operated without a licence under the protection of corrupt police or criminal gangs; only about 60% of gambling establishments operated with an official licence. Following a fire in a gambling club in which a number of people died, the government introduced a ban on all forms of gambling (see Markovska and Zabyelina, 2016). Since the 2009 ban, therefore, the demand for gambling has been met by an underground economy of illegal establishments.

9.2 Methodology

Any research into organised crime starts with a definition of organised crime, and as such is limited by the official labels used. We deviate from these official definitions, of which there are many, and approach our subject from a behavioural, dynamic angle: namely criminals organis*ing* crime. Naturally, such research is also limited by the data available for analysis. For example, Campana and Varese (2013) discussed the use of phone intercepts in Italy as a way of studying its criminal networks; Kleemans and de Bunt (2008) analysed official data from the Dutch Organised Crime *Monitor*; and Morselli and Tremblay (2004) conducted a study on a sample of incarcerated offenders in Canada to understand their criminal earnings. In one way or another, all these studies depend on a functioning criminal justice system and the data produced by that system. This is challenging when applied to a country where endemic corruption has resulted in the criminalisation and politicisation of both police and judiciary. Discussing organised crime in Ukraine poses a number of important methodological problems regarding the validity of data obtained from corrupt organisations, namely:

1 Police corruption: official statistics available on organised crime relate only to violent underworld criminal groups. This is only a subsection of the whole of organised crime. Over the last twenty years, the police have largely failed to investigate upper-world criminal organisations. Where such investigations do occur, they are often launched to meet official targets and demonstrate that 'something is being done' (Markovska and Serdyuk, 2013).
2 Judicial corruption and strong political influence which take precedence over the justice can be considered a serious problem in Ukraine (Kupatadze, 2012). In response to significant pressure exerted by the West, in 2015 the Ukrainian government established the National Anti-Corruption Bureau (NABU), an independent law enforcement organisation with significant powers to investigate high-level corruption in Ukraine. It works in conjunction with the Specialised Anti-Corruption Prosecution Office (SAPO), which has powers to prosecute upper-level criminality. However, the data

available (or lack of it) thus far do not show that the whole approach is efficient and effective.[1]

The above issues make the analysis of the standard data sets really problematic because cases in which high-level state officials are investigated are still rare. Nevertheless, qualitative studies can provide an important insight into those situations where obtaining reliable official data is difficult. Whilst this chapter aims to elaborate on available academic and official data on organised crime in Ukraine, our assessment of it will be supported by empirical research conducted in one Ukrainian city and with one organiser of illegal gambling clubs.

Between spring of 2015 and autumn of 2017, interviews were conducted with one organiser (called Guy here) of illegal gambling clubs. The interviews provide an account of the experience of a businessman who witnessed the criminalisation of gambling in 2009, so that after 2009 his business activities became illegal. Our interviews were used in conjunction with the participatory mapping method, in which the respondent was asked to present schematically the structure of the networks in which he participated and to comment on the nature of the links established within and outside of them. We have previously reported on the different models of operations employed by illegal gambling clubs (Markovska and Zabyelina, 2016) and on the negotiated nature of prohibition in Ukraine (Markovska and Zabyelina, 2019). Negotiated prohibition is defined by a special relationship between power holders and banned service providers where both parties participate in a subjective conception of what is legal and illegal (Ibid.).

Obviously, anecdotal narratives such as Guy's have their limitations even though over the last three years we have observed the networks being established and promoted by him. We have, however, employed the triangulation method to increase the reliability of our data. Data from additional open sources, as well as information from police reports for comparison, have further strengthened our conclusion. Of course, the use of open source and police data must be treated with caution. We accept that due to a lack of systematic research on organised illegal gambling clubs, our findings must be limited to the context of a specific city.

Our interviews can be divided into three stages. In stage one, in spring of 2015, we conducted interviews and used 'participatory mapping' to establish the basic characteristics of each gambling network, including the respective numbers of organisers and their clients. Emmel and Clark (2009) discuss participatory mapping as an effective visual data-gathering approach that 'enables participants to move from description of spatial practices, to their elaboration and theorization' (p. 16). Participatory mapping provided us with an opportunity to produce a more detailed elaboration of the nature and structure of the gambling networks.

1 There is a discrepancy between the concerns expressed about corruption and evidence of subsequent appropriate actions and results by law enforcement, for example, in Serbia (see Van Duyne, P. et al. (2012), casting doubt on the degree to which the concern expressed is genuine.

In the next stage, in spring of 2016, we conducted a second series of interviews with the aim of analysing specific links and connections between networks in order to create an adequate narrative description of them. In stage three, which occurred in the autumn of 2017, we discussed the financial viability of each of the networks, the extent of trust within them and the role of the power exercised by authoritative figures in the provision and protection of illegal gambling services.

We begin by briefly outlining the meaning of the term 'organised crime' in the Ukrainian context. We then discuss some conceptual issues of trust in organised crime literature before moving on to describe the criminalisation of the gambling industry in Ukraine. We discuss the qualitative data regarding factors that are conducive to the development of illegal gambling networks and will relate these to our empirical research on the development of gambling networks in one Ukrainian city.

9.3 Organising crime in Ukraine

The post-Soviet Ukraine inherited many features of the Soviet criminal past: the traditional 'thieves-in-law', black market operations, a corrupt nomenclature, a large shadow economy and a substantial group of well-trained security personnel (Williams and Picarelli, 2001) who could add 'muscle' to criminal networks. Glazov (2002) discusses 'thieves' as being a powerful underground crime institution, 'an esoteric order of professional outlaws', living under strict thieves' laws (p. 31) with a history stretching back to the days of the 1917 Revolution and the first years of the Gulag. Once in Stalin's prisons, the thieves declined any co-operation with the authorities as one of their strict rules of conduct, consequently, the state used the method of so-called 'bitch-making' in an attempt to re-educate them. 'Transformation of the thieves into "bitches" was actually an adaptation of the thieves' community to a new social environment, which required the splitting of their personality whereby the supremacy of the individual ego gives way to the supremacy of the state' (Glazov, 2002, p. 44). In fact, instead of their successful re-education to form part of society, the 'bitches' formed in effect new criminal groups, now trained to co-operate with the corrupt authorities. To Glazov (2002), this is an example of the strength of the state in that it managed to control all sections of the society, 'even the most stubborn and independent' (Ibid., p. 46).

Nikiforov (1993) argues that organised crime in the former USSR was different from that in the West because its figures occupied 'key positions within the state bureaucracy' (p. 217). A more accurate qualification of them, he suggests, would be 'white-collar gangsters' (p. 217). Nikiforov notes that in the West, organised criminals 'strive for a monopoly in the field of their business, in the former USSR, organized "white-collars" have already had this monopoly since October 1917' (p. 218). It is thus essential in the post-USSR context to understand 'the co-operation of "businessmen" and "criminals" [that] ensures the coordination of their criminal activities, mutual support while confronting society...' (Nikiforov, 1993, p. 218).

The idea of negotiated prohibition is relevant here to the post-USSR situation in that there was no political will to challenge the corrupt system and stop negotiations between 'illegal' businessmen, criminals and politicians. Effectively, all parties that engaged in the negotiation of 'business' interests disregarded the law (knowing that the intention of the law was unrealisable).

Writing on organised white-collar criminality in Soviet times, Shelley (1994) argues that embezzlement was 'the most pervasive crime in the Soviet period and was not perceived as being criminal by most citizens' (p. 224). The theft of state social property was still increasing by 1988, with three republics, Russia, Ukraine and Kazakhstan, together accounting for around 86% of all such thefts (Butler, 1992). Butler (1992) notes that the crimes of appropriation, embezzlement and the abuse of official position increased steadily from 1980 to 1986. This increase has largely been attributed to the involvement of law enforcement agencies (Ibid.). However, official statistics showing a subsequent decrease in these crimes from 1986 to 1989 do not imply a reduction of criminal activity, but rather an operational decision of the police not to investigate it. Later, in post-Soviet organised criminality, the attitude towards state property did not change. The large-scale embezzlement of state property and associated fraud continued to be the most lucrative criminal activity (Shelley, 1994).

Organised criminality amongst the upper political classes has been a difficult issue to tackle in the Soviet and post-Soviet period. Globalisation and liberalisation of financial markets led to new ways of hiding the wealth of politically exposed people in the successor states such as Ukraine. According to the NABU, as of the end of 2017 they had 'opened 543 criminal proceedings and issued 181 notices of suspicion' and had ... seized more than UAH 650 million and USD 160 million. In addition, there are currently 120 NABU criminal investigations pending' (NABU, 2018, p. 8). However, as soon as proceedings begin, the momentum towards prosecution fades. Indeed, an unreformed judiciary remains a major problem; as of September 2017, only one conviction had been secured by the NABU (Ibid.). In principle, however, the NABU and SAPO have the potential to investigate and prosecute upper-level criminality, a resource that Ukraine has not had before.

9.4 Trust and power

How do you know whom to trust? This question is especially important to individuals and groups engaged in organis*ing* crime, be it crime committed by underworld figures or by the legitimate upper-world. Essential to organising crime is information regarding ongoing *risk management*. Such risk management concerns mainly people: whom to trust and whom not to? Trust is vital in this context because many elements of the crime business have to be outsourced to trusted others over whom the crime entrepreneur must exert some power. The concept of trust is an interesting and multidimensional one. Bicchieri, Xiao and Muldoon (2011) distinguish between 'trusting as a behaviour that is norm driven versus trusting as behaviour that is predicated on the anticipation of profit through reciprocation' (p. 171). It is also important to consider personal trust against generalised trust. 'The breeding ground of trust, cooperative habits, and solidarity is always the small group, and the move to generalised trust is something that happens almost by default, as a habit one does not shed just because the situation is unusual or different' (Ibid., p. 171).

Ukraine is an example of a society where people may display high levels of trust among the family members but show mainly mistrust towards authorities and institutions. A survey conducted by the Democratic Initiatives Foundation reported that only 10% of respondents trusted the courts in Ukraine and only 35% reported any trust in the work of the NABU (Democratic Initiatives Foundation, 2017). According to Yamagishi (2001), we need to separate trust from trustworthiness. Trust is 'meaningful only in situations characterised by a high level of social uncertainty, in which there are incentives to act dishonestly and the consequences of being the target of dishonesty are costly' (Bicchieri, 2011, p. 172). Bicchieri, Xiao and Muldoon (2011) conclude that 'it is a presence of a norm of reciprocity that elicits trusting behaviour in impersonal context' (p. 182). The problem is that the norm of reciprocity becomes problematic in a highly volatile environment, such as criminalised markets, and may depend on the balance of power between individuals. If you generally do not trust the police, but have to buy protection from them, how much trust will you have in the police offering illegal protection? This is one of the dilemmas that operators of illegal gambling clubs deal with on a daily basis.

Von Lampe and Ole Johansen (2004) isolated the issue of trust and elaborated its position in the organised crime literature. The authors propose considering trust to be 'a property of dyadic relations that forms the basic elements of criminal networks' (p. 167) and developed a typology of trust that includes the following:

1 Individualised trust, where 'the expectation of agreeable behaviour relates specifically to the trustee as an individual' (p. 168);
2 Trust as based on reputation, 'the trustor relies on publicly formed and held opinion about the trustees' (p. 169);
3 Trust based on generalisation where trust is linked to social groups and not individuals;
4 Abstract trust, 'trust that is based in abstract systems that set and maintain certain basic conditions, for example the government, the monetary system or the medical system in society at large' (p. 170).

These types of trust are not mutually exclusive (Ibid.).

Individualised trust is very important and can be said to be a building block for a trust based on reputation. Charette and Papachristos (2017) argue that the 'search for suitable co-offenders is a constant concern during offender's trajectory' (p. 11). The authors observe that once a good partner is found, 'you stick with him' (Ibid.). Thus trust is built on the basis of previous experience with each other, and a successful past criminal experience is a factor in identifying potential criminal partners in the future.

In order to apply Von Lampe and Ole Johansen's (2004) typology to our Ukrainian study, we need to discuss the cultural context and social settings of organising criminals. Kleemans and Van de Bunt (2008) pointed to the importance of applying the routine and opportunity theories to explore the social context, opportunities and structures dictating the conduct of organised criminals. To organise your business, be it legal or illegal, you have to engage in social exchange. This exchange can bring with it certain vulnerabilities and uncertainties, but it also offers the promise of reward. In the example of dodging a prohibition regime, the two parties that are most likely to co-operate are (a) those who offer and (b) those who are in need of protection. So, the latter will seek to create some sort of trustful relationship with the providers in order to secure long-term security. In the Ukrainian context, there are two groups of those offering illegal protection: state officials (upper-level criminality) and criminals (underworld criminality). In this chapter, we investigate the relationships established between these parties and the choices made by those in need of protection.

A number of studies have recently explored criminal connections with state officials. For example, Garay-Salamanca and Salcedo-Albaran (2012) report on the nature of Co-opted State Reconfiguration (CStR) in both Mexico and Columbia, where lawful and unlawful groups seek to unlawfully modify the political regime and thereby influence the decision-making process. Diviak, Dijkstra and Snijders (2018) investigate the corrupt politicians in the Czech Republic who constructed criminal networks through which to embezzle state resources. To complement these studies, following Kleemans and Van de Bunt (2008), the settings of organised crime in Ukraine are best understood within the structure of the state institutions themselves. For example, Markovska and van Duyne (2018) discuss the structure of and the opportunities for white-collar and corporate crime within the gas industry in Ukraine, arguing that politicians effectively used regulatory and structural opportunities within different ministries to create one of the most effective embezzlement schemes, where state resources and bureaucratic procedures were misused to enrich certain individuals. The Council of Europe (2017) investigated such criminality within the Ukrainian natural gas sector using the example of a case going back to 2013 which featured state officials and criminals working together to embezzle state funds. 'From January 2013 to June 2016, it is alleged that this group illegally took possession of funds received from the sale of natural gas to the amount of UAH 1,613,224,251.69 (€ 52,886,443.57). This is estimated to have caused losses to the state of UAH 740,065,924 (€ 24,261,632.99). It is alleged that an official of the state enterprise, acting on instructions, laundered the proceeds by transferring funds to accounts of fictitious enterprises. Subsequently, these funds are said to have been converted into cash or transferred to accounts abroad' (Ibid., p. 61). The special protection in this case was offered by the officials who instructed the business about the steps to follow in order to avoid being detected. This implies that the use of a corporate vehicle for the purpose of corruption was sanctioned by state officials.

There are two levels of power within organised criminality in Ukraine. One is apparent in the level of underworld criminality as recorded by the police, for example, in statistics related to armed robberies. Violent organised criminality has been on the rise since 2014. In 2016, 3,900 robberies were registered in Ukraine, including 196 robberies involving the use of the firearms (Knyazev, as discussed (in Bodnya, 2017)). Another level is that of *upper-world criminality*, as investigated by the NABU.

Legislation intends to move the gambling sector from its legal to an illegal status, or from the 'upper-world' to the 'underworld'. But this did not occur. Effectively, it has remained 'dovetailed' into the upper-world. In the first place, the market for gambling services did not end but has continued to thrive informally due to the continued demand of normal rather than marginal or criminal citizens as customers. In the second place, the supply of gambling services has remained more or less intact. This is not only due to the many ordinary non-criminal customers, as mentioned above, but is also the result of new forms of trust and power relationships which have developed between the authorities, criminal entrepreneurs and the establishment of interfaces wherever a demand occurs.

The two questions remain: How does the organisation of these illegal services relate to the issue of trust and what does power mean in this context? As far as power is concerned, the crime-entrepreneur is able to fall back on a trusted practice. As we have seen earlier in this discussion, the trust and power relationships in the traditional underworld or thieves-in-law, with their strict codes of conduct, were challenged during the 1950s–1960s to bolster the role of the 'legitimate' but corrupt power and authority in order to achieve illegal gains.

Power and trust in these relationships are never far apart, though they do not necessarily overlap. If an illegal industry looks for, or is forced to accept protection, its entrepreneurs must trust that they are dealing with the real protector. If the police appoints itself as an illegal protector, the protected gambling operator has no option but to trust the police. We will see that the police can be just as unreliable in its illegal as in its legal function. For the illegal gambling service providers, this means two things: (1) they are at the mercy of their protectors; but (2) the status of those protectors can be a significant factor in determining the level of their trust. Indeed, protectors and protectees become mutually dependent and vulnerable: the protector may be misled concerning the earnings of the protectee, and the latter may be deceived because the protector does not perform their function. Whether or not the protected entrepreneur is free to leave the agreement depends on the power of the protector, whose protection turns effectively into extortion. When power replaces trust, there is no 'free shopping' (Gambetta, 1993).

9.5 The present illegal gambling sector in Ukraine exemplified by a biography

Given the scarcity of data, we chose an ethnographic approach to study the current state of the sector through a narrative supplied by one participant who acted as an 'informant'. We call him 'Guy'. He is a man in his early 30s, with a university degree, who comes from a stable background. Guy has no criminal record. He views the organisation of illegal gambling clubs as a business and himself as a businessman. He worked for three years for a legal poker club until it was closed down in 2009. Following the state ban on gambling since March 2012, Guy has been involved in the activities of seven different clubs that offer facilities to play poker illegally. Here we discuss the different stages in the development of Guy's 'business' and address issues of trust and the power exercised by authorities and criminals, both within the underworld and the upper-world.

9.5.1 The beginning: fresher's years

Guy argues that beginning in 2011, two years after the criminalisation of gambling, a fashionable trend emerged for the establishment of underground poker clubs in Ukraine. In our study, Club 1 represents the first attempt of two friends, Guy and another person, to organise an illegal gambling facility. At this stage, a gambling facility or underground poker club usually signified a studio flat rented illegally. According to Guy, in 2012, a total of four individuals were involved in the operation of this small gambling Club 1: Guy and Y were responsible for the organisation and daily running of the club; while W and Z invested funds and provided necessary equipment (poker table, chairs and mini bar).

We have calculated that around 50 clients were on the books to make the club profitable: 15 clients were on Guy's list and the rest, 35, on Y's list. The profit was shared equally between the two groups of organisers: Guy and Y on one side, and W and Z on the other. The agreement was that each organiser would get 25% of the profits.

The club faced both internal and external threats. Internal threats came from a lack of trust amongst the four entrepreneurs: each group suspected the other of concealing profit or not sharing profit according to the agreement. In Club 1, only Guy and Y were working with the clients. This lack of trust among the organisers was not, however, considered to be a serious threat to the sustainability of the club. The external threats mainly concerned protection. This club operated in rented flats, so the main danger of discovery came from neighbours. This was one of the reasons why the role of X and Y was critically important: they were tasked to only invite clients who would not engage in violent conduct and would not carry firearms. It was also important that the members of the club were not connected to any of the established organised criminal groups in the city (who might later demand protection money). The club did not pay protection money to the police or to any other authorities in the city. The club survived for six months but it had to be disbanded after a violent confrontation between Y and one client. This event also marked the end of Guy's friendship with Y. Club 1 had very little inherent power of its own and was subject to an obvious lack of mutual trust amongst its organisers. Powerless crime-entrepreneurs with little mutual trust must keep their heads down and remain as invisible as possible.

Club 2 was formed by four individuals: Guy, W, Z and T. Z was a close friend of Guy whom Z invited to join the business he had already started with T and W. All four organisers invested money in the club, each contributing roughly 25% of the total investment. Guy took on the crucial role of inviting clients and thus established about 60% of the client database. This club also operated for six months and ended due to a lack of suitable premises and increasing threats of police raids. This situation corresponds to the increasing number of police raids then being reported by local media.

Most of such Ukrainian news regarding successful police operations against illegal gambling clubs was based on the discovery of clubs such as the one above. Guy explained that a number of their competitors at the time had made the crucial mistake of paying the police for protection. Largely operated by amateur or semi-professional gamblers with no connection to the criminal underworld, these clubs were easy targets for the police, even if the police had previously been receiving protection payments from those clubs. In such cases, the police appeared to be working according to a 'fleece first, bust later' strategy.

Of the 13 police raids reported by the local news agency for the period 2015–2017, five were raids targeting private properties and clubs where one poker table was in operation (Onews, 2017). The rest involved raids resulting in the confiscation of computers used in the provision of gambling services. According to Guy, protection payments made to police by these clubs are useless, as the police generally do not heed their protection duties.

Both Clubs 1 and 2 operated on the basis of mutual trust between the organisers (Von Lampe and Ole Johansen, 2004), a trust based on friendship and shared norms of behaviour, but also based in the context of a general lack of trust in society at large and, ironically, a lack of trust in the police. Once such mutual trust was broken, the actors separated and usually no opportunity occurred to mend the trust (which would have been risky in view of increasing police scrutiny).

9.5.2 *Club 3: in search of protection*

In the winter of 2015, Guy considered new strategies to continue the business of illegal poker. Both Clubs 1 and 2 had operated underground with no protection payments being made. Guy decided to change tactics and approached the boss of a well-known criminal group, still referred to locally as the thieves-in-law. Guy proposed to open a poker club in the district controlled by this group. He knew the Boss, having been introduced to him during a poker tournament in another club. This Boss, who enjoyed playing poker himself, agreed to offer protection in return for monthly payments of 10% of profits. Club 3 had three main organisers: Guy, Z and T. By this stage, Guy himself was able to supply about 80% of the required investment, with Z and T providing the rest. Z and T looked after the clients and day-to-day running of the club. Profit was shared between the three organisers, with 10% paid for protection.

Such a connection to the criminal underworld elevated Guy's activities to a different level, offering opportunities for establishing a wider client base of higher-status organisers and players. According to Guy, even rumours that they were working with the Boss helped to create an aura of untouchability due to the power of his criminal authority. Interestingly, these arrangements were not without disadvantage. Ironically, the Boss himself represented a big problem for the club: he was an alcoholic and substance abuser, displaying unpredictable and violent behaviour, and regularly carried a gun. So, whilst the Boss protected Guy's business from others (including the police), no one protected Guy from the Boss. Trust based on the reputation of the Boss was essential to build the reputation of the club as being untouchable, however, it also led to the club's having a reputation for violent conduct during games. Although in Club 3 reputational trust became a major issue for Guy, it is clear that when reputational trust is not strongly supported by individual trust, the organisational network will struggle to survive.

9.5.3 The ultimate power

While working for Club 3 under the Boss's protection, Guy was beginning to be involved in the operation of a much larger illegal gambling club. We call it Club 4. In 2013, Guy was employed there on a shift basis and received a monthly salary. This illegal gambling establishment operated openly and in the city centre. It provided not only poker facilities but all other casino services. According to Guy, once a big gambling establishment is open, the smaller ones go out of business, as clients prefer to play as part of a bigger organisation.

Club 4 operated on a highly professional level: it invested in professional safety measures, installed metal detectors, enforced a no-firearms regime and even had police officers patrolling its entrance. In view of these provisions, it was clear to Guy in 2013 that the club was backed by very powerful investors.

However, during winter–spring of 2013/2014, the environment in which the clubs operated changed. Political events in Ukraine and armed conflict in the East of the country led to the formation of a number of armed units that offered to protect the country from external aggression and from internal corruption. These units presented a real operational threat to the gambling clubs. In the spring of 2015, Club 4 was closed down after violent encounters with one of these armed groups. Ultimately, power came from the barrel of a gun.

By the winter of 2017, new gambling clubs re-appeared in the city centre, often employing their previous staff and offering poker tables and other casino facilities. Guy considered Club 4 to be once again a well-protected working environment due to protection offered by the upper-world and accepted an invitation to oversee the play in its poker halls. The senior manager viewed this club as a business venture and never discussed issues of legality with its personnel. According to Guy, to operate such an illegal establishment so openly requires a level of protection that goes beyond the remit of the local authorities and the police and involves senior officials in the capital Kiev. In its first months of operation, the club made protection payments in the region of $100,000 per month. However, six months later, this payment was reviewed, as the gambling hall was not making enough money to cover the cost of protection. Such a negotiation of protection payment rates is highly significant. Gambetta (1988) points out that protection payments should not be extortionate but affordable and credible.

Bouchard and Morselli (2014) discuss the efficiency of a criminal organisation. In the case of Guy, the nature of his organising criminal conduct is dependent on his ability, as a risk manager, to form long-term trusting relationships.

9.6 Conclusion: the law, trust and the powerful

It can be argued that the criminal protection offered by the authorities to Club 4 is based on abstract trust (Von Lampe and Ole Johansen, 2004), trust in authoritative figures within the government. Such trust in the criminal authority of the government has been developing in the Ukraine over a number of years and has peaked within the last ten years.

His involvement in Club 4 made Guy aware of the operational reach of governmental power, which could overrule subordinate foci of power. He also learned that power unaccompanied by trust will soon result in coercion and violence, basically undermining itself. Thus, ironically, Guy was able to rebuild his trust within state institutions even if his activities remained obviously criminal. It implies that corrupt officials are the best in providing protection for the very services that they had criminalised in the first place! This is reminiscent of a similar situation during Soviet times when state officials negotiated with a criminal business underworld to ensure the supply of scarce goods in exchange for protection.

This account of the four illegal gambling clubs organised by Guy offers an insight into the world of organising illegal businesses and the associated interaction between the criminal and political worlds through the lens of their trust and power relationships. The ban on gambling created a social context wherein advantage is contested by legal and illegal players. In effect, the concept of legality becomes irrelevant, and instead, relationships are facilitated by the power to negotiate interests and maintain trust in that power on a long-term basis.

In our research on illegal gambling in Ukraine, we examined the organised crime landscape in the country and focused on one of the coveted services previously regulated by the public administration, which became suddenly outlawed: gambling. This prohibition of what was a popular service in the country, already plagued by a weak rule of law and endemic corruption led, as was to be expected, to illegal substitutes offering the now-illegal services. In effect, such services mushroomed even though faced with a variety of risks or even direct threat.

At the micro level, we identified small-scale entrepreneurs with little power, forced to remain within networks of fellow-entrepreneurs at a similar level, according to the notion that those who have no power had better remain rather invisible. However, working through and within such networks remains inefficient and small-scale. Real trustworthiness within such networks remains a scarce 'commodity' and the fear of their participants of being cheated remains a threat to their continuity. Because of the unavoidable distance between many of the network nodes, control and risk management within such networks is difficult.

In gambling-related trading networks, trust, though important, is not crucial, but a lack of trust leads to volatility; such short-lived operations re-structure frequently. Consequently, the co-offending relationships within them are short-lived.

This observation agrees with the findings of Charette and Papachristos (2017) who conclude that 'partnerships between co-offenders are short-term, most of them ending after their first experience' (p. 10). Considering Guy's career trajectory, it is possible to argue that his best criminal partner in gambling was the larger club, which could offer reliable protection. In the case of Club 4, Guy had become a member of a powerful network operating under effective protection. Subsequently, this protection was allegedly provided by a real, that is, central power, which involved itself in the organised illegality of the prohibited gambling industry. We might say that the supposed defenders of legality showed themselves to have the power to create a 'protective dovetail' with organised crime enterprises who had confidence in the protection thus obtained. Indeed, it might be said that trust and power relations are as important in organised crime as they are in any successful legal enterprise.

References

Bicchieri, C., Xiao, E., Muldoon, R. (2011) Trustworthiness is a social norm, but trusting is not. *Politics, Philosophy and Economics*, Vol. 10, No. 2, pp. 170–187.

Bodnya, T. (2017) Head of the Criminal Investigation Department: 'The number of crimes has risen last year. And this year is not going to be easier'. In Russian (Глава Департамента уголовного розыска Сергей Князев: "Количество преступлений в прошлом году выросло. И этот год не будет легче") [On-line]. Available at: https://censor.net.ua/resonance/423591/glava_departamenta_ugolovnogo_rozyska_sergeyi_knyazev_kolichestvo_prestupleniyi_v_proshlom_godu_vyroslo.

Bouchard, M., Morselli, C. (2014) Opportunistic structures of organised crime. In: Paoli, L. (ed.) *Oxford Handbook of Organised Crime*. Oxford: OUP. pp. 288–302.

Butler, W. E (1992) Crime in the Soviet Union: early glimpses of the true story. *British Journal of Criminology*, 31, pp.144–159

Campana, P., Varese, F. (2013) Cooperation in criminal organisations: kinship, violence as credible commitments. *Rationality and Society*, Vol. 25, No. 3, pp. 263–289.

Charette, Y., Papachristos, A. V. (2017) The network dynamic of co-offending careers. *Social Networks*, Vol. 51, pp. 3–13.

Democratic Initiatives Foundation. (2017) National Survey [On-line]. Available at: https://dif.org.ua/category/opinion-polls.

Diviak, T., Dijkstra, J. K., Snijders, T. A. (2018) Structure, multiplexity, and centrality in a corruption network: The Czech Rath affair. *Trends in Organised Crime*. https://doi.org/10.1007/s12117-018-9334-y.

Gambetta, D. (1988) Fragments of an economic theory of mafia. *European Journal of Sociology*, Vol. XXIX, No. 1, pp. 127–145.

Gambetta, D. (1993) *The Sicilian Mafia: The Business of Private Protection*. Harvard: Harvard University Press.

Garay-Salamanca, L. J., Salcedo-Albarán, E. (2012) Institutional impact of criminal networks in Columbia and Mexico. *Crime, Law and Social Change*, Vol. 57, No. 2, pp. 177–194.

Glazov, Y. (2002) 'Thieves' in the USSR – A social phenomenon. In: Galeotti, M. (ed.) *Russian and Post-Soviet Organised Crime.* Aldershot: Dartmouth Publishing Company. pp. 141–156.

Emmel, C., Clark, A. (2009) The methods used in connected lives: investigating networks, neighborhoods, and communities. Working Paper. ESRC National Centre for Research Methods. [On-line]. Available at: http://eprints.ncrm.ac.uk/800/1/2009_connected_lives_methods_emmel_clark.pdf

Handelman, S. (2002) The Russian Mafiya. In: Galeotti, M. (ed.) *Russian and Post-Soviet Organised Crime.* Aldershot: Dartmouth Publishing Company. pp. 83–96.

Keller, B. (1988) Brezhnev Son-in-Law Gets 12-Year Term [On-line]. Available at: www.nytimes.com/1988/12/31/world/brezhnev-son-in-law-gets-12-year-term.html.

Kleemans, E. R., Van de Bunt, H. G. (2008) Organised crime, occupations and opportunity. *Global Crime*, Vol. 9, No. 3, pp. 185–197.

Kupatadze, A. (2012) Organised crime, political transitions and state formations in post-Soviet Eurasia. New York: Palgrave Macmillan.

Markovska, A., Serdyuk, A. (2013) Dysfunctional social institutions as an obstacle to tackle crime: Exploring the dilemma of a good Ukrainian policeman. In: Van Duyne P. (ed.) *Human Dimensions in Organised Crime: Money Laundering and Corruption.* Oisterwijk: Wolf Legal Publishing. pp. 425–440.

Markovska, A., Van Duyne, P. (2018) Contextualising corporate criminality in different cultural settings: The case of the gas industry in Ukraine. In: Campbell, L., Lord, N. (eds.) *Corruption in Commercial Enterprise: Law, Theory and Practice.* Abingdon: Routledge. pp. 143–160.

Markovska, A., Zabyelina, Y. (2016) Enforcing prohibitions in weak states: Gambling in Ukraine. In: Van Duyne, P.C. (ed.) *Narratives on Organised Crime in Europe: Criminals, Corruptors and Policy.* Oisterwijk: Wolf Legal Publishing. pp. 89–116.

Markovska, A., Zabyelina, Y. (2019) Negotiated prohibition: The organisation of illegal gambling businesses in Ukraine. In: Polese, A., Russo, A., and Strazzari, F. edition *Governance Beyond the Law: The Immoral, The Illegal, The Criminal.* International Political Economy Series. Cham: Palgrave Macmillan. pp. 105–124.

Morselli, C., and Tremblay, P. (2004) Criminal achievement, offender networks and the benefits of low self-control. Criminology, 42, pp. 773-804

NABU. (2018) Technical assessment of the anti-corruption Bureau of Ukraine [On-line]. Available at: https://nabu.gov.ua/technical-assessment-bureaus-first-3-years-activity.

Nikiforov, A. S. (1993) Organised crime in the West and in the Former USSR: An attempted comparison. *International Journal of Offender Therapy and Comparative Criminology*, Vol. 37, No. 1, pp. 5–15.

Onews. (2017) On-line search for the cases reported. Available at: http://uanews.odessa.ua/.

Shelley, L I (1994) Post- Soviet Organised Crime: Implications for Economic, Social and Political Development, Demokratizatsiya, 2, pp. 341–358.

Van Duyne, P., Stocco, E. (2012) *Corruption in Serbia, from Black Box to Transparent Policy Making.* Oisterwijk: Wolf Legal Publisher.

Varese, F. (2002) The Society of the Vory-v-Zakone, 1930s–1950s. In: Galeotti, M. (ed.) *Russian and Post-Soviet Organised Crime.* Aldershot: Dartmouth Publishing Company. pp. 7–30.

Von Lampe, K., Ole Johansen, P. (2004) Organized crime and trust: On the conceptualisation and empirical relevance of trust in the context of criminal networks. *Global Crime*, Vol. 6, No. 2, pp. 159–184.

Williams, P., Picarelli, J. (2001) Organised crime in Ukraine: Challenges and responses. *Trends in Organised Crime*, Vol. 6, No. 3&4, pp. 100–142.

Yamagishi, T. (2001) Trust as a form of social intelligence. In: Cook, K. (ed.) *Trust in Society*. NY: Russel Sage Foundation. pp. 121–147.

10 The social organisation of treason

Anti-Hitler networks in the Third Reich

Robert R. Faulkner and Eric R. Cheney

10.1 Introduction

Since Plutarch and the assassination of Caesar in 44 BC, the course of history has often hinged on conspiracy and treason. In Nazi-Germany, on July 20, 1944, the plot to assassinate Hitler and stage a coup d'état remains one of the most dramatic events of the 20th century. The assassination of Caesar was successful; the assassination of Hitler was not. Failed conspiracy plots offer many lessons for the study of political lethality, as well as the examination of the structure of social networks of treason.

Treason consists of subverting governmental, political and military institutions through coup d'état, insurrection, sabotage, espionage, disclosure of top-secret information, and other means designed to undermine, overthrow, and replace the leadership and personnel of a political regime. Because the regime possesses a monopoly of the means of surveillance and violence, a political conspiracy exists in a state of constant potential threat (of attack or accident), and it is only by making the responses routine that the conspirators can go about their work of orchestrating, concealing, and effectively carrying out high-risk anti-state action. We do not pursue a value judgement of the plotters' treasonous actions in the Nazi-Germany context. Instead, we use this case of treason as a laboratory to study the extraordinary acts of attempted assassination and coup d'état within an extreme secret society.

Our context for study is the network of anti-Hitler and anti-Nazi conspirators who created multiple conspiracies or plots. These network structures are dynamic, heterogeneous, and contingent (White, 1992). We focus on these three features, especially the contingent, i.e., those features upon which the rise of illegal political networks in an authoritarian regime depend. We provide a sketch of the rise of anti-Hitler networks and a network analysis of the intersection of ties of treason and the overall structure of this secret 'social circle' [Simmel, 1906, 1950, 1955; see Bendix in Simmel, 1955, p. 125].

We reconstructed the network from biographies, memoirs, and historical sources that include every plotter who participated in every plot from 1938 to 1944. These data also include vital time-varying information on the military and political successes or failures of the Third Reich, the network characteristics of the plot teams, and measures of collaboration on treasonous strategies and tactics. We want to emphasise that by 'anti-Hitler' we mean collective beliefs and practices supporting the primary goal of leader-focused lethality through the assassination of Hitler.

The numerous plots against Hitler and the Nazi regime are among the most famous and well-chronicled subversive activities in 20th-century history. Initially, the conspirators attempt pursuing a coup d'état while opening secret channels of diplomacy with the West. They only fitfully venture into contemplating plans to murder Hitler and his Nazi leadership. These plans or combinations of plans are kept within a 'secret circle' (Churchill, 1948, p. 311), a 'tiny group' (Shirer, 2011, p. 372) with an 'innermost circle' of conspirators (Fest, 1996, p. 89; Reitlinger, 1957). Opposition plans are worked out in and across clandestine meetings of Hitler's expert advisers and top generals. There is an 'intense, unceasing struggle' within the army staff that soon moves down the chain of command while spreading into the upper echelons of Germany's political and diplomatic professions. The assassination of Hitler soon achieves high salience in the conspiracies. This form of 'hot' treason – high lethality – is one among a set of alternative treasonous techniques.

In the initial stages, the networks are not aligned into a focused organisation (Feld, 1981). They are not yet a 'growing concern.' There is disunity with 'perhaps only a number of functionaries set to cooperate in prescribed ways at a certain conjuncture' (Sumner in Hughes, 1971b, p. 53). An active nucleus forms with a 'defined situation' of how and when they are to act (Hughes, 1971b, pp. 54–55). Yet, as noted above, in overcoming objections to treason and in working out focused definitions of it, disjunctures appear. There is a 'gap between the military and civilians' (Shirer, 2011, pp. 374–375) and a gap between the persistent core and the precarious periphery of the conspiracies, characterised by the following cleavages and misunderstandings: (a) about how formal and hierarchical the conspiratorial plots should be; (b) over the proper role of the military officers (generals, lieutenants, corporals) and civilians (diplomats, lawyers, pastors, intellectuals) in treason; (c) about killing others and the specific direction and timing of proposed murders and coup; (d) about who can be depended on to simultaneously implement the Berlin, Paris, and Prague takeover of the SS and Gestapo; and (e) about time. By the summer of 1944, the plotters know time was closing in on Hitler and on them. Allied and Russian troops invade the homeland. Deadlines loom. Deadlines create 'overload.' Misunderstandings and overload push the plotters into impatience (Gibson, 2012; Weiner, 1976). The bomb failure in the 1945 Valkyrie plot is an accident. It ignites a catastrophic breakdown of coordination and quickly results in the collapse of hierarchy, cohesion, efficient decision-making, and role responsibility (Perrow, 1999; Vaughan, 1996). Misunderstanding, deadline, and accident feed directly into the tragedy that was to come.

As we know, Valkyrie as assassination and coup fails. The violent murder and the non-violent putsch collapse. The bomb placed by Stauffenberg in the briefing room at the Wolf's Lair (Wolfschanze) detonates but does not kill Hitler. While the cadre of plotters refined Valkyrie, they made no allowance for Hitler surviving an assassination attempt (Jones, 2008, p. 287). The coup in Berlin wastes valuable time awaiting confirmation of Hitler's assassination; the core cannot mobilise the top levels of the military and police forces upon which it depends; promises and expectations of combat readiness for military seizure of power quickly evaporate; key plotters fail to cut the communication lines from Hitler's headquarters to the centres of power. At the nerve centre of the coup at Home Army Command on the Bendlerstrasse, we find only uncertainty, hesitation, and inaction. Hitler's propaganda chief steps into the void and takes over. The four core activists are arrested, taken out into the courtyard in Berlin's war ministry, and shot by a firing squad. Orders to murder them are issued by a general who knew about and 'wavered' in his support of the coup. Opportunism and defection set in. The conspiracy is now in disarray. The Nazis pounce and restore order. The Führer orders lethality and retribution. Show trials and execution of central and peripheral conspirators unfold.

Yet, in the run up to Valkyrie, and despite the distrust, impatience, and differences in tactics, meeting after secret meeting take place. Often the same people show up at the meetings. There is a chain of repeated ties (Simmel, 1906). Programmes of action are proposed, choices dissected, tactics mapped out, problems ejected, forks in the road reached, decisions made, promises announced, and personnel mobilised. The course of treason, worked out in its skeletal form in 1938, ebbs and flows, and begins to take shape in 1943 and 1944. The objectives are to kill Hitler, cordon off the main centres of power, isolate and disable Hitler's SS, seize the government through a non-violent coup, and form a provisional government. The conspirators coalesce around a core or nucleus of highly active and zealous plotters. Organisational command shifts from older-line generals – Beck, Goerdeler, Hassell, and Popitz – to a network of mid-level colonels, key civilians and police, and urban control personnel with reputations for dependability.

To foreshadow our themes, the plotters vary in their connectedness, their persistent attendance in plot events, endorsement of assassination and coup, and commitment to treasonous action. Within political conspiracies, under constant threat of detection and death, lack of persistence in group ties, mistrust of colleagues, misalignment of objectives, and impatience with achieving them not only impede concerted action, they can be fatal.

10.2 Exogenous social ties and network construction

Anti-Nazi plotters actively opposing the regime drew on pre-existing association ties to mobilise for treason. Social ties form among senior army officers concerned about what they saw as Hitler's rashness in risking a general European war by the invasion of Czechoslovakia. A worried former ambassador to Italy, Ulrich von Hassell, brings together a small number of like-minded Foreign

Ministry officials, including State Secretary Ernst von Weizsacker, Adam von Trott zu Solz, and Hans-Bernd von Haeftenstaff (Evans, 2008). Specialised cavalry officers, superintendents of police, for example, become a basis for recruitment of 'like-minded men who would put the moral duty of ridding Germany of Hitler ahead of their professional job as soldiers' (Jones, 2008, p. 123). Prior professional, occupational, and social associations among pastors, justice officials, lawyers, and intellectuals become cooptable associational ties – a resource for plotters in creating and organising sustained anti-regime action. In short, prevailing legal social ties provide opportunities for organising secret meetings, airing grievances, focusing anger, and hatching illegal plans against Hitler and the Third Reich. However, prevailing professional and military roles can inhibit treason against the regime. Prussian officers abhor disobedience to authority and to their superior's orders; Protestant and Catholic ministers and pastors abhor murder; diplomatic foreign officers detest and resist clandestine and dangerous negotiations with Britain. These tensions exert a push-pull dynamic on the plotters and their plots.

An overlap between legal associational ties and illegal ties between plotters may facilitate the rise and persistence of treasonous groups; however, at the same time, an overlap between official roles and unofficial roles may inhibit treason, 'whose whole raison d'etre is deception, disobedience and defiance' (Jones, 2008, p. 114). Yet, despite the paralysis and lethargy that may set in, a 'tiny nucleus' (Shirer, 2011, p. 374) of plotters forms. In these fledgling anti-regime networks – called 'circles,' cells,' 'nests,' 'rings,' or 'plots' – a small set of conspirators overcome their ambivalence, even abhorrence towards anti-regime action.

10.3 Plotter orientation and network construction

The anti-Hitler conspirators differ in their commitment to holding and attending secret meetings. They have different interests, voices, stakes, focal concerns, and competencies in manoeuvring themselves and others into implementing a strategy of treason by violent or non-violent means. One important source of the plotters' variation is their individual beliefs in appropriate strategic action to successfully overthrow the regime. Some of the plotters saw assassinating Hitler as a necessary action to overthrow the regime; others were opposed to assassination on moral grounds. Some of the plotters were so committed to the overthrow of the regime by means of assassination that they offered to sacrifice their own life in various scenarios of suicide missions – from suicide bombs hidden in overcoats to proposing smuggling bombs on planes to be detonated while flying with Hitler. The necessity of a coup d'état was a widely held strategic view. Other plotters saw sharing war secrets with the Allies and the Soviets as part of the key to the plot's success. Still others believed in the importance of diplomacy with the Allies and Soviets as part of plot success. These strategic orientations were not mutually exclusive and many of the plotters held multiple plot strategies as part of their outlook of the ingredients for success.

10.4 Hypotheses

The historical record indicates that actor social attributes such as membership in the military, civil service, or religious organisations, or as members of the aristocracy were resources for the plotters in the initial formation of the anti-Hitler networks. We draw from research that implies that locations in social institutions are recourses for network mobilisation (Gould, 1991, 1996) to formulate the following hypothesis:

Hypothesis One: Plotters' exogenous social attributes such as being a civilian or military officer partially explains the formation of the anti-Hitler networks within the Third Reich.

The historical record also shows that the anti-Hitler plotters were oriented to five basic strategies: (1) coup d'état, (2) assassination, (3) assassination with zealotry, (4) diplomacy, and (5) espionage. We hypothesise that these strategic orientations form an endogenous cultural code within the conspiracy that plays an important role in network formation.

Hypothesis Two: Plotters' actor attributes, such as their plot orientation, partially explain the formation of the anti-Hitler networks within the Third Reich.

10.5 Sources and data

It should be emphasised that we are studying clandestine plots and their plotters. These are of course not public events, such as petitions, legal briefs, public demonstrations by regime opponents, and violence by police or counter demonstration tactics by armed squads of state actors. We are not studying protest activities and social movement events that are accessible through newspapers of record, such as *The New York Times* or, in this case, the Berlin, Paris, or Prague press. To be sure, the show trials of the plotters were public and famously recorded events; they too, however, are not a focus of our data collection. We seek to illuminate a dark corner of 20th-century Europe. Our principal sources of data about anti-Nazi plot events in a six-year time period culminating in the Valkyrie debacle are numerous, multi-layered, and wide-ranging – from memoir to archive. The data sources are: *Plotting Hitler's Death* (Fest, 1996); *They Plotted Against Hitler* (Kahle, 1944); *Target Hitler: The Plots to Kill Hitler* (Duffy, 1992); Killing Hitler (Moorhouse, 2006); *Kill Hitler* (Short, 2013); *Kill the Fuhrer* (Astridge, 2009); *To Kill the Devil* (Mason, 1978); *The Secret Plot to Kill Hitler* (Noack, 2005); *The Men Who Tried to Kill Hitler* (Manvell and Fraenkel, 2008); and *Hitler Must Die* (Mason, 1985).

Supplementing the 'kill Hitler' genre is the 'plan hatching' and 'plot unfolding' genre chronicled in the following books: *The Conspirators* (Manvell, 1971); *No Ordinary Men* (Sifton and Stern, 2013); *Valkyrie: The Story of the Plot to Kill Hitler, By Its Last Member* (Boeselager, 2009); *Valkyrie: An Insider's Account of the Plot to Kill Hitler* (Gisevius, 2009, 1947); *Operation Valkyrie: The German Generals' Plot Against Hitler* (Galante, 2002); *Codename Valkyrie* (Schrader, 2009); *The Canaris Conspiracy* (Manvell and Fraenkel, 2008); *Hitler's Spy Chief: The Wilhelm Canaris Mystery* (Bassett, 2005); and *The Oster Conspiracy* (Parssinen, 2012).

Invaluable background on the Third Reich is found in Kershaw's book on Hitler (2000), Michael Burleigh's *The Third Reich: A New History* (2000), and Shirer's *The Rise and Fall of The Third Reich* (2011 [1959]), as well as incisive writing of Nigel Jones (2008). Shirer and Jones, among the other writers cited above, provide uneven but thick detail on what we have called the first stage or the 'birth of a conspiracy against Hitler' (Jones, 2008, pp. 42–93; Shirer, 2011, pp. 372–382) and the middle stage conspiracies (Jones, 2008, p. 112–144; Shirer, 2011, pp. 647–659), as well as the assassination and coup plots of 1942 (Shirer, 2011, pp. 1018–1028) and 1944 (Shirer, 2011, pp. 1044–1082, 2008, pp. 172–235). Nearly all these sources take note of the 'bloody vengeance' that followed the fall of Valkyrie. Sweeping historical treatments reveal the hidden traces of the regime's depravity and the roads to resistance (Ainsztein, 1974; Churchill, 1948; Gallin, 1961; Grunberger, 1971; Hoffmann, 1988, 2008, 2011; Remak, 1969; Rothfels, 1962; von Schlabrendorff, 2005; Suhl, 1968; Thomsett, 1997; Wheeler-Bennett, 2005).

10.6 Coding co-conspirators and keywords

A heroic resistance narrative deployed by writers on Germany under the Third Reich emphasises the collective exploits and courage of Oster, Caranis, Tresckow, Schlabrendorff, Hassell, Goerdeler, Dohnanyi, Bonhoeffer, and Stauffenberg, to name a few. For purposes of content analysis and keywords, names overlap and connections and keywords duplicate one another. A similarity of links among conspirators across conspiracies facilitates the compilation and mapping of linkages between them (Krebs, 2001; Sparrow, 1991). This in turn facilitates inter-rater reliability in depicting the plot paths to Valkyrie. It multiplies redundancy among the historical sources, over-representation of highly visible military and civilian plotters, and tolerable levels of low overlap for one-shot or low-visibility participants.

We discarded two plots because they involved a lone bomber; despite decades of speculation by scholars, we could find no evidence that a plot event was at work in these two solo assassination attempts. Finally, our inter-rater reliability for the remaining plots and their plotters using Cronbach's alpha is .82. The final data network is 178 plotters and 18 plots.

10.7 Coding plotter orientations

Anti-Hitler plotters had a variety of conceptions of how a plot against Hitler might be successful. We judge that there were five major plotter orientations among the plotters in the anti-Nazi networks. The five plotter orientations described below are not mutually exclusive; conspirators often espoused multiple of these orientations, while some only espoused one.

Some of the plotters met and discussed their beliefs in turning over war plan secrets to the Soviets or Allies to hasten the inevitable defeat of the Third Reich. We code these anti-Nazi plotters with the label 'espionage.'

Some of the plotters met and discussed their belief that secretly meeting with the Allies or Soviets to organise a diplomatic solution to the war's end, without the consent of the official Nazi government, was a necessary strategy to either ending the war or resisting Nazi rule, or both. We code these anti-Nazi plotters as 'diplomats.'

Some of the plotters met and discussed their support for a coup d'état. These plotters believed arresting Nazi government leaders and forming a new German government out of anti-Nazi high ranking military leaders was a necessary strategy to ending Nazi rule. We code these anti-Nazi plotters with the label 'coup.'

Some of the plotters met and discussed their beliefs that assassinating Hitler was a necessary strategy to ending Nazi rule. Some of the religious civilian plotters were opposed to assassination. We code the anti-Nazi plotters favourable to Hitler's assassination with the label 'assassination.'

Finally, some of the plotters met and discussed their belief that assassinating Hitler was a necessary strategy to ending Nazi rule could be distinguished from the other 'assassination' code discussed above because they were willing to die in the act thought necessary to kill Hitler. There was variation in the ways that the conspirators conceived of their own death if it meant the death of Hitler – from detonating their bomb-loaded overcoats in Hitler's presence to exploding bombs on airplanes while traveling with the Führer. We code these anti-Nazi plotters with the label 'zealots.'

10.8 The Kreisau Circle

The so-called Kreisau Circle is mentioned, even highlighted, in virtually every book on resistance to the Nazi-regime, and then includes Shirer, Jones, Evans, and all our sources (which we have listed in the reference section). It is important because in 1938 and even before it was a social circle that informally brought together the cream of the Prussian aristocracy, young Prussian officers, intellectuals, and others who were disenchanted with Hitler and the Nazi regime.

Two coders went through the sources and listed the names of those nominated as being in the circle – Hofacker, Schulenberg, Trott, Schwerin, Yorck, Moltke, Qirnheim, Harnacks (husband and wife), Schlabrendorff, Father Delp, and then Finckh, and of course both B. Stauffenberg and C. Stauffenberg. There was high inter-rater agreement with the exception of Harnack (the wife), Finckh (who arrives later), and ÜxKüll (due to confusion over the name and spelling of Üxküll-Gyllenband (full name).

The Kreisau Circle is heterogeneous in its composition; it contains impatient and action-oriented actors like Stauffenberg (who later became the proponent of assassination) and those opposed to any form of killing such as Father Delp.

10.9 Data

The above codes led to a series of sociomatrices and sociographs that form the data for the analysis. The sociomatrices are bipartite matrices where the columns of the matrix represent the eighteen (18) major plots during the years 1938 through 1945 and the rows are the 178 plotters involved in attempts to assassinate Hitler, overthrow the Nazi regime, or both. A one (1) in the intersection of the ith row and jth column means that the ith plotter collaborated on the jth plot. A zero (0) in the intersection of the ith row and jth column means that the ith plotter did not collaborate on the jth plot. We present all data in the form of graphs, or sociomatrices. The line in the graph, or sociomatrix, in a bipartite graph means that a plotter collaborated on a plot. In our graphs, we depict the plotters as circles and the plots as squares.

Figure 10.1 depicts the social organisation of the eighteen (18) anti-Hitler plots. The appendix lists the plotters listed in the graph. Figure 10.1 forms the dependent variable for this study. Figure 10.1 is comprised of 178 anti-Hitler plotters and eighteen (18) anti-Hitler plots. There are 387 lines or 'edges' in the graph – or, in other words, there are 387 connections between plotters and plots. The research question is: What accounts for the social formation of the network shown in Figure 10.1? One of our hypotheses is that exogenous social attributes such as military rank, civilian status, or membership in the aristocracy accounts for the formation of Figure 10.1. A second hypothesis is that the plotter orientations account for the social formation of network shown in Figure 10.1.

Figure 10.2 shows the distribution of degree centrality for each plotter. For these data, degree centrality for the *plotters* is simply the count of the number of times a plotter participates in the plots. Figure 10.1 shows that ninety-five (95) conspirators only collaborated on one (1) of the plots; thirty (30) conspirators collaborated on two (2) plots; twenty-seven (27) plotters collaborated on three (3) plots; all the way down until we see that one (1) plotter collaborated on a total of ten (10) anti-Hitler plots. Figure 10.2 shows that the plotters shown in the sociomatrix of the anti-Hitler network (Figure 10.1) were not evenly distributed, with a few of the plotters participating in much more of the plots than others, and the majority of the plotters involved in just one, two, or a few plots.

Figure 10.3 shows the distribution of degree centrality for each plot. For these data, degree centrality for the *plots* is simply the count of the number of plotters who collaborated on a plot. Figure 10.3 shows that the first plot had twenty-five (25) plotters; the second had eight (8) plotters; the third plot had nine (9) plotters; all the way up until the eighteenth Valkyrie plot, which has a degree centrality (frequency) of eighty-four (84) plotters. The number of plotters per plot ranges from a low of eight (8) plotters to a high of eighty-four (84) plotters.

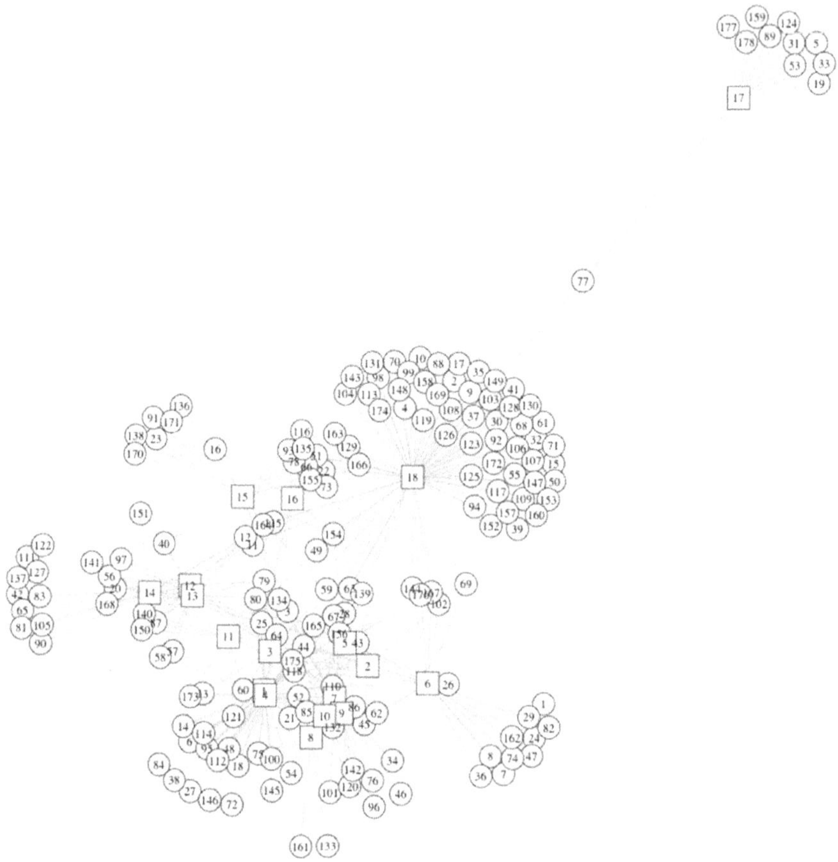

Figure 10.1 All plotters by all anti-Hitler plots (circles = plotters; squares = plots)

10.10 Measures: actor social attributes as independent variables

Figure 10.4 presents the plotters who were civilian members of religious organisations or state bureaucracies in black. Our hypothesis is that the civilian social attribute of the plotters shown in Figure 10.4 is an independent variable that is statistically related to the formation of Figure 10.1.

Figure 10.5 presents the plotters who were members of the Kreisau Circle in black. Our hypothesis is that the Kreisau social attribute of the plotters shown in Figure 10.5 is an independent variable that is statistically related to the formation of Figure 10.1.

Figure 10.6 presents the plotters who were military officers in black. Our hypothesis is that the military officer social attribute of the plotters shown in

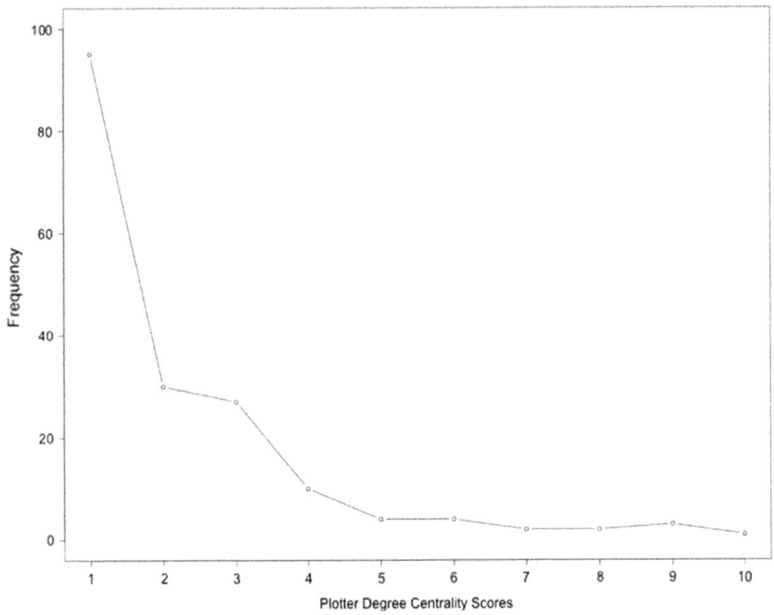

Figure 10.2 Distribution of plotter degree centrality scores across all anti-Hitler plots

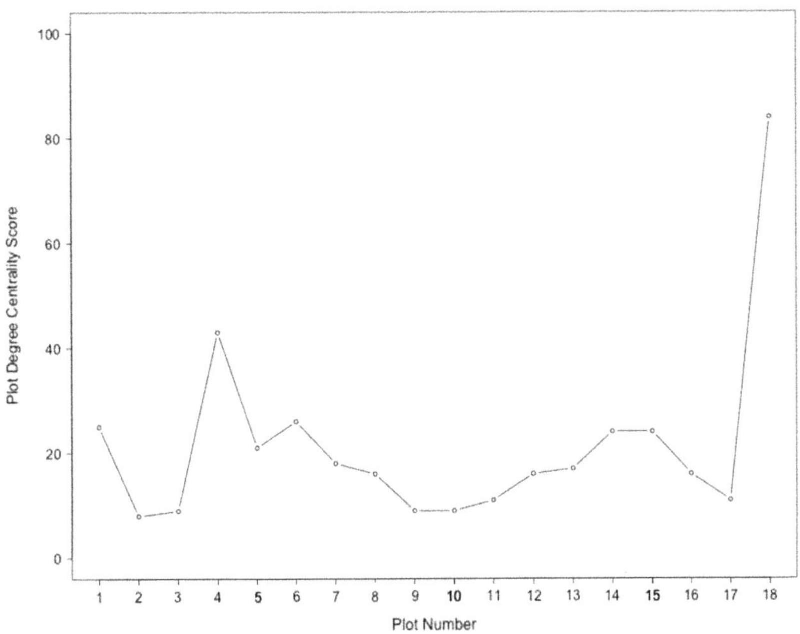

Figure 10.3 Plot degree centrality scores across all fifteen anti-Hitler plots

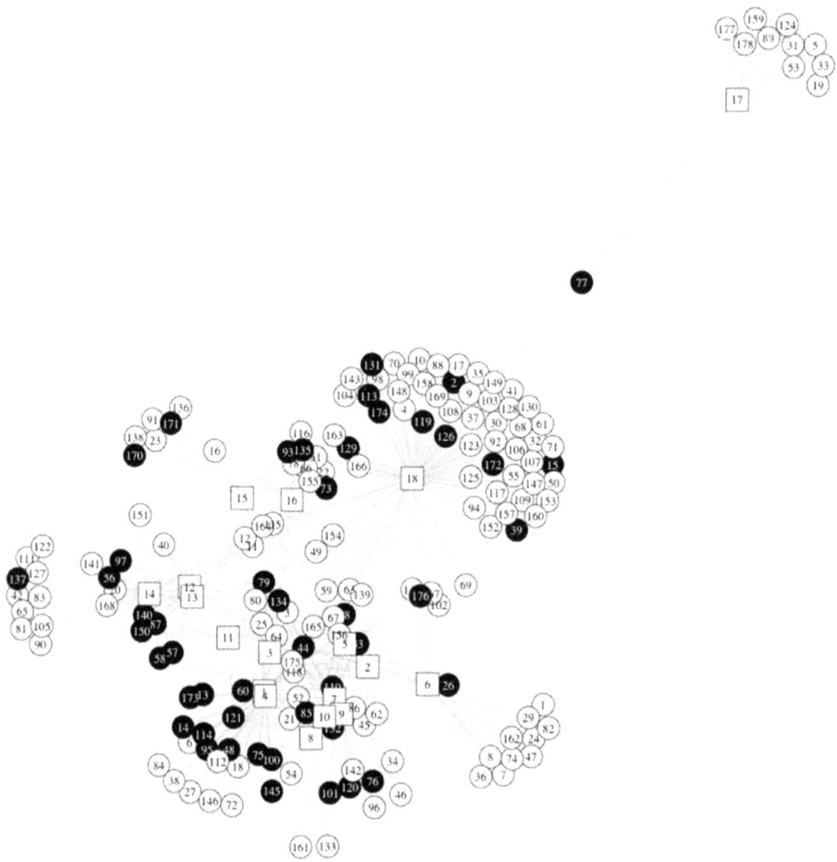

Figure 10.4 All plotters by all anti-Hitler plots with civilian members in black (circles = plotters; squares = plots)

Figure 10.6 is an independent variable that is statistically related to the formation of Figure 10.1.

Figure 10.7 presents the plotters who were military officers, specifically generals and field marshals, in black. Our hypothesis is that the general or field marshal social attribute of the plotters shown in Figure 10.7 is an independent variable that is statistically related to the formation of Figure 10.1.

Figure 10.8 presents the plotters who were military officers other than general or field marshal in black. Our hypothesis is that plotters with the social attribute of being a military officer other than general or field marshal, as shown in Figure 10.8, is an independent variable that is statistically related to the formation of Figure 10.1.

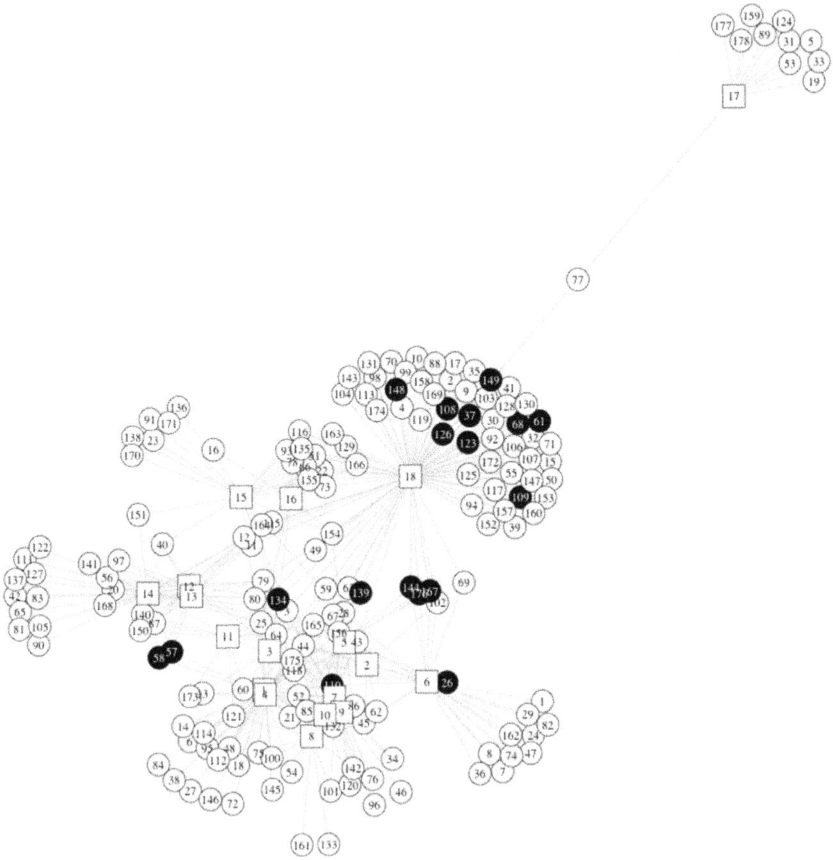

Figure 10.5 All plotters by all Anti-Hitler Plots with Kreisau Circle Members in Black (Circles = Plotters; Squares = Plots)

10.11 Plotter orientation attributes as endogenous independent variable

Figure 10.9 presents the plotters who were oriented towards the strategy of a coup d'état. Our hypothesis is that plotters with the attribute of being oriented to the plot strategy of coup d'état, as shown in Figure 10.9, is an independent variable that is statistically related to the formation of Figure 10.1.

Figure 10.10 presents the plotters who were oriented towards the strategy which we coded 'diplomacy.' Our hypothesis is that plotters with the attribute of being oriented to the plot strategy of diplomacy, as shown in Figure 10.10, is an independent variable that is statistically related to the formation of Figure 10.1.

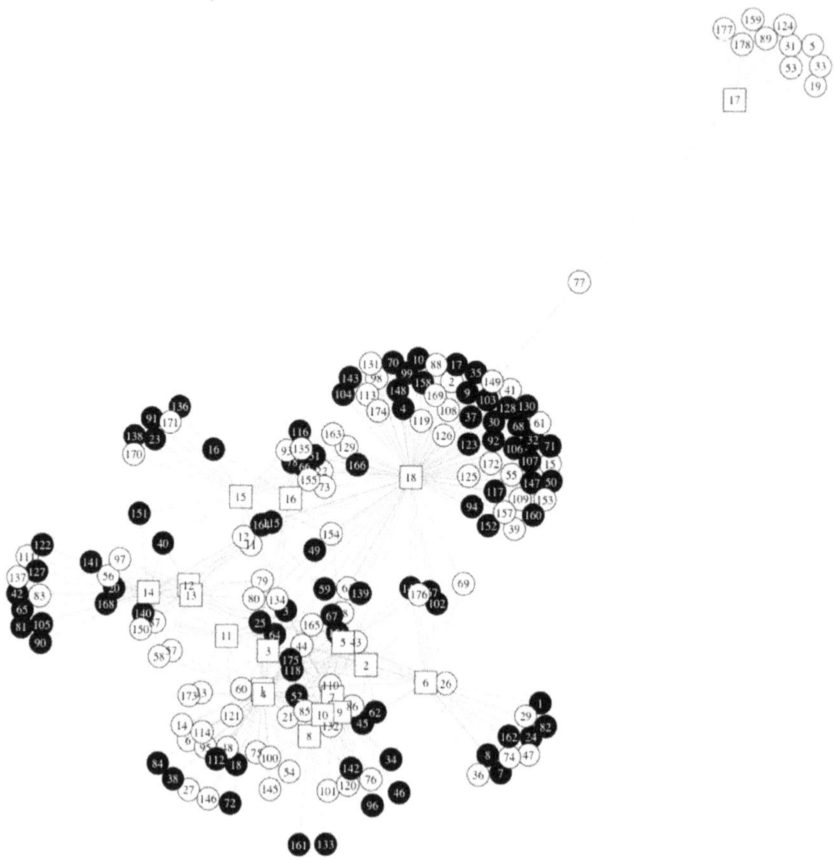

Figure 10.6 All plotters by all anti-Hitler plots with military officers in black (circles = plotters; squares = plots)

Figure 10.11 presents the plotters who were oriented towards the strategy which we coded 'espionage.' Our hypothesis is that plotters with the attribute of being oriented to the plot strategy of espionage, as shown in Figure 10.11, is an independent variable that is statistically related to the formation of Figure 10.1.

Figure 10.12 presents the plotters who were oriented towards the strategy which we coded 'assassination.' Our hypothesis is that plotters with the attribute of being oriented to the plot strategy of assassination, as shown in Figure 10.12, is an independent variable that is statistically related to the formation of Figure 10.1.

Figure 10.13 presents the plotters who were oriented towards the strategy which we coded assassination with 'zealotry.' Our hypothesis is that plotters with the attribute of being oriented to the plot strategy of assassination with zealotry,

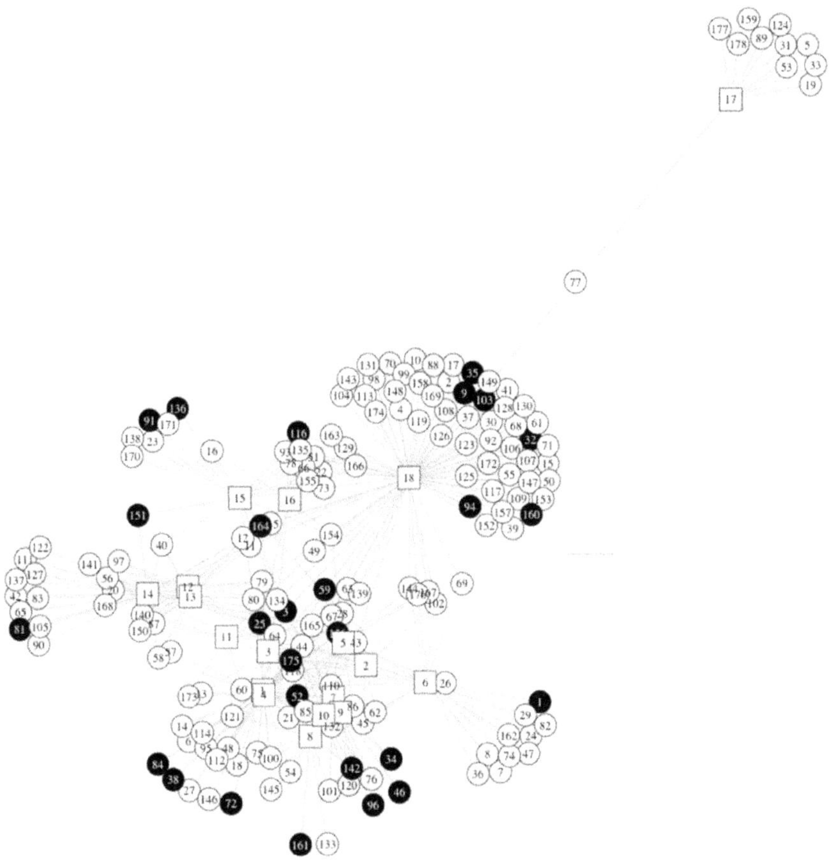

Figure 10.7 All plotters by all anti-Hitler plots with generals and field marshals in black (circles = plotters; squares = plots)

as shown in Figure 10.13, is an independent variable that is statistically related to the formation of Figure 10.1.

10.12 Exponential random graph modelling

Exponential Random Graph Models (ERGMs) are used to model endogenous network effects, exogenous actor attributes, and exogenous network effects on the likelihood of an edge in a dyad among conspirators. ERGMs can be thought of as something like general linear models, with the important distinction that ERGMs model network dependency, whereas general linear models (like logistic regression) assume independence. (See Lusher, Koskinen, and Robins, 2013 for a discussion of ERGM modelling.)

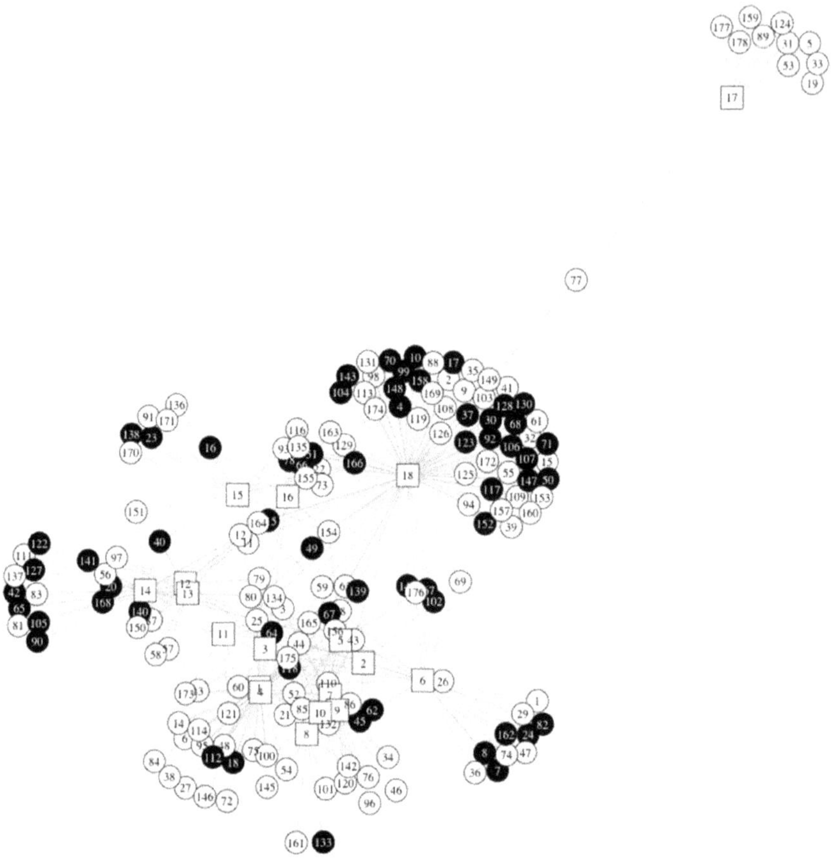

Figure 10.8 All plotters by all anti-Hitler plots with military officers excluding generals or field marshals in black (circles = plotters; squares = plots)

For the analysis here, the edges in Figure 10.1 form the dependent variable. The social attributes of the plotters shown in Figures 10.1–10.8 are the independent variables and are entered into the ERG-model as 0,1 indicator variables. Further, the plotter orientations as shown in Figures 10.9–10.13 are also treated as independent variables and are entered into the ERG-model as 0,1 indicator variables.

10.13 Distribution of plotter orientations findings

Table 10.1 presents the distribution of frequencies and percentages of the plotter orientations. Table 10.1 shows that seventy-eight (78) or 43.82% of the plotters supported an assassination strategy. Eighty-nine (89) or 50.00% of

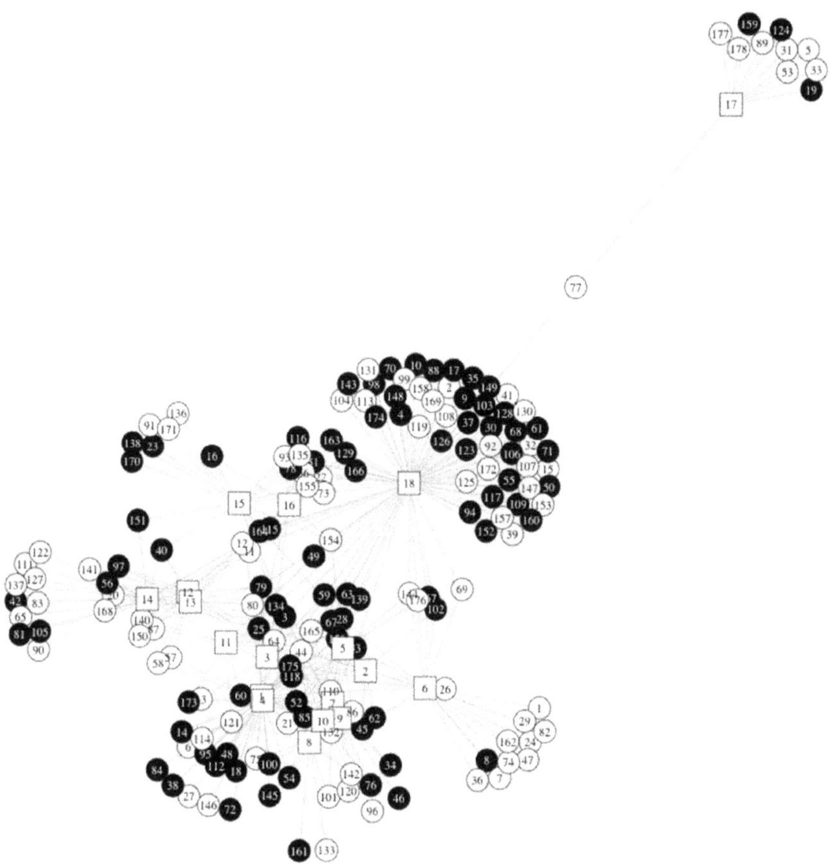

Figure 10.9 All plotters by all anti-Hitler plots with plotters oriented to coup d'état action in black (circles = plotters; squares = plots)

the plotters supported a coup strategy. Thirty-seven (37) or 20.79% of the plotters supported a diplomacy as an anti-Hitler strategy. Eighteen (18) or 10.11% of the plotters supported an espionage strategy. Finally, Table 10.1 shows that thirty-nine (39) or 21.91% of the plotters supported assassination with zealotry.

10.14 Distribution of plotter social attribute findings

Table 10.2 presents the distribution of frequencies and percentages of the plotter social attributes. Table 10.2 shows that forty-eight (48) or 26.97% of the plotters were civilians. Eighteen (18) or 10.11% of the plotters were members of the

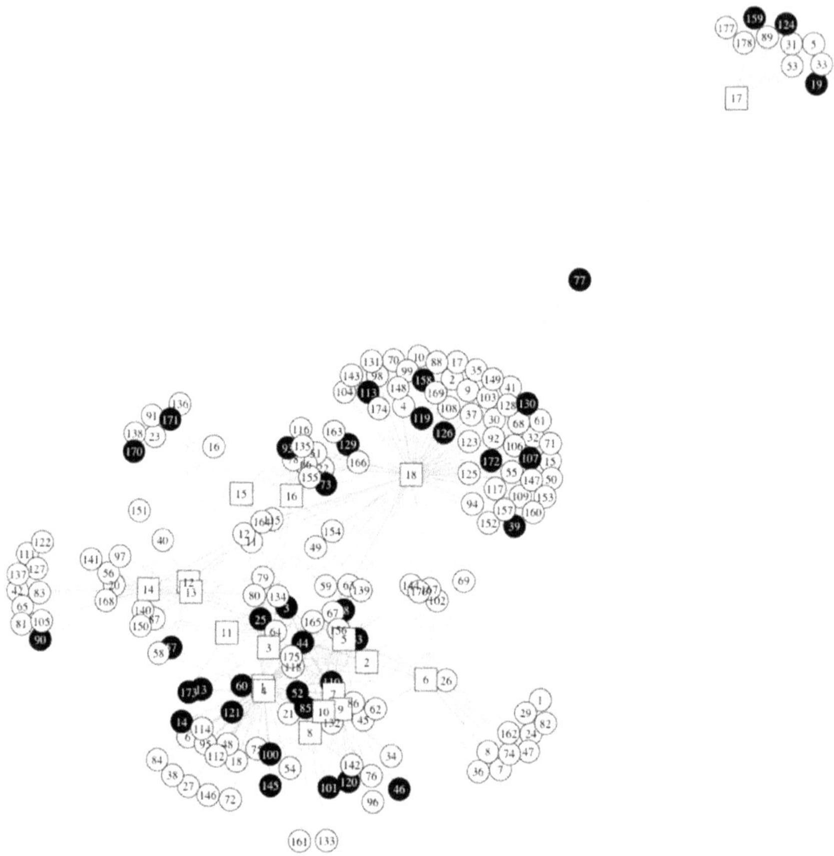

Figure 10.10 All plotters by all anti-Hitler plots with plotters oriented to diplomacy action in black (circles = plotters; squares = plots)

Kreisau Circle. Eighty-seven (87) or 48.88% of the plotters were military officers. Sixty (60) or 33.71% of the plotters were lower ranking military officers. Finally, Table 10.2 shows that twenty-seven (27) or 15.17% of the plotters were either generals or field marshals.

10.15 ERGM findings

Table 10.3 presents the coefficients for the ERG-model. Model One in Table 10.3 reports the full ERG-model, including all variables discussed as potential independent variables explaining the formation of the ties constituting the network. Model Two in Table 10.3 reports the reduced ERG-model consisting of only significant variables and their estimated effects.

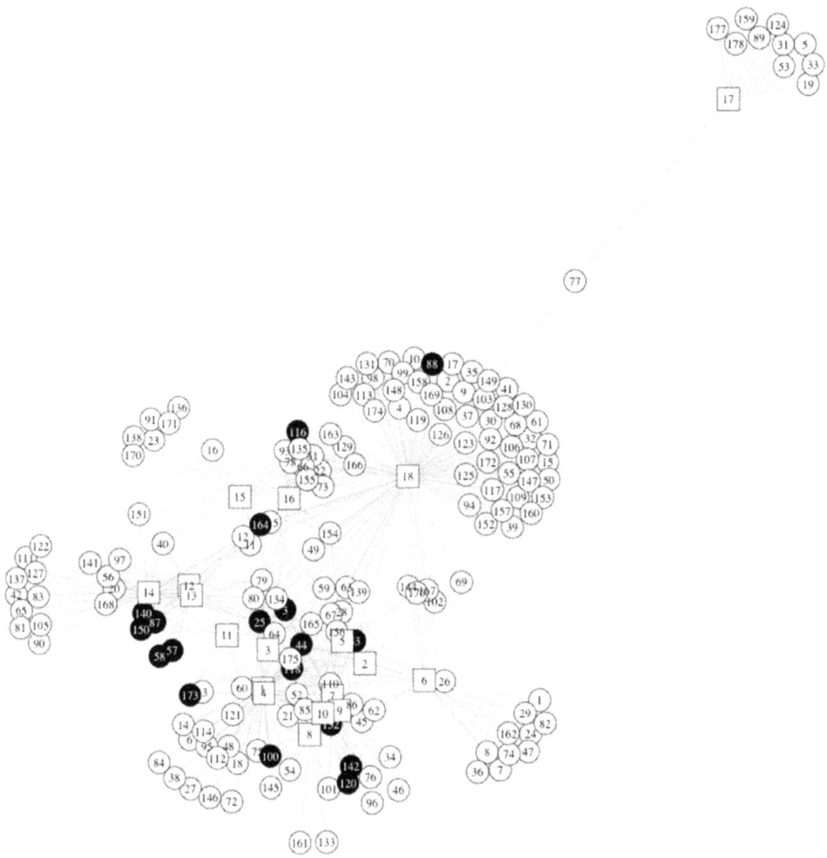

Figure 10.11 All plotters by all anti-Hitler plots with plotters oriented to espionage action in black (circles = plotters; squares = plots)

Both Models One and Two in Table 10.3 report a negative and statistically significant estimate for the 'edges' coefficient. The edges effect can be thought of as a baseline to which all the other coefficients either raise or lower the baseline probability of a tie in the anti-Hitler network. The negative value for edges can be interpreted to mean that the sociomatrix of the anti-Hitler plotters and plots shown in Figure 10.1 has fewer edges (lines) in the graph than we would expect if the graph were just random. This makes sense: Secret societies must be small to contain their secrecy and so would have an incentive to have fewer edges to maximise concealment (Baker and Faulkner, 1993).

Model One in Table 10.3 presents a positive but insignificant coefficient for Assassination.

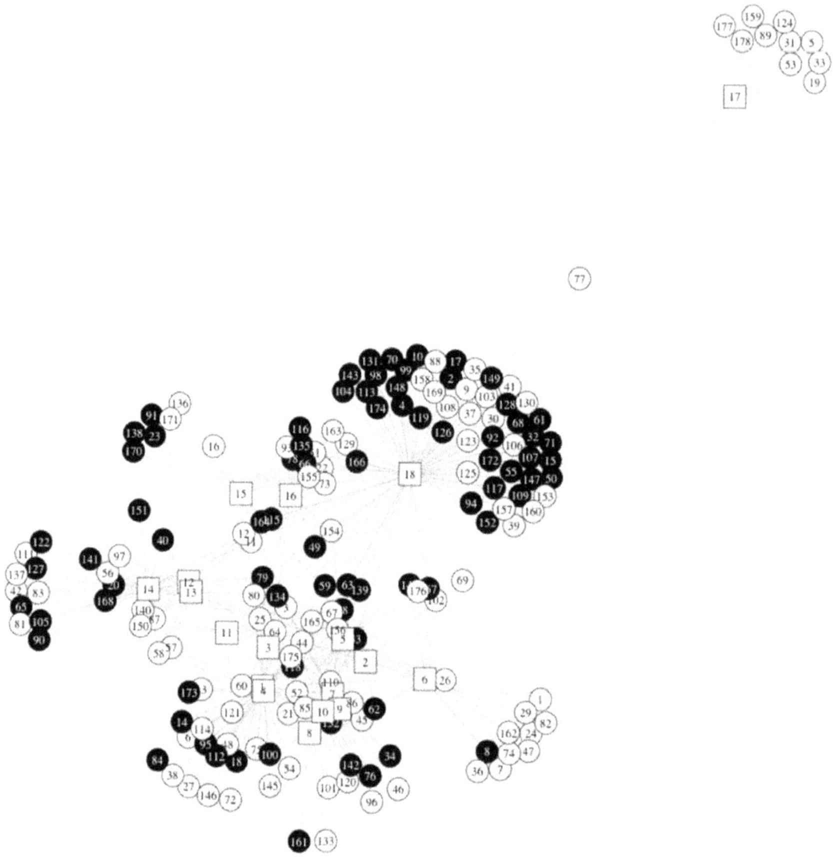

Figure 10.12 All plotters by all anti-Hitler plots with plotters oriented to assassination action in black (circles = plotters; squares = plots)

Both Models One and Two in Table 10.3 present a positive and significant coefficient for Coup, indicating that plotter orientation of coup d'état increased the likelihood of a tie in Figure 10.1's sociomatrix of anti-Hitler plots and plotters, net the effects of the other independent variables.

Model One in Table 10.3 presents a negative coefficient for Diplomacy, but the effect is insignificant.

Both Models One and Two in Table 10.3 present a positive and significant coefficient for Espionage, indicating that plotter orientation of Espionage increased the likelihood of a tie in Figure 10.1's sociomatrix of anti-Hitler plots and plotters, net the effects of the other independent variables.

Both Models One and Two in Table 10.3 present a negative and significant coefficient for assassination with zealotry. These negative coefficients imply that

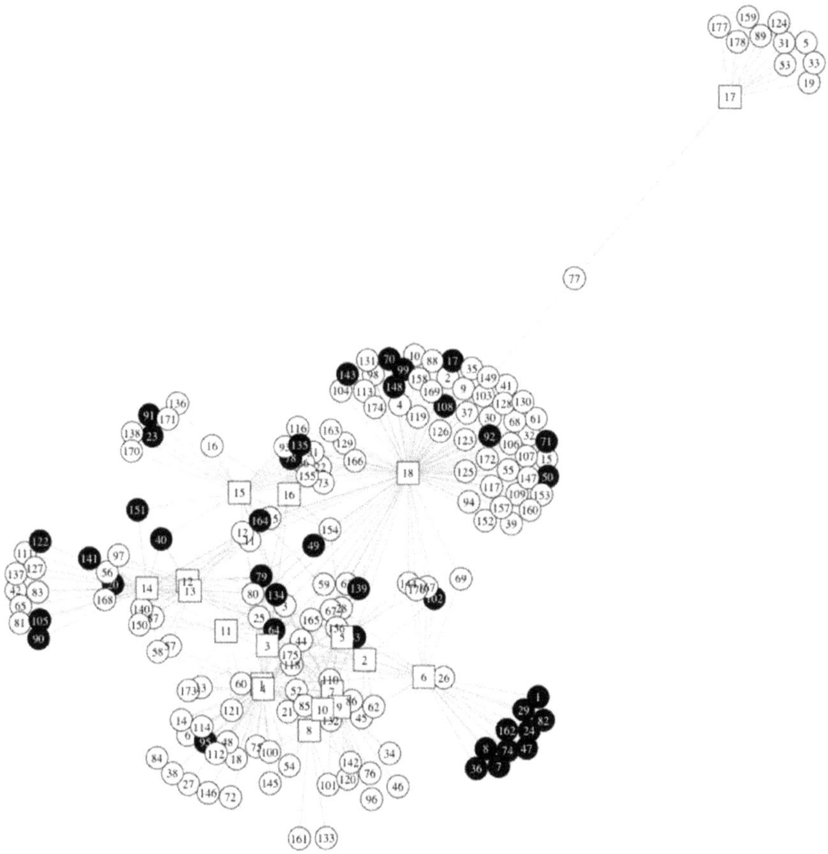

Figure 10.13 All plotters by all anti-Hitler plots with plotters oriented to assassination with zealotry in black (circles = plotters; squares = plots)

assassination with zealotry-oriented plotters reduced the likelihood of a tie in anti-Hitler network as depicted in Figure 10.1, net the effect of the other independent variables.

Both Models One and Two in Table 10.3 present positive coefficients for civilians, indicating that civilian plotter social status increased the likelihood of a tie in Figure 10.1's sociomatrix of anti-Hitler plots and plotters, net the effects of the other independent variables.

Model One in Table 10.3 presents a positive coefficient for Kreisau Circle, but the effect is insignificant.

Model One in Table 10.3 presents a negative coefficient for all military officers, but the effect is insignificant.

Table 10.1 Distribution of plotter orientations

Orientation	*Frequency*	*Percentage*
Assassination	78	43.82
Coup	89	50.00
Diplomacy	37	20.79
Espionage	18	10.11
Zealotry	39	21.91

Table 10.2 Distribution of plotter social attributes

Orientation	*Frequency*	*Percentage*
Civilian	48	26.97
Kreisau Circle	18	10.11
All military	87	48.88
Military *not* generals or field marshals (lower ranking military officers)	60	33.71
Generals and field marshals	27	15.17

Table 10.3 Exponential Random Graph Model (ERGM) coefficients[1]

	Model One	*Model Two*
Edges	–2.47***	–2.57***
	(0.17)	(0.13)
Assassination	0.05	.
	(0.10)	.
Coup	0.24*	0.19*
	(0.11)	(0.09)
Diplomacy	–0.16	.
	(0.13)	.
Espionage	0.56***	0.45***
	(0.15)	(0.14)
Assassination with zealotry	–0.19*	–0.20*
	(0.13)	(0.10)
Civilian	0.24*	0.27**
	(0.14)	(0.09)
Kreisau Circle	0.10	.
	(0.17)	.
All military officers	–0.17	.
	(0.18)	.
Lower ranking military officers (military *not* generals or field marshals)	0.35**	0.31**
	(0.15)	(0.10)

[1]Standard errors in parentheses. ***p<.001, **p<.01, *p<.05.

Both Models One and Two in Table 10.3 present a positive and significant coefficient for plotters coded as lower ranking military officers (that is, military, *not* generals or field marshals). These positive coefficients imply that lower ranking military officer status increased the likelihood of a tie in the anti-Hitler network as depicted in Figure 10.1, net the effect of the other independent variables.

10.16 Discussion

The ERG-model shows that some of the plotters' plot orientations and pre-existing social attributes partially contributed to the formation of the anti-Hitler networks of 1938 through 1945. Net of the effects of the other variables, plotter orientations of coup d'état, and espionage significantly increased the ties in the sociomatrix of anti-Hitler plots and plotters as shown in Figure 10.1. Moreover, the pre-existing social attributes of being a civilian or of being a lower ranking military officer – a lieutenant, colonel, or lieutenant colonel, for example – had a positive and significant effect on the tie formation of anti-Hitler plots and plotters shown in Figure 10.1. Assassination with zealotry lowered the likelihood of tie formation, net the effects of the other variables.

The ERG-model shows some of the orientation variables increased the likelihood of tie formation while others decreased the likelihood of tie formation. In terms of plotter orientations and commitment to specific plot strategies, coup d'état and espionage led to increased tie formation, net the effects of the other variables, while assassination with zealotry led to a reduction in the likelihood of tie formation. These conflicting effects imply conflicting views and tensions among the conspirators. Some plot orientations were less controversial and led to an increase in the likelihood of tie formation, while other plot orientations were indeed controversial and led to a decrease in the likelihood of tie formation.

Similarly, the ERG-model shows interesting effects for the social attributes of the plotters. Specifically, the effect for being a lower ranking officer raises the likelihood of tie formation in the anti-Hitler network, while the effect for higher ranking military officers is negative, although weak and not significant, net the effect of the other variables, including the effect for lower ranking officers. The result of these effects reflects the historical record of these plots, particularly the final Valkyrie plot – a large number of lower ranking officers and a lesser number of the highest rank. The eagerness of lower ranking officers to join the plots led to an increase in tie formation, but it created a conspiracy without the sufficient social hierarchy necessary to execute its intended actions.

10.17 Conclusion

We chose the network of a political conspiracy that failed. This famous debacle reveals in retrospect the career of the conspiracy as well as its collapse, a topic of interest to not only historians and biographers but also to social scientists, game theorists, and even film and television writers-producers-directors. In the post-mortem that accompanies any political or military disaster, a post-factum narrative misses an important point: Conspiracies are mysteries wrapped inside institutions. Breakdown and failure reveals: (a) the institutional context in which illegal or covert networks unfold; (b) the ways plotters coordinate and organise their covert plots; and (c) the external and internal dynamics of network destabilisation.

Why did Valkyrie collapse? The answer now widely accepted but clearly not appreciated sufficiently is that the July 1944 crisis and plot was made possible by an extremely fragile treasonous network in which military and civilian plotters indulged in too much reliance on the military chain of command as well as hazardous reliance on a hastily rebuilt network of plotters, along with lax supervision by its leaders. That there is wide agreement on the causes of the breakdown following the failed assassination attempt should not be surprising. It is hardly novel to recognise, for example, that dismantling an illegal or 'dark' network from the outside can result in the destruction or impairment of persons, group arrangements, facilities, and the like. It is less well acknowledged that covert network ties can be affected from both without *and* from within – a phenomenon we call 'co-dismantling.' Conspiratorial group arrangements, planned plots, and their network ties can be delayed, impaired, or severed. Erosion and replacement of key conspirators inside the plots affect the internal organisation of anti-Nazi networks leading to operation Valkyrie. The basic problem, however, was not ignorance of such dangers but that the plotters in the crucial stages of assassination and coup were not sufficiently vigilant in anticipating and controlling them.

We draw on historical sources and network analysis to identify structural conditions that lead to social order and the persistence of ties across secret plots or to their breakdown and collapse. First, we show that anti-regime networks are not static but dynamically changing in structure over time. We reconstruct the covert network core or centre of the anti-Hitler and anti-Nazi Valkyrie plot. The conspirators on the periphery, by contrast, have few connections to one another and weak connections to the core.

Second, this political conspiracy is structurally fragile. The plots and their plotters are capable of being disrupted and destroyed from the *outside* by arrest, detention, and imprisonment by the regime's internal security forces and the Gestapo. They are capable of being dismantled from the *inside* as conspirators avoid one another to enhance secrecy and replace their older and more cautious colleagues. 'Co-dismantling' from the inside and outside, by conspirators and Gestapo, effectively undermines the cohesion of the conspiracy in its final event of operation Valkyrie. Not only was the Gestapo closing in, but Himmler had warned Canaris and others that the SS knew that a rebellion was being planned. Gestapo pressure against anti-Nazi plotters left deep fissures inside those secret bodies, sowed the seeds of suspicion and distrust, squeezed out formerly influential plotters, and led to an internal shake up on the eve of operation Valkyrie. Close surveillance was soon followed by arrest of 'the old guard' and key plotters such as Beck, Goerdeler, Hassell, and Witzleben. Plotters started to implicate one another.

Moltke fingers Kiep; Canaris implicates Dohnany. This dual-dismantling – internal forces followed by internal changes – had an immediate and chilling effect on the other plotters and their plans.

The diffusion of context of suspicion (Glaser and Strauss, 1964) spread within the conspiracy. Secrecy is heightened, caution is raised, and fear of detection dampens coordination by making plotters more and more cautious about meeting with one another to plan assassination and coup attempts.

Third, external and internal forces combine to disrupt the persistence of plot meetings and interrupt the continuity of treasonous plans. These changes begin to disrupt the internal social organisation, revealing how small changes in local network structure (delaying plot meetings, squeezing out 'old line' influential plotters, shifting the center of gravity from upper level military to a middle level military officer) has profound effects at the organisational level of the overall network.

Finally, in June 1944, in the run up to bomb and putsch attempts, the plotters saw that time was running out (Shirer, 2011, pp. 1035–1036). Concealment was more and more difficult to achieve. The anti-Nazi plotters became increasingly impatient: with Stauffenberg, with his tight-core of mid-level military followers, with the sidelining and replacement of the 'old guard,' with civilian envoys and their peace attempts with the Allies, and with leftists and their deteriorating alliances with the communists. Combined, these directions heightened tensions and increased mistrust. Impatience under conditions of secrecy undermines collective action.

Political and economic conspiracies are wrapped inside institutional contexts. Anti-Nazi networks as political conspiracies should be seen as small-scale secret societies (Simmel, 1906, 1950) embedded in a particular *type* of society – a highly militarised dictatorial state. The conspiracies' structure was driven by the need to maximise secrecy or concealment while adapting to a hierarchical authoritarian system. On the one hand, the plotters had to coordinate their plots and constantly solve complex, non-routine, rapidly changing, and dangerous 'problems' of assassination, coup, and covert diplomacy. On the other hand, they had to prevent discovery of these treasonous plans to stay hidden from the regime (the Third Reich's Gestapo, SS, and its nest of informers) and to maximise the security of their 'secret society.' They faced the constant danger of becoming targets of suspicion and objects of detention, arrest, torture, and execution.

References

Ainsztein, R. (1974) *Jewish Resistance in Nazi-Occupied Eastern Europe*. New York: Barnes and Noble.

Astridge, P. (2009) *Kill the Fuhrer*. Warriewood, NSW: Woodslane Press.

Baker, W.E. and Faulkner, R.R. (1993) 'The Social Organization of Conspiracy: Illegal Networks in the Heavy Electrical Industry.' *American Sociological Review* 58: 837–960.

Bassett, Richard. (2005) Hitler's Spy Chief: The Wilhelm Canaris Mystery. London: Cassell.

Burleigh, M. (2000) *The Third Reich: A New History.* New York: Hill and Wang.

Churchill, W.S. (1948) *The Gathering Storm.* Boston: Houghton Mifflin Company.

Duffy, J. (1992) *Target Hitler: The Plots to Kill Hitler.* New York: Greenwood Publishing Group.

Evans, R.J. (2008) *The Third Reich at War.* New York: Penguin Books.

Feld, S.L. (1981) 'The Focused Organization of Social Ties.' *American Journal of Sociology* 86: 1015–1035.

Fest, J. (1996) *Plotting Hitler's Death: The Story of German Resistance.* New York: Henry Holt and Company.

Galante, P. (2002) *Operation Valkyrie: The German Generals' Plot against Hitler.* With Eugene Silianoff. Translated from the French by Mark Howson and Cary Ryan. New York: Cooper Square Press.

Gallin, M.A. (1961) *German Resistance to Hitler.* Washington, DC: Catholic University of America Press.

Gibson, D.R. (2012) *Talk at the Brink: Deliberation and Decision During the Cuban Missile Crisis.* Princeton, NJ: Princeton University Press.

Gisevius, H.B. (1947) *To the Bitter End.* Cambridge, MA: Da Capo Press.

Gisevius, H.B. (2009) *Valkyrie: An Insider's Account of the Plot to Kill Hitler.* Translated by Richard and Clara Winston. Cambridge, MA: Da Capo Press.

Glaser, B. and Strauss, A. (1964) Awareness Contexts. American Sociological Review. Vol. 29. No. 5 (Oct. 1964), pp. 669–679.

Gould, R.V. (1991) 'Multiple Networks and Mobilization in the Paris Commune, 1871.' *American Sociological Review* 56(6): 716–729.

Gould, R.V. (1996) 'Patron-Client Ties, State Centralization and the Whiskey Rebellion.' *American Journal of Sociology* 102(2): 400–429.

Grunberger, R. (1971) *A Social History of the Third Reich.* London: Weidenfeld and Nicolson.

Hoffman, P. (1988) *German Resistance to Hitler.* Cambridge, MA: Harvard University Press.

Hoffman, P. (2008) *Stauffenberg.* Montreal, QC and Kingston, ON: McGill-Queen's University Press.

Hoffman, P. (2011) *Behind Valkyrie: German Resistance to Hitler.* Montreal, QC and Kingston, ON: McGill-Queen's University Press.

Hughes, E.C. (1971a) 'Bastard Institutions.' In: *The Sociological Eye: Selected Papers.* Chicago: Aldine-Atherton, pp. 98–105.

Hughes, E.C. (1971b) 'Going Concerns: The Study of American Institutions.' In: *The Sociological Eye: Selected Papers.* Chicago: Adline-Atherton, pp. 52–64.

Jones, N. (2008) *Countdown to Valkyrie: The July Plot to Assassinate Hitler.* London: Frontline Books.

Kahle, H. (1944) *They Plotted Against Hitler.* London: I.N.G. Publications.

Krebs, V. (2001) 'Mapping Networks of Criminal Cells.' *Connections* 24: 43–52.

Lusher, D., Koskinen, J. and Robins, G. (2013) *Exponential Random Graph Modelsfor Social Networks: Theory Methods and Applications.* New York: Cambridge University Press.

Manvell, R. (1971) *The Conspirators: 20 July 1944.* New York: Ballantine Books.

Manvell, R. and Fraenkel, H. (1969) *The Canaris Conspiracy: The Secret Resistance to Hitler in the German Army.* New York: David McKay Company.

Manvell, R. and Fraenkel, H. (2008) *The Men Who Tried to Kill Hitler. Foreword by Roger Moorhouse.* New York: Skyhorse Publishing Inc.

Mason, H.M. (1978) *To Kill the Devil.* New York: Norton.

Mason, H.M. (1985) *Hitler Must Die.* New York: Penguin Group.

Moorhouse, Roger. (2006) Killing Hitler: The Plots, The Assassins and The Dictator Who Cheated Death. New York: Bantam.

Noack, Dunja. (2005) The Secret Plot to Kill Hitler. New York: Cerberus.

Parssinen, T. (2012) *The Oster Conspiracy of 1938.* New York: Random House.

Perrow, C. (1999) *Normal Accidents: Living with High Risk Technologyies.* Princeton, NJ: Princeton University Press.

Reitlinger, G. (1957) *The SS – Alibi of a Nation.* New York: The Viking Press.

Remak, J. (ed.) (1969) *The Nazi Years.* Englewood Cliffs, NJ: Prentice-Hall.

Rothfels, H. (1962) *The German Opposition to Hitler.* Chicago: Regnery.

Schrader, H. (2009) *Codename Valkyrie: General Friedrich and the Plot Against Hitler.* London: Haynes Publication PLC.

Shirer, W. (2011) *The Rise and Fall of the Third Reich*, New Edition. New York: Simon and Schuster.

Short, N. (2013) *Kill Hitler.* Oxford: Osprey Publishing.

Sifton, E. and Stern, F. (2013) *No Ordinary Men: Dietrich Bonhoeffer and Has von Dohnanyi, Resisters Against Hitler in Church and State.* New York: New York Review Books.

Simmel, G. (1906) 'The Sociology of Secrecy and of Secret Societies.' *American Journal of Sociology* 11: 441–498.

Simmel, G. (1950) *The Sociology of Georg Simmel.* Edited by Kurt H. Wolff. Glencoe, Ill.: The Free Press.

Simmel, G. (1955) *Conflict and the Web of Group Affiliations.* New York: Free Press.

Sparrow, M.K. (1991) 'The Application of Network Analysis to Criminal Intelligence: An Assessment of the Prospects.' *Social Networks* 13: 251–274.

Suhl, Y. (1968) *They Fought Back: The Story of Jewish Resistance in Nazi Europe.* London, UK: MacGibbon and Kee.

Thomsett, M.C. (1997) *The German Opposition to Hitler: The Resistance, the Underground, and Assassination Plots, 1938–1945.* London: McFarland & Company, Inc.

Vaughan, D. (1996) *The Challenger Launch Decision: Risky Technology, Culture, and Deviance at NASA.* Chicago and London: University of Chicago Press.

von Boeselanger, P.F. (2009) *Valkyrie: The Story of the Plot to Kill Hitler, by Its Last Member.* Trans. by Steven Rendall. New York: Alfred A. Knopf.

von Schlabrendorff, F. (2005) *They Almost Killed Hitler.* New York: Kessinger Publishing.

Weiner, S.S. (1976) 'Participation, Deadlines, and Choice.' In: James G. March and Johan P. Olsen (eds.), *Ambiguity and Choice in Organizations.* Bergen: Universitetsforlager. pp. 225–250.

Wheeler-Bennett, J.W. (2005) *The Nemesis of Power: The German Army in Politics*, 1918–1945. New York: Palgrave Macmillan.

White, H.C. (1992) *Identity and Control: A Structural Theory of Social Action.* Princeton, NJ: Princeton University Press.

Appendix

Actor key for figures

1. Adams, 2. Bargatzy, 3. Beck, 4. Bernardis, 5. Bernstorff. A., 6. Bernstorff. J., 7. Bistrick, 8. Blumenthal, 9. Blumentritt, 10. Boehmer, 11. Boeslager, G., 12. Boeslager, P., 13. Bohm-Tettelbach, 14. Bonhoeffer, 15. Borhoefferil, 16. Bose, 17. Brandt, 18. Brauchitsch, 19. Bredow, 20. Breitenbuch, 21. Brockdorff, 22. Burckhardt, 23. Bussche, 24. Buttlar-Brandenfels, 25. Canaris, 26. Delp, 27. Deschel-Deuffenstetten, 28. Dohnanyi, 29. Einsiedel, 30. Erdmann, 31. Erxlenbren, 32. Esebeck, 33. Fallestrom, 34. Faulkenhusen, 35. Fellgiebel, 36. Finckenstein, 37. Finckh, 38. Fritsch, 39. Galen, 40. Gersdorff, 41. Gerstenmeier, 42. Gigas, 43. Gisevius, 44. Goerdeler, 45. Groscurth, 46. Guderian, 47. Gunther, 48. Guttenberg, 49. Haeften, 50. Hagen, 51. Hahn, 52. Halder, 53. Halem, 54. Hammerstein, 55. Hansen, 56. Hardenberg, 57. Harnack. A., 58. Harnack. M., 59. Hase, 60. Hassell, 61. Haubach, 62. Heinz, 63. Helldorf, 64. Herzner, 65. Hidding, 66. Hitzfeld, 67. Hoepner, 68. Hofacker, 69. Hoffmann, 70. Jacob, 71. Jaeger, 72. Jodl, 73. John, 74. Junker, 75. Kaiser, 76. Kessel, 77. Kiep, 78. Klausing, 79. Kleist-Schmenzin. E., 80. Kleist. H., 81. Kluge, 82. Knaack, 83. Koenig, 84. Koerber, 85. Kordt. E., 86. Kordt. T., 87. Kuckhoff, 88. Kuebart, 89. Kuenzer, 90. Kuhn, 91. Lahousen, 92. Lancken, 93. Langbehn, 94. Lanz, 95. Leber, 96. Leeb, 97. Lehndorff, 98. Lengsfeld, 99. Leonrod, 100. Leuschner, 101. Lieber, 102. Liedig, 103. Lindemann, 104. Linstow, 105. Loringhoven, 106. Marogna-Redwitz, 107. Matuschka, 108. Meichssner, 109. Mierendoff, 110. Moltke, 111. Muller, 112. Nebe, 113. Neurath, 114. Niekisch, 115. Oertzen, 116. Olbricht, 117. Oppen, 118. Oster, 119. Oven, 120. Pechel, 121. Popitz, 122. Pretzell, 123. Quirnheim, 124. Reckse, 125. Reichmann, 126. Reichwein, 127. Retel, 128. Roenne, 129. Sack, 130. Saefkow, 131. Schaal, 132. Schacht, 133. Schaired, 134. Schlabrendorff, 135. Schmidt-Salzmann, 136. Schmundt, 137. Schoenfeld, 138. Schrader, 139. Schulenburg, 140. Schulze-Boysen, 141. Schulze-Buttger, 142. Schwarnefeld, 143. Schweizer, 144. Schwerin, 145. Seizsacker, 146. Soderstein, 147. Speidel, 148. Stauffenberg. B., 149. Stauffenberg. C., 150. Stennes, 151. Stieff, 152. Strachwitz, 153. Strolin, 154. Strunk. E., 155. Strunk. T., 156. Stulpnagel, 157. Tauengen, 158. Teuchert, 159. Thadden, 160. Thiele, 161. Thomas, 162. Thun-Hohenstein, 163. Tresckow. E., 164. Tresckow. H., 165. Trott, 166. Unger, 167. Uxkull-Gyllenbrand, 168. Voss, 169. Wager, 170. Wallenberg. J., 171. Wallenberg. M., 172. Warterburg, 173. Weizsacker, 174. Wirmer, 175. Witzleben, 176. Yorck, 177. Zarden. A., 178. Zarden. I.

Part V

Advancing the field

11 Organised crime research 1985–2014

Mapping research dynamics through social network analysis

Panos Kostakos

11.1 Introduction

Since the Prohibition Era, when the term 'organised crime' made its debut into the public discourse, the volume of knowledge on the topic has increased exponentially. The growth of international literature that can be found focusing its research in this field testifies to that fact. Indicatively, from the 1960s onwards, the amount of information on organised crime has been doubling and even tripling approximately every ten years (Figure 11.1).

This growth is part of a global phenomenon which is often attributed to the new technologies and the methods used to assist in the flow of information in modern society (de Solla Price, 1986; Bornmann and Mutz, 2015). In this

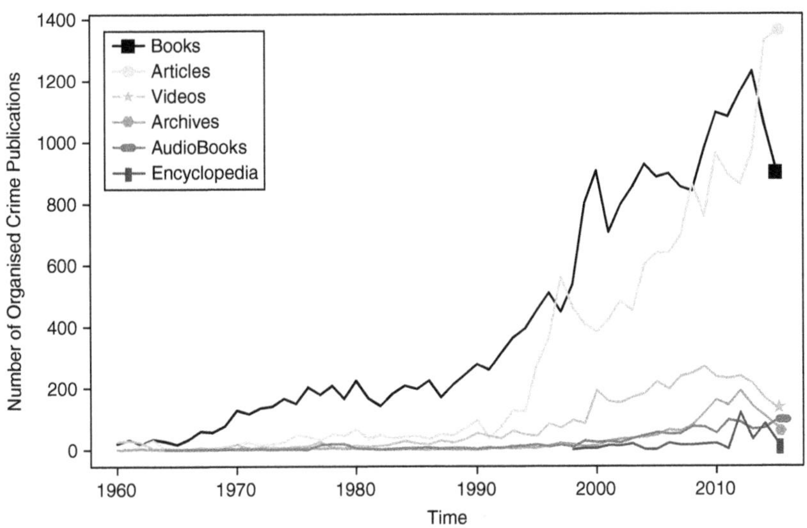

Figure 11.1 Historical frequency in which publications on 'Organized Crime' are recorded in WorldCat.Org

Source: Wordcat.org

context, an increasing difficulty for scholars to identify emerging themes and linkages between topics has been noticed, along with the challenging task for policymakers to apply research findings to effective policy-planning strategies (He, 1999). Early detection and monitoring of research themes is not only highly important for organised crime researchers who produce novel research findings and advance current knowledge to new frontiers, but also for policymakers who need to make informed decisions on the allocation of human and financial resources, and for civil society actors whose role is key in raising public awareness.

Traditionally, review articles that have gauged the literature on organised crime have relied on a small selection of manuscripts that had been created by a select few expert scholars or authorities (Maltz, 1976; Finckenauer, 2005; Hagan, 2006). While qualitative content analysis of scholarly works on organised crime has produced some intuitive results, the Internet now accumulates knowledge at volumes that exceed the limits of human memory and prohibit *close reading*. This is why a large number of publications, outside the field of organised crime, employ *distant reading* tools (Michel et al., 2011; Moretti, 2013). These include quantitative techniques like topic modelling (Schmidt, 2012), machine learning (Witten and Frank, 2002), and co-word analysis (Liu et al., 2014), tools that can effectively grasp the expanding knowledge structure of science by aggregating and analysing considerable amounts of data (He, 1999).

To be more specific, previous studies have shown that online academic indexes (like Scopus, Google Scholar, and Web of Science) can be used as proxies for knowledge discovery (Bar-Ilan, 2008; Falagas et al., 2008). Bibliographic metadata from reference lists, titles, and abstracts have been shown to serve as valid data sources for measuring the semantic cohesion, evolution, and maturity of research (Whittaker, 1989; Bar-Ilan, 2008; Fanelli and Glänzel, 2013). Additionally, it has been shown that topic modelling and co-word networks are effective tools for mapping out the development and maturity of various research domains (Schmidt, 2012; Liu et al., 2014; Wang et al., 2015). These tools can help us improve understanding of organised crime, which is a complex and volatile phenomenon, preying on glocal dynamics, legal asymmetries, institutional weaknesses, and loopholes. In addition, a *distant reading* approach can enable researchers to highlight latent patterns in the way the scientific knowledge on organised crime grows and highlight novel avenues for both exploratory and critical scholarship.

In this paper, we collected a corpus of research articles on organised crime and evaluated their bibliometric and co-word network parameters. We measured bibliometric parameters as described in Fanelli and Glänzel (2013), and used the co-word analysis tool developed in Liu et al. (2014). We demonstrate how these tools could readily be utilised by organised crime researchers to measure the evolution of scientific knowledge longitudinally.

We collected articles published from 1985 to 2014 in the Web of Knowledge index. These articles were collected by filtering them using a series of specific keywords. We extracted key bibliometric information and measured the cohesion of the research domain. We divided the corpus into two decades, and for each decade we explored their network topology. We measured the density and centrality for each topic network and used strategic diagrams to visualise the evolution of their knowledge structure longitudinally.

11.2 Related concepts

Scholars have used various techniques as proxies for capturing the processes of knowledge production, development, and growth. These methods include citation analysis, bibliometrics, impact factor, topic modelling, and co-word analysis. In this section, we briefly explain the main concepts used in the study, while in the next section we discuss the quantities that we have measured.

The current version of globalisation is enabled by the rapid flow of knowledge across territorial borders, professional sectors, and frontiers. Previous research has shown that global knowledge-flows critically affect economic development, competition, and employment (Jaffe, 1999). For instance, shifts in knowledge production and knowledge-flows have been shown to provoke global shifts in power and wealth (Stewart, 1997). This causal relationship between knowledge and economic performance is evident not only in the more advanced Organisation for Economic Co-operation and Development (OECD) countries, which are predominantly knowledge- and information-based economies, but also in transitioning economies (OECD, 1996). But what exactly is the knowledge structure of organised crime, and how can it be measured and studied?

A *knowledge structure* can be simply defined as the collection of interrelated facts, knowledge, or information about a subject that can be graphically depicted as a semantic network (Galambos et al., 1986). For illustration purposes, in Figure 11.2 we have provided a simple semantic network deduced from the official definition of organised crime provided by the US Federal Bureau of Investigations (FBI). Note that the semantic network used here for illustration captures only a small amount of information pertaining to how the FBI defines organised crime. The greyed-out documents, or the branches, of the semantic web indicate a possible knowledge discovery based on a simple binary selection. In other words, we can extract multiple documents and concepts (activities, internal structure of groups) from the FBI discourse about organised crime to study the evolution of the phenomena from an institutional perspective.

Generally speaking, *documents* are the texts used for extracting meaning. These can be single documents (e.g. a book, a webpage, a newspaper article, or a journal article) or shorter text snippets (e.g. a legal definition, a quote, an email, or a tweet). A corpus (corpora in plural) is the collection of documents used in each analysis.

Keywords are the proper words used in texts that convey meaning. In the knowledge structure extracted from document 3 in our example from Figure 11.2, we manually identified a set of keywords (FBI, Organized Crime,

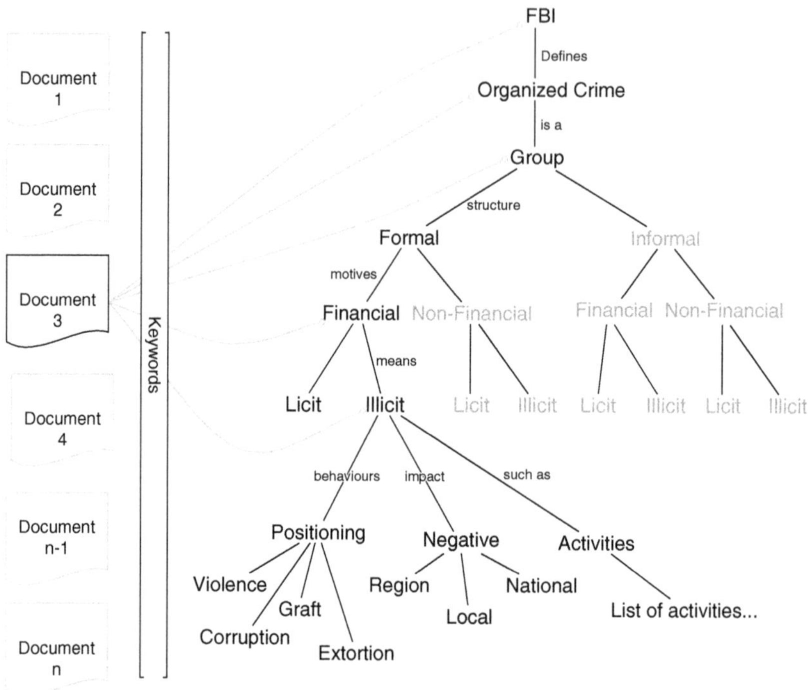

Figure 11.2 After manually extracting keywords from a document, we can develop a semantic network for a given concept. This figure graphs a simple semantic network taken from the following definition of organised crime: 'The FBI defines organized crime as any group having some manner of a formalized structure, and whose primary objective is to obtain money through illegal activities. Such groups maintain their position using actual or threatened violence, corrupt public officials, graft, or extortion, and generally have a significant impact on the people in their locales, region, or the country as a whole'

Source: www.fbi.gov

Group, Formal Structure, Obtain Money). One fundamental property of keywords is their tendency to co-occur with other keywords within text corpora (ex. 'Italian'+'Mafia') and thereby enable texts, documents, and corpora to effectively communicate meaning.

Co-words are keywords that co-occur in the same document or corpus. This is why the study of 'co-words' has been central in knowledge discovery and information retrieval. Co-words can be modelled and analysed as networks of keywords. Density and centrality are two concepts from graph theory that we apply to analyse co-word networks (Callon et al., 1991, 1983).

Density is the strength of links that tie together clusters of co-words or a research theme/topic/discourse. This measure relates to a theme's development and semantic coherence. Poor themes have low density compared with strong themes, which have higher density and stronger connections to the wider community of clusters (Callon et al., 1991; Coulter et al., 1998; Hu et al., 2013; Liu et al., 2014). A relatively new research theme like illicit human organ harvesting where the theories, methods, and data sources are sparse is more likely to produce low density scientific discourse compared to the more established topics like drug trafficking where the discourse is anticipated to have a stronger internal coherence.

Centrality denotes the extent to which a node in each graph is important. When calculating degree centrality, the importance of nodes is measured by counting the number of direct links each node has to other nodes in the network. The centrality of a cluster of nodes (i.e. a research theme) signifies the centrality of concepts and how the field develops. Emerging and declining themes have low centrality, while themes with high centrality can be conceived as having a much greater maturity. Case in point: because the economic models of organised crime are widely adopted by end-users and extensively discussed in the literature, their degree centrality is also expected to be high. By plotting density and centrality in the same graph, we create a two-dimensional Cartesian system which is divided into four regions/quadrants, forming what is known as strategic diagrams (Liu et al., 2014).

Strategic diagrams have been used to study the dynamic growth of keywords and discourse networks due to their ability to combine centrality and density measures (Callon et al., 1991; Coulter et al., 1998; He, 1999; Liu et al., 2014). The four regions contain research themes with the following properties (Figure 11.3):

- **Quadrant I:** Have high centrality and density, meaning that the theme is mature; it has the potential to influence other themes and has strong internal cohesion.
- **Quadrant II:** Themes with high density/internal coherence but lacking centrality that would otherwise shift them in the mainstream themes. Themes in quadrant II are also known as Ivory Towers due to their internal cohesion and isolation from other themes.
- **Quadrant III:** Themes that shift away from the centre of a scientific discourse have low centrality and density. Accordingly, new themes that might be emerging can also be found in this area. The final trajectory of a given topic in this quadrant is explored by comparing the evolution of the knowledge structure over time.
- **Quadrant IV:** General and transversal research themes with high centrality but weakly structured might eventually have a considerable impact in the overall knowledge structure. Topics residing within this knowledge system often create a bandwagon effect where the adoption of a problem, or theoretical perspective, is directly linked to the perceived uptake by other researchers in the community.

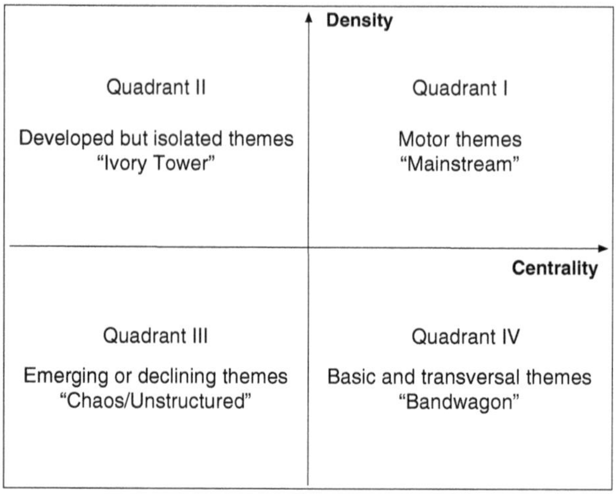

Figure 11.3 Sample strategic diagram divided into four quadrants

Source: Liu et al. (2014)

Table 11.1 List of top 10 journal titles included in the database, and the absolute frequency of journal articles per title

No of Art.	*Name of Journal*
108	Crime, Law and Social Change
25	The British Journal of Criminology
16	Terrorism and Political Violence
11	The European Journal on Criminal Policy and Research
11	Studies in Conflict & Terrorism
10	Journal of Modern Italian Studies
9	Australian and New Zealand Journal of Criminology
9	Journal of Drug Issues
9	Policing
8	European Journal of Criminology

11.3 Data

In order to retain the consistency and reproducibility of the results, the sample used in this study is limited to peer-reviewed articles published in journals indexed by the Web of Science. In the remainder of this section, we present in detail the data collection protocol and bibliometric parameters used to quantify the evolution of the organised crime knowledge structure.

11.3.1 Documents

We collected 850 journal articles (documents) from Web of Science, and included articles published between 1985 and 2014 internationally.[1] We selected the Web of Science due to the reported consistency and coverage (Falagas et al., 2008). Table 11.1 presents the top ten journals and the frequency of articles that we have collected for bibliometric analysis. In terms of absolute frequencies, Figure 11.4 shows an increase in the number of published articles discussing extensively organised crime topics. Scholars and practitioners have a large number of outlets to consider when publishing their work making the journal literature on a particulate subject scattered across differ titles. Because many journal articles, books and other published material are missing from the Web of Science

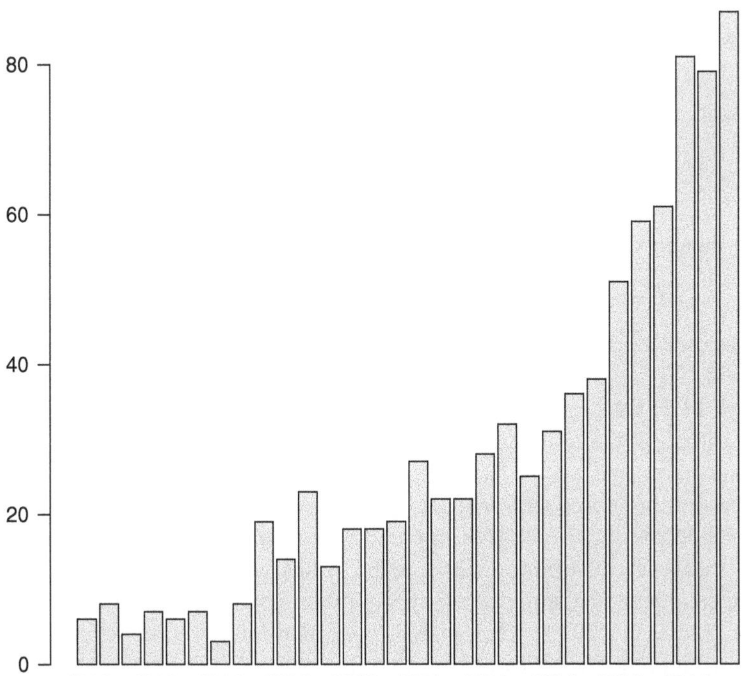

Figure 11.4 Number of articles on OC from Web of Science, from 1985–2014

1 The following string was used to retrieve the results: TOPIC: ("organized crime" OR "organised crime" OR "transnational organized crime" OR "transnational organised crime" OR "criminal networks" OR "Illicit networks" OR "mafia*" OR "illicit enterprise" OR "criminal organisations" OR "criminal organizations") Refined by: DOCUMENT TYPES: (ARTICLE) AND LANGUAGES: (ENGLISH) Timespan: All years. Indexes: SSCI, A&HCI.

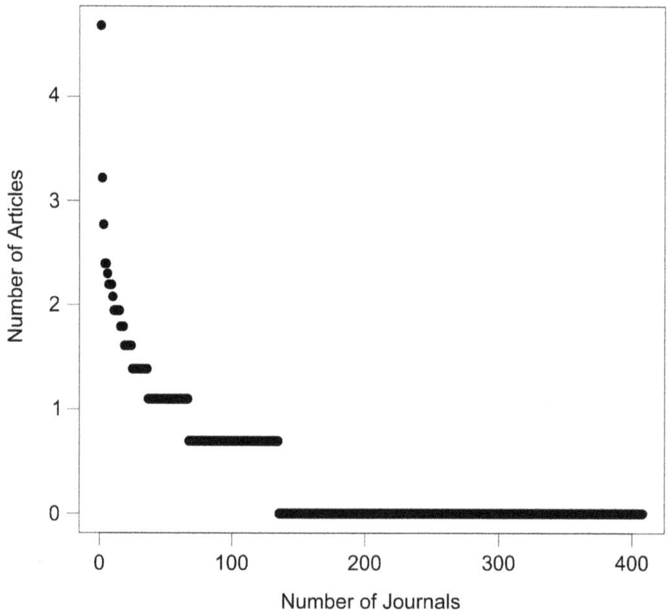

Figure 11.5 Frequency distribution of journal titles

platform, we used a popularity index to test if our sample captured core journals from the field.

In Figure 11.5, we present the ranked frequency of the popularity of journals, as measured by the number of articles published in each journal title. The index demonstrates that about 10% of the journals have published 60% of the articles collected for subsequent analysis. Thus, while at least two core journals were not included in our sample (*Global Crime* and *Trends in Organized Crime*), the ranked frequency distribution seems to be in line with Bradford's law, and thus we are confident that some of the core publications have been included in our sample (Liu et al., 2014). Our analysis is divided into two parts. First, we extracted key bibliometric indicators from the large sample of articles (N=850). However, a significant number of journal articles from this sample come with no keywords. In the second part of the analysis, the co-word networks included only articles with keywords supplied from the authors. Consequently, the second part of the analysis considered 62 papers from 1994 to 2003, and 448 papers from 2004 to 2014 (total N=510). After splitting our data into different databases in a chronological order, we measured the following bibliometric and co-word graph parameters.

11.3.2 Bibliometric parameters (N=850 articles)

Several recent studies have shown that descriptive bibliometric statistics can yield valuable insight for studying the evolution and structure of research areas (Falagas et al., 2013; Fanelli and Glänzel, 2013). Here we will consider the following indicators:

- **Number of authors:** More authors per paper and larger research teams means greater scope for interdisciplinarity and consensus on theories, topics, methods, and approaches. Measure: Number of authors.
- **Length of article:** The length of article indicates that more needs to be said to justify the arguments made in a paper. While the length of a paper is determined also by publishers' requirements, research notes and short technical papers might for example signal a dormant sift in the knowledge structure. Measure: Word count or number of pages.
- **Number of references:** Longer lists of references are necessary to justify ideas and approaches that might otherwise be contested. Measure: Number of references.
- **Volume of journal:** Articles that appear in the early or later stage of a journal's trajectory are likely to signify the development of a community. Measure: Volume number of journals.
- **Relative length of title:** Ability to convey research findings or a social problem in the most parsimonious way. Measure: Total number of words in the title divided by the number of pages.
- **Age of references (Price index)**: It has been shown that consolidated fields with strong community consensus can easily metabolise new research findings, leading to a negatively skewed distribution in the age of references (de Solla Price, 1986). Measure: Price index.
- **Diversity of cited source (Shannon div. index):** Established research communities publish in a few core outlets leading to a reduced diversity of sources in reference lists. Measure: Shannon diversity of sources (Simpson, 1949).

11.3.3 Co-word graph parameters (N=510 articles)

Networks of keywords have been shown to be effective tools for assessing the development of research themes. To achieve similar results for our sample, we replicated the co-word analysis tool developed by Liu et al. (2014) and implemented their code in R environment. The code uses the following concepts from graph theory and social network analysis.

- **Co-word networks:** For each article in our database, we extracted the keywords supplied by the authors. In this context, a keyword is analysed as a node within a network, and the size of the node is determined by its

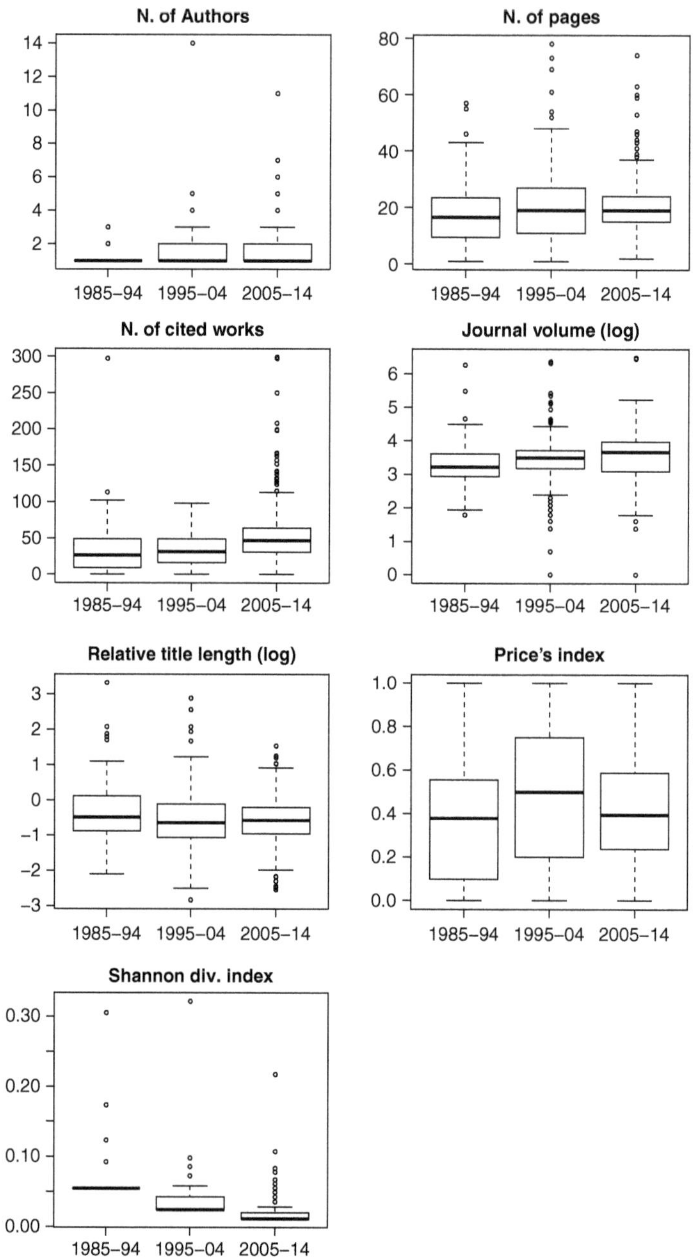

Figure 11.6 Characteristics of papers (N=850) published from 1985–2014, hypothesised to reflect the level of community maturity and consensus

frequency in our database. The links in the network are formed when two keywords appear in the same paper. We extracted 322 keywords/nodes for 1994–2003 and 3,551 keywords/nodes for 2004–2013.

- **Clusters:** Using the co-word analysis tool, hierarchical clustering was conducted using Ward's method and taking Squared Euclidean Distance as the distance measurement. We created 12 clusters for the period 1994–2003 and 14 clusters for the period 2004–2014. To achieve an optimal number of clusters, we explored different settings and ran numerous iterations of the code.

11.4 Results

Figure 11.6 presents some general bibliometric statistics from our first sample (N=850). The metrics have been hypothesised to measure the levels of community development and are divided into three samples, one per decade. We present the data in box-plots, as it is easier to graphically depict variation across different categories of indicators (Fanelli and Glänzel, 2013). Many conclusions can be drawn.

First, the number of scholars and research teams working together has increased dramatically over the past 30 years. This increase is already noted in the period between 1994 and 2003, where compared to previous years, more researchers were working together to produce research outputs. Larger research teams indicate the need for interdisciplinary approaches. This also denotes the fact that there is a growing consensus over research objectives, methods, and theories. Nevertheless, from 1994 onwards this trend has plateaued. Second, the length of articles remains constant, and only recently do we notice a slow reduction in this indicator, suggesting the slow development of research consensus. This is also reflected when looking at the number of cited works and their relative title length. Third, the Price index suggests the ability of the community to metabolise new literature. The faster the integration of new literature, the greater the consensus. The Price index for 2005–2014 is at the same level as it was in 1985–1994. Finally, the diversity of sources one finds in the reference lists of the journal articles has improved, from 3.59 in 1985–1994 to 4.19 in 1995–2004, followed by another increase to 5.23 in 2005–2014. This implies that the community considers multiple publication outlets.

General knowledge of organised crime has increased substantially; however, we have yet to consider the themes and research topics. After splitting the sample of 510 papers that contained keywords into two groups, we explored the research themes for the two time periods. We extracted all the keywords supplied by the authors of each paper in our database, conducted clustering analysis, and developed a co-word graph to map out the themes discussed by the research community. Based on the data from Table 11.2 and Table 11.3, we plotted two strategic diagrams to visualise the cohesion and maturity of the field. As explained in the previous section, Figure 11.7 was created using the centrality and density measures of each cluster of keywords.

Table 11.2 Major research themes during 1994–2003 ID, keyword, size, frequency (F), co-word frequency (CWF), centrality (C), density (D)

ID	*Keywords*	*Size*	*F*	*CWF*	*C*	*D*
A1	risk, assault, city, death, disorders, epidemiology, factors, mortality, new york, physical, psychiatric, rates, states, suicide, united, violent	17	17	272	0	1
A2	piracy, against, armed, Asia, Malacca, robbery, ships, singapore, southeast, strait	10	11	90	0	1
A3	clientelism, business, crisis, economy, family, international, Italy, legitimacy, party, relations, system, welfare	12	17	176	0.09	1.01
A4	globalization, competition, democracy, growth, location, policies, pressure, reform, taxes	9	11	75	0.03	1
A5	minority, adjustment, assimilation, children, patterns	5	5	45	0.05	1
A6	friendships, deviant, drug, use	4	4	36	0.06	1
A7	alcohol, americans, drinking, school	4	9	74	0.14	2
A8	illicit, gains fine, learning, loosely, offenders, optimal, repeat	8	8	80	0.03	1
A9	capital, cults, cultural, ethnicity, fundamentalism, globalization, possession, religious	8	9	73	0.03	1
A10	crime, dynamics, conventions, inertial, policy, social, state, support	8	29	152	0.52	1.14
A11	mafia, criminal, development, justice, legal, mass	6	16	29	0.18	0.26
A12	behavior, culture, economic, performance, political	5	16	56	0.32	1.1

Table 11.3 Major research themes during 2004–2013 (ID, keyword, size, frequency (F), co-word frequency (CWF), centrality (C), density (D)

ID	*Keywords*	*Size*	*F*	*CWF*	*C*	*D*
B1	diaspora, ethnic, immigration, collective, history, new, organization, studies, urban	9	46	200	0.49	0.75
B2	Network, analysis, law, enforcement, investigation	5	91	435	0.68	4.2
B3	cybercrime, financial, fraud, governance, illegal, internet, mafia, media, political, reporting, self, state, systems	13	140	502	0.82	0.61
B4	justice, procedural, punishment	3	16	77	0.24	2
B5	criminal, careers, chicago, social, social, networks, theory	7	139	548	0.83	2.42
B6	business, community, criminology, deterrence, economics, gangs, impact, information, knowledge, management, model, organizations, police, policing, power, protection, research, risk, states, united, violence, work	22	221	768	0.84	0.38
B7	eastern, europe, organizational, structure	4	20	103	0.26	1.5
B8	africa, conflict, illicit, industry, market, national, security, smuggling, terrorism, trade, transnational, west	13	165	673	0.88	0.88
B9	border, civil, corruption, democracy, drug, drugs, globalization, human, international, italy, mexico, migration, piracy, policy, regional, soc, trafficking, use	18	281	1171	0.91	1.20
B10	laundering, money	2	12	44	0.07	6
B11	risk, assessment, crime, organised, serious, threat	6	398	1394	0.97	12
B12	china, institutions, politics, reform, rights, russia, transition	7	60	257	0.62	2.04
B13	development, european, union	3	21	100	0.29	4
B14	black, cooperation, economic, economy, markets	5	45	174	0.57	1.1

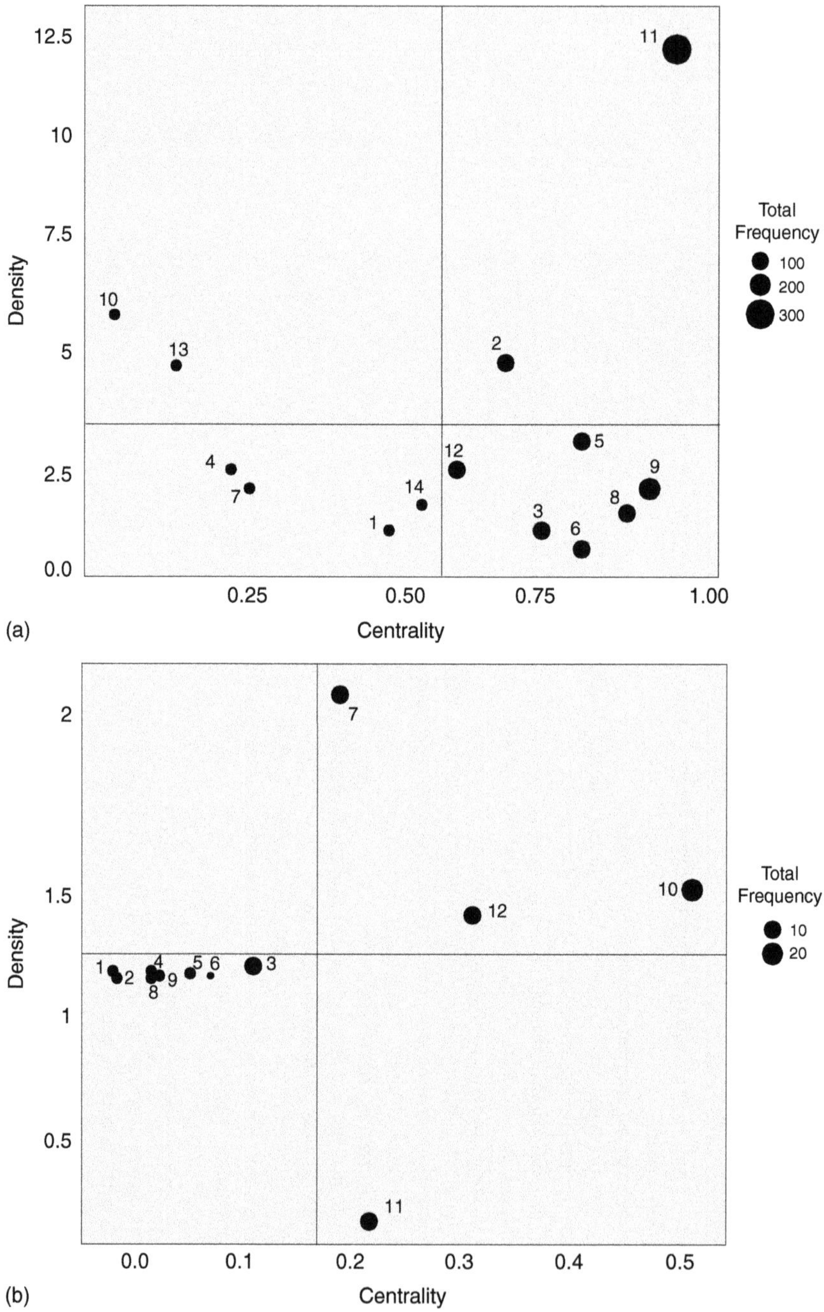

Figure 11.7 Strategic diagrams for the periods 1994-2003 (top) and 2004–2013 (bottom)

11.5 Discussion

Previous research on organised crime has proposed various themes, models, and discourses by subjectively analysing selected key texts. The novelty of the quantitative approach developed in this paper is based on the use of *distant reading* tools to provide a bird's eye view. Using bibliometric indicators, co-work analysis, and clustering of keywords into research themes, the paper provides an alternative way to map out the academic discourse on organised crime. While our sample is limited, we can risk making several generalisations and forecasts.

Organised crime research has over the past years become more coherent and interdisciplinary. The number of papers published on organised crime has increased dramatically, and research teams have become larger. The scope for collaboration on different facets of organised crime has improved. Similarly, the diversity of bibliographical sources has increased notably, with the Shannon index shifting from 3.59 in 1985–1994 and 4.19 in 1995–2004, to 5.23 in 2005–2014. The analysis of co-word networks is also in line with these trends. The average centrality and density across all the clusters increased from the period 1994–2003 (0.571, 2.305) to the period 2004–2013 (0.635, 3.127). Below we look closely at the shifting research themes using the strategic diagrams (Figure 11.7) that we created from data in Tables 11.2 and 11.3.

11.5.1 Organised crime research: 1994–2003

In Figure 11.7a (quadrant III) we observe clusters A1 (risk), A2 (piracy), A3 (clientelism), A4 (globalisation), A5 (minority), A6 (friendship), and A8 (illicit gains) with low density and centrality. These are topics that either emerge or decline. In hindsight, and given that we have data for two consecutive decades, we can observe the development of these topics over time. While it may seem that most of these topics have faded out, a closer look indicates that these clusters have morphed into more coherent topics/discourses. For example, cluster A1 (risk) was assimilated by cluster B11 (risk assessment), and cluster A5 (minority) morphed into cluster B1 (ethnic diaspora).

Similarly, in quadrant I we observe clusters A7 (alcohol), A12 (behavior), and A10 (crime dynamics). These are mainstream clusters in the 1990s with high centrality and network density. Interestingly, these are rather generic topics that have either disappeared or have achieved a narrower semantic granularity in the following decade. At first glance, this implies that in the first decade of our sample, the research community lacked effective basic research themes whose impact can be easily traced to future research endeavours.

Finally, in quadrant IV we observe cluster A11 (mafia-criminal-justice) which has relative high centrality but low density, a sign of an important but immature research theme. While clusters in this quadrant hold significant potential due to their high centrality value and bandwagon effect, in hindsight we see that cluster A11 is assimilated by cluster B3 (cybercrime-financial-mafia).

11.5.2 Organised crime research: 2004–2014

The research themes in the second period are marked by various high-density topics which are directly related to law enforcement and practitioners' needs. In Figure 11.7b (quadrant I), we locate clusters B11 (risk assessment) and B2 (network analysis), which are the mainstream topics for the given time period. These are clusters with high density and high centrality, and are expected to become the motor themes in future research.

In quadrant II we locate clusters B10 (money laundering) and B13 (european union) with high density but low centrality. These are fairly well-developed topics, but remain isolated from all the other clusters. These clusters are not yet well connected to other themes, and their links remain rather weak.

Placed in quadrant III are research topics that are either emerging or declining and might contribute to new academic discourses in the future. Clusters B4 (justice), B7 (eastern, europe, organizational structure), B1 (ethnic diaspora), and B14 (black economy) have low centrality and density.

Finally, in quadrant IV we encounter themes with high frequency and centrality, yet with low density and internal cohesion. Specifically, we intuitively observe several research topics: Criminal careers (B5), China-Russia (B12), corruption-globalization (B9), Africa-smuggling-terrorism (B8), cyber-economic-crime-mafia (B3), and business-community (B6).

11.6 Conclusion

Scholars have traditionally used textual interpretation by carefully examining brief passages of texts extracted from newspapers, policy reports, and academic sources. However, the Internet accumulates new research at such rapid and immense volumes that *close reading* of all available material is unfeasible, making it challenging to trace the knowledge-flow in scientific domains (Michel et al., 2011; Moretti, 2013). This paper sampled over 850 papers in the field of organised crime published during 1985–2014, and measured parameters that previous studies suggested would show the evolution of the knowledge structure. We have combined bibliometric analysis, social network analysis, hierarchical cluster, and graph theory, and used artefacts such as strategic diagrams to map out the evolution of academic discourse on organised crime.

There are many limitations as more effort is required to improve the size and balance of our sample. Based on the current results, we put forward several concluding remarks.

1 The number of published papers in journals has increased as the research community has grown. Research teams are growing, and the diversity of primary and secondary sources in bibliographies is improving. This trend signposts the interdisciplinary nature of the organised crime research domain. Exploring ways to advance the interdisciplinarity of the field can be very productive for young researchers who are seeking to engage with the literature.

2 A key tradition in the study of organised crime is the large number of emerging topics and the lack of overarching theories and methodologies. The driving themes of the 1990s (clusters A7, A10, and A12) evolved into new research themes (B2, B11). In particular, the uptake of social and cultural models in the 1990s has morphed into a more structured discourse about 'social networks' in the 2000s. Correspondingly, the ambiguous discourse about 'criminal dynamics' is now taking a more rigid shape as 'risk assessments'. The sociocultural dynamics driving this *methodologisation* of organised crime in the journal literature offers a very fruitful research path for future explorations.
3 Another equally important key tradition is that accumulated knowledge in organised crime is rooted in official discourses. Many of the focal topics we have extracted are directly linked to governments' and law enforcement needs and agendas. Overall, the distribution of research themes in the second period of the sample (2004–2013) underlines the tendency of the community to put practitioners' needs above researchers'. Themes with high density and centrality are explicitly linked to the needs of policing and home affairs. These are also research themes with promising potential for becoming main themes in the future. Finally, the community gives preference to economic models, and social network analysis seems to be the motor theme that will drive the knowledge structure in the years to come.

References

Bar-Ilan, J. (2008) Which h-index? — A comparison of WoS, Scopus and Google Scholar, *Scientometrics*, 74(2), pp. 257–271.

Bornmann, L., and Mutz, R. (2015) Growth rates of modern science: A bibliometric analysis based on the number of publications and cited references, *Journal of the Association for Information Science and Technology*, 66(11), pp. 2215–2222.

Callon, M., Courtial, J.P., and Laville, F. (1991) Co-word analysis as a tool for describing the network of interactions between basic and technological research: The case of polymer chemistry, *Scientometrics*, 22(1), pp. 155–205.

Callon, M., Courtial, J.-P., Turner, W.A., and Bauin, S. (1983) From translations to problematic networks: An introduction to co-word analysis, *Social Science Information*, 22(2), pp. 191–235.

Coulter, N., Monarch, I., and Konda, S. (1998) Software engineering as seen through its research literature: A study in co-word analysis, *Journal of the American Society for Information Science*, 49(13), pp. 1206–1223.

de Solla Price, D.J. (1986) *Little Science, Big Science… and Beyond*. Columbia University Press: New York.

Falagas, M.E., Pitsouni, E.I., Malietzis, G.A., and Pappas, G. (2008) Comparison of PubMed, Scopus, web of science, and Google Scholar: Strengths and weaknesses, *FASEB Journal*, 22(2), pp. 338–342.

Falagas, M.E., Zarkali, A., Karageorgopoulos, D.E., Bardakas, V., and Mavros, M.N. (2013) The impact of article length on the number of future citations: A bibliometric analysis of general medicine journals, *PLOS ONE*, 8(2), p. e49476.

Fanelli, D., and Glänzel, W. (2013) Bibliometric evidence for a hierarchy of the sciences, *PLOS ONE*, 8(6), p. e66938.

Finckenauer, J.O. (2005) Problems of definition: What is organized crime?, *Trends in Organized Crime*, 8(3), pp. 63–83.

Galambos, J., Abelson, R., and Black, J. (1986) *Knowledge Structures*. LEA: London.

Hagan, F.E. (2006) 'Organized crime' and 'organized crime': Indeterminate problems of definition, *Trends in Organized Crime*, 9(4), pp. 127–137.

He, Q. (1999) Knowledge discovery through co-word analysis, *Library Trends*, 48(1), pp. 133–159.

Hu, C.-P., Hu, J.-M., Deng, S.-L., and Liu, Y. (2013) A co-word analysis of library and information science in China, *Scientometrics*, 97(2), 369–382.

Jaffe, A.B., and Trajtenberg, M. (1999) International knowledge flows: Evidence from patent citations, *Economics of Innovation and New Technology*, 8(1–2), pp. 105–136.

Liu, Y., Goncalves, J., Ferreira, D., Xiao, B., Hosio, S., and Kostakos, V. (2014) CHI 1994–2013: Mapping two decades of intellectual progress through co-word analysis. In: Proceedings of the Conference on Human Factors in Computing Systems (CHI), Toronto, Canada, pp. 3553–3562.

Maltz, M.D. (1976) On defining "organized grime": The development of a definition and a typology, *Crime and Delinquency*, 22(3), pp. 338–346.

Michel, J.-B., Shen, Y., Aiden, A., Veres, V., Gray, M., The Google Books Team,... and Lieberman Aiden, E. (2011) Quantitative analysis of culture using millions of digitized books, *Science*, 14, pp. 176–182.

Moretti, F. (2013) *Distant Reading*. Verso: London.

OECD. (1996) The knowledge-based economy, general distribution OCED/GD (96)102.

Schmidt, B. (2012) Words alone: Dismantling topic models in the humanities, *The Journal of Digital Humanities*, 2(1) Winter.

Simpson, E.H. (1949) Measurement of diversity, *Nature*, 163(4148), pp. 688–688.

Stewart, T.A. (1997) *Intellectual Capital*. Bantam Doubleday Dell: New York.

Wang, Z., Zhao, H., and Wang, Y. (2015) Social networks in marketing research 2001–2014: A co-word analysis, *Scientometrics*, 105(1), pp. 65–82.

Whittaker, J. (1989) Creativity and conformity in science: Titles, keywords and co-word analysis, *Social Studies of Science*, 19(3), pp. 473–496.

Witten, I.H., and Frank, E. (2002) *Data Mining: Practical Machine Learning Tools and Techniques*, 2nd Edition. Elsevier: London.

12 Network analysis – Quo vadis?

A look at future developments in the field

Saskia Hufnagel and Anton Moiseienko

12.1 Introduction

A major challenge in putting together an edited volume is ensuring coherence in what may be an eclectic collection of chapters. This is particularly true in a field as diverse as analysis of criminal networks. With an international and interdisciplinary cohort of contributors, chapters brought together under this cover were limited to neither a single continent nor even a single time period. They spanned a broad range of geographies, from Norway to the Indo-Pacific region, and brought network analysis to bear on covert groups ranging from early 20th-century British suffragettes to modern-day mafia in Rome.

For all the variety of the contributions brought together in this book, several key themes emerge that point to promising directions for future work. These are the examination of historical case studies to better understand the criminal networks of today; the application of social network analysis (SNA) to the study of ties between not only individuals, but also objects and companies; and the use of methods other than SNA to shed light on the operation and evolution of criminal networks.

This concluding chapter looks back at past analyses and discusses in turn avenues for further research in the field. We aim to offer some comments on the features of criminal networks that this book has identified. While the list of possible directions for future work identified here is by no means exhaustive or definitive, it highlights the potential that the study of criminal networks continues to have for improving our understanding of organised crime and, it is hoped, will stimulate a discussion on academic horizons that lie ahead. We furthermore hope to provide some insights from a disciplinary perspective rarely involved in network analysis research: law and legal studies. We argue that network analysis is potentially very useful for lawyers, be they practitioners or academics, and could be used for (court) case analysis and training purposes, for example in organised crime and other joint enterprise cases.

12.2 Lessons from history

The attraction of historical case studies to researchers is evident throughout the book. In discussing the formation of criminal networks and patterns of co-offending, the chapter by Chiara Broccatelli, Martin Everett and Johan Koskinen compared four clandestine networks, including two networks of British suffragettes and two modern terrorist groups. Their work discerns common tendencies in different types of networks perceived as criminal by their contemporaries, although the qualifier 'criminal' may appear misplaced in relation to suffragettes from today's perspective.[1] Similarly, Siobhan Lawler and David Bright resort to analysing an Australian drug syndicate active in the 1970s in order to examine how leaders in criminal networks manage the risk of detection by law enforcement. Historical analysis is also used by Robert R. Faulkner and Eric R. Cheney to explore how the personal background of anti-Nazi plotters in the Third Reich determined their favoured strategy of resistance.

The relatively distant past can appeal to researchers by virtue of the availability of information that is far more detailed, and may well be more reliable, than that in relation to recent events. The inevitable question, however, is the extent to which the insights derived from historical examination apply to contemporary criminal networks. L.P. Hartley famously said that 'the past is a foreign country; they do things differently there'; and although he spoke of Victorian schoolboys rather than organised criminals, his dictum should be borne in mind by all those who expect the present to emulate the past. Continuity in the mindset, practices and objectives of criminals cannot simply be assumed, especially if the research *does* concern a country that is foreign to the reader as well as a different time period. Yet to assume the irrelevance of all analyses that draw on dated, foreign or otherwise uncommon sources would risk impoverishing the field and unnecessarily constraining the creativity of scholars.

There is therefore a need for an appraisal of the opportunities and challenges inherent in conducting research on criminal networks by examining historical examples. To that end, both empirical and conceptual work is valuable. Empirical studies can conduct comparative analysis of the similarities and differences in the way criminal networks operate across various time periods, as well as proffer theories that explain those similarities and differences. An idea similar to this one is expressed by Chiara Broccatelli et al., who argue that few publications so far have taken account of the temporal dimension of activities within criminal networks, namely of the development of co-offending partnerships with time. In like vein, there is merit to examining how comparable criminal networks operate in various time periods and what lessons that holds for policy-makers and law enforcement agencies. The issue of what makes a comparable network will be central to such research.

On a conceptual level, future work could assess the contribution that the study of historical networks could make to developing knowledge in the field even in the absence of immediate relevance to law enforcement imperatives of the day.

1 As emphasised in the introduction, the word 'criminal' here is used in a morally agnostic sense of breaking a state's law, with the consequence that criminal activities – such as those of anti-Nazi resistance organisations – may nonetheless be morally commendable.

Some, including the present authors, would argue that research on criminal networks should aim to be useful to law enforcement agencies, as well as to prosecutors and judges in current cases, on the basis that the study of crime ought to be practice-oriented and contribute to practical solutions to crime rather than ideological constructs. It would be immensely helpful for law enforcement agencies to be provided examples of past criminal networks on the basis of network analysis to pursue and inform avenues of investigations. Furthermore, judges and prosecutors would benefit from such studies to see through the invariably complex cases of organised crime and – more generally – accessorial liability in trials. Future studies that focus on the provision of knowledge to practitioners or the 'translation' of past studies into the language and processes of legal practitioners and law enforcement would hence be immensely valuable and very likely appreciated by research funding bodies. On the other hand, it is arguable that an understanding of how criminal networks come into existence and operate is valuable regardless of whether it can be operationalised by law enforcement agencies. A focus on the lessons learned from historical case studies therefore holds out the opportunity to advance a conversation on the objectives that research in the area can – and should – pursue.

12.3 Application of SNA in novel settings

While four out of the five chapters in this book that use SNA do so in order to analyse ties between individuals in a criminal network, SNA can be applied to any linked objects or events (Home Office, 2016, p. 7). The benefits of conducting SNA in an innovative setting are showcased in the chapter by Panos Kostakos, who traces the development of academic literature on organised crime by analysing the density and centrality of keywords used by authors. By turning the observer into the observed, he thus employs SNA to study those who study crime and provide a bird's eye view of the ebbs and flows in scholarly discourse. Also, assessing the research using network analysis could be a very fruitful exercise, helping to take stock of existing research and determining future research needs and potentials.

The range of objects that can be subjected to SNA with a view to studying crime is wide and varied, and the use of the method is far from being the exclusive preserve of academics. For instance, investigative journalists apply SNA to discern connections between corporate structures, such as those used by the rich and powerful of this world to keep private the extent of their wealth (International Consortium of Investigative Journalists, 2016). Anti-money laundering supervisors establish links between companies and/or bank accounts to investigate possible fraud or money laundering (Kraft, 2018, pp. 17–19). Analyses of North Korean nuclear proliferation networks have drawn on the connections between companies and various maritime vessels allegedly used to ship goods to and from North Korea (C4ADS and the Asian Institute for International Studies, 2016). Identifying connections between stolen objects of art, such as them transiting via the same geographical locations, can elucidate the extent and operation of trafficking networks (Tijhuis, 2006; Brodie, Doole and Renfrew, 2001; Lane, Bromley, Hicks and Mahoney, 2008); and so on. By identifying different areas where network analysis could be used, future research fields can be identified, for example, in the area of art crime, where networks have been analysed, but network analysis as a method so far not been used. By analysing the usefulness of network analysis in different crime areas for practitioners and academics, different network analysis approaches could furthermore be developed that fit the various crime areas more specifically.

The fact that much of such work is being done outside of academia is to some extent a consequence of the challenges of getting access to relevant data. Reliable in-depth information on the operation of criminal groups is a scarce commodity; as already mentioned, reliance on studies from the past is one of the coping mechanisms that researchers have developed in response. Yet, depending on the availability of sources, such as indictments or court documents, these difficulties may not be insurmountable. For instance, Italian court documents used by Anna Sergi in her chapter provide a deep insight into the workings of criminals, as do many of the indictments published by the US Department of Justice. Even though such documents tend to be most useful for understanding interactions between individuals, scholars would do well to be alert to the opportunities offered by studying links between other types of network nodes, such as those described in the previous paragraph.

Apart from access to data, another reason why SNA predominantly looks at individuals is the formulation of academic research questions, which typically revolve around the choices made by criminals in forming, maintaining and terminating co-offending partnerships with other criminals, or around the tactics they use to perpetrate crime. Such research involves postulating and verifying theories about criminals' behaviour. In contrast, the work done outside the academia often aims to identify the composition and extent of criminal networks, and thus tends to be investigative rather than explanatory in nature.

However, the distinction is not rigid, and academic research too can expand our knowledge of how criminals operate, in addition to explaining why they do what they do. For instance, establishing that corporate structures incorporated in certain jurisdictions frequently play a pivotal role in facilitating economic crime can be a valuable finding and ultimately lead to policy change, as was the case with the reform of the law on Scottish Limited Partnerships in Scotland (Department for Business, Energy & Industrial Strategy, 2017). In short, there is merit to examining all information that has the potential to explain criminal modi operandi, and SNA has the potential to be a key component of the effort to do so.

One way of breaking through the distinction between practitioner and academic network analysis research is to involve both parties in each other's studies. As already mentioned, access to government data is for academics often limited due to data protection and other security concerns. However, there are ways for government, law enforcement and legal practitioners to involve academics in areas of work benefitting from network analysis. Academics could, for example, be involved in government reporting responsibilities, training of practitioners in need of network analysis skills and on a regular basis be given final judgements in court cases to develop new insights on criminal networks relevant to practitioners in other cases and related investigations. Vice versa, it is easy and desirable for academics to involve practitioners in research projects, thereby enriching their studies with insider knowledge and practitioner expertise. Involving practitioners in academic studies furthermore helps to tailor research more closely to practitioner needs.

12.4 Use of methods other than SNA

At the same time, SNA is not the only tool in the armoury of those who study criminal networks. A wide variety of methods can be usefully applied, as the chapters in this book demonstrate. These range from Synøve N. Andersen's statistical analysis of co-offending in Norway, to qualitative analysis of interviews with 'money mules' carried out by Rutger Leukfeldt and Edward Kleemans, to Samuel Hardy's open-source review of online communications between metal detectorists operating in South-East Asia; to the application by Jade Lindley and Erika Techera of routine activity theory to explain the persistent appeal of illicit fishing to criminals groups in the Indo-Pacific region; to interviews and 'participatory mapping' used by Anna Markovska and Petrus C. van Duyne to explain the role of trust in the interaction between illicit entrepreneurs and corrupt state officials in Ukraine.

These chapters demonstrate the diversity of methods that can advance our understanding of criminal networks. By approaching criminal networks from a different angle, they can complement SNA and address issues that might otherwise elude researchers' attention. In particular, while the use of SNA discloses the structure of criminal networks and identifies their key nodes, a complete understanding of their operation often requires the analysis of factors that are either intrinsic to its nodes, such as the motivations of individual offenders, or exogenous to the network, such as the political or economic context within which it functions. Beyond practitioner-academic cooperation, the cross-fertilisation of network analysis with other academic disciplines is hence another way of advancing network analysis research.

It therefore comes as no surprise that two chapters in the book use SNA in conjunction with qualitative content analysis of the data at hand. For instance, Siobhan Lawler and David Bright come to the conclusion that the leaders of the drug trafficking syndicate considered in their chapter managed risks of detection not by strategic positioning within the criminal network but by resorting to behavioural risk-management strategies, which they analyse on the basis of two detailed non-fiction publications. Similarly, in Anna Sergi's chapter, SNA is combined with content analysis of intercepted materials that contain clues as to how the leaders of the mafia group in question viewed its strengths and sought to capitalise on them.

By showing how a variety of methods can improve on our understanding of criminal networks, this book underscores the need for a 360-degree view of criminal networks in their contexts, which requires making use of insights that SNA can produce, while at the same time venturing beyond the study of network structures.

As with the use of SNA, ingenuity and innovation in making use of novel data sources is likely to be essential to the success of this endeavour. For instance, while some researchers may have access to materials of police interrogations or the ability to interview convicted criminals, others may rely on the ever-increasing amount of publicly available information, such as conversations on open or closed internet forums that are being increasingly used in academic research. Just as open-source investigative journalism by the likes of Bellingcat shows the utility of open-source analysis,[2] academics too already use publicly accessible information, such as surface web forums, dark net forums and social network pages to gather data, but the potential of these sources for crime research is only beginning to be exploited. Our recommendation would be for academics to join forces and enrich their research with methods and data from colleagues to advance the findings of network analysis studies.

12.5 Insights into criminal networks

This book's sections looked in turn at the formation of criminal networks; their management; their involvement in various types of illicit trafficking; and the interplay of criminal networks and politics.

The two chapters on the formation of criminal networks considered how, why and how often criminals join their forces to offend. The research on the management of criminal networks, in turn, presented conflicting perspectives on how criminal leaders achieve their needs through criminal networks while at the same time managing the risks of detection or betrayal. While Australian drug traffickers of the 1970s relied predominantly on behavioural tactics such as intimidation to avoid detection, contemporary cybercriminals structure a criminal network in such a way as to entrust the most perilous task – the 'cashing out' of proceeds – to a 'money mule' who will often be unaware of the cybercriminal's identity.

Both approaches, the behavioural and the structural one, are likely to be employed by high-ranking criminals in various degrees to limit their exposure to risks. They go some way towards explaining how criminals overcome their lack of trust in each other, the ability to do so being indispensable to co-offending over an extended period of time.

Yet, depending on how a criminal network is structured, the problem of trust may not be as acute as in the foregoing examples. Illicit metal detectorists described by Samuel Hardy are a case in point. Rather than working together as a coordinated network, they provide each other with advice on the internet and thereby form a loose support community while each being guarded by their relative online anonymity. Although innocuous in comparison to organised criminal

2 See https://www.bellingcat.com/.

groups, such networks too can wreak significant damage on the cultural heritage of countries where their participants operate. Similarly, the analysis of illegal fishing in the Indo-Pacific region demonstrates that fishers engaged in breaking the law can be either members of organised gangs, up to the point of exploiting forced labour, or disparate opportunists. It follows that the lines from licit to illicit, from criminal to legal and from criminal network to tolerated interest group can be seriously blurred.

These examples highlight the related questions of, first, what a criminal network is in the first place and, second, how the ability to communicate over long distances in real-time transforms criminal networks and their modus operandi. Although ever more attention is being paid to cybercrime and the opportunities that internet forums offer for budding cybercriminals, it is important to recognise the implications of seamless cross-border communication for all sorts of criminal networks, such as those engaged in illicit metal detecting and looting of cultural property. In our view, the implications of technology should feature prominently in future research given the realistic possibility that criminal networks formed online may differ significantly from those networks that interact in the offline world.

Furthermore, both the ability of law enforcement to intercept the communications of such networks and of researchers to use their open-source data for network analysis and other research are extensive. This is due to the fact that participants feel protected by their online anonymity and therefore converse much more freely, making online forums a rich source of data for investigations and research. At the same time, anonymity on the internet is only relative and law enforcement agencies have little difficulty intercepting suspicious conversations and tracking the real-life names of participants. Collaboration of academics and practitioners in analysing criminal activity in online forums would therefore be an ideal starting point for fostering more interaction between the worlds of academia and practice, while respecting data protection and national security interests.

In addition to the fluid nature of networks in a technically interconnected world, this book shone light on the obvious but easily neglected fact that criminal networks are not self-contained but operate within legitimate political structures with which they necessarily interact to some extent. The section of politics catalogued several modalities of such interaction, namely: criminal entrepreneurs enjoying the protection and patronage of state authorities in Ukraine; an organised criminal group acting as a conduit between local politicians and the criminal underworld in Rome; and a community of plotters seeking to overthrow their state's antidemocratic political order in Nazi Germany.

Each of these chapters is a study of criminal networks in context, and in some cases the ability to forge connections with outside groups has proved essential to such networks' success and longevity. In some cases, the familiar theme of trust and honour among thieves emerges, as it did in the case of corrupt officials exercising patronage over illicit gambling activities in Ukraine. Given the variety of possible interactions between criminal networks and exogenous actors, ranging from symbiosis to opposition, this represents a crucial area in the study of criminal networks that is ripe for continuing exploration. As argued earlier, it is in this area that non-SNA methods can be particularly valuable.

Both of these research directions – the changing nature and modus operandi of networks in an internet-connected world, and the interaction of criminal networks with outside actors – are of direct relevance to law enforcement efforts in some contexts. One example is the efforts of Europol and domestic police forces in EU member states to disrupt the use of money mules, which are a fixture of many cybercrime and fraud cases (Europol, 2018). Given that low-level money mules typically know little of the identity of 'mastermind' criminals, better information on key nodes in the network – so-called mule herders, who arrange for the recruitment of money mules – can be of considerable value. Or, to take a different example, understanding that a criminal group draws its strength from connections with the political establishment can serve to underscore the need for anti-corruption measures so as to alter structural societal conditions conducive to criminality.

In short, future work on criminal networks can span the entire gamut from replicating the results of existing research in novel settings, such as new geographical locations, and putting conventional wisdom to test; all the way to examining the ramifications of technology for criminal modi operandi and exploring the application of new methods to the study of criminal networks. A combination of practical relevance and creativity, as well as a mixture of robust quantitative methodologies and bold hypotheses, are key to further advancement of this expansive and dynamic area of criminology.

One of the most important developments we would like to promote in this final chapter of the book is the cooperation between academics from different disciplines and methodological backgrounds to inform network analysis, as well as the more practice-oriented forms this research should take. For the latter, it is crucial that academics and practitioners work together, facilitating access to data and practitioner expertise, as well as articulating the most prominent practitioner needs. While this is not a new proposal, it is nevertheless one that should be kept in mind when looking at the future of network analysis and many other methods and research areas.

Lastly, it should be stressed that even in the legal field, and particularly for prosecutors and judges in criminal cases, network analysis could be a valuable tool for better understanding current and future cases of organised crime and more generally accessorial liability, considering that cases in this field are invariably complex and not analysed in a systematic way until long after the final judgement has been handed down. Training on network analysis and engagement with network analysts in this field could hence be vastly beneficial to the working of criminal justice systems in the areas of organised crime and other cases of accessorial liability.

Bibliography

Brodie, N., Doole, J. and Renfrew, C. (eds.) (2001) *Trading in Illicit Antiquities: The Destruction of the World's Archaeological Heritage*. Cambridge, UK: Cambridge University Press.

C4ADS and the Asian Institute for International Studies (2016) In China's Shadow: Exposing North Korean Overseas Networks. https://c4ads.org/s/In-Chinas-Shadow.pdf.

Department for Business, Energy & Industrial Strategy (2017) Scottish Limited Partnerships to Reveal Identity of Owners Thanks to New Laws. www.gov.uk/government/news/scottish-limited-partnerships-to-reveal-identity-of-owners-thanks-to-new-laws.

Europol (2018) Over 1500 Money Mules Identified in Worldwide Money Laundering Sting. www.europol.europa.eu/newsroom/news/over-1500-money-mules-identified-in-worldwide-money-laundering-sting.

Home Office (2016) *Social Network Analysis: 'How to Guide'*, p. 7. https://www.gov.uk/government/publications/social-network-analysis-how-to-guide

International Consortium of Investigative Journalists (2016) The Power Players. www.icij.org/investigations/panama-papers/the-power-players/.

Kraft, O. (2018) Sharpening the Money-Laundering Risk Picture: How Data Analytics Can Support Financial Intelligence, Supervision and Enforcement, RUSI Occasional Paper.

Lane, D. C., Bromley, D. G., Hicks, R. D. and Mahoney, J. S. (2008) Time Crime: The Transnational Organization of Art and Antiquities Theft. *Journal of Contemporary Criminal Justice*, 24(3): 243.

Tijhuis, E. (2006) *Transnational Crime and the Interface between Legal and Illegal Actors: The Case of the Illicit Art and Antiquities Trade*. Nijmegen, the Netherlands: Wolf Legal.

Index

***Page numbers in bold are in tables

For Product Safety Concerns and Information please contact our EU representative GPSR@taylorandfrancis.com
Taylor & Francis Verlag GmbH, Kaufingerstraße 24, 80331 München, Germany

www.ingramcontent.com/pod-product-compliance
Ingram Content Group UK Ltd.
Pitfield, Milton Keynes, MK11 3LW, UK
UKHW011001180926
475701UK00004B/509
* 9 7 8 0 3 6 7 7 2 6 9 7 3 *